COMPLETE EDITION

UKULELE

Beginning • Intermediate • Mastering

GREG HORNE & SHANA AISENBERG
EDITED BY DANIEL HO

CONTENTS

Alfred Music
P.O. Box 10003
Van Nuys, CA 91410-0003
alfred.com

ISBN-10: 1-4706-1768-4 (Book & CD)
ISBN-13: 978-1-4706-1768-4 (Book & CD)

Cover photograph of Daniel Ho by Larry Lytle
Interior photographs by Greg Horne and Paige M. Travis

 Alfred Cares. Contents printed on environmentally responsible paper.

BEGINNING UKULELE

CONTENTS

ABOUT THE AUTHORS

PHOTO BY BILL FOSTER

Greg Horne is a multi-instrumentalist, songwriter, author, and teacher in Knoxville, Tennessee. He is the author of several books and DVDs published by Alfred Music, including the *Complete Acoustic Guitar Method*, *Teach Yourself Songwriting*, two volumes of the *Complete Mandolin Method*, and the *Couch Potato Guitarist/Bassist* books. Greg holds a bachelor of arts in music from the College of Wooster, and pursued graduate studies at the University of Mississippi. To contact Greg, hear his music, or see his videos, visit: www.greghornemusic.com

PHOTO BY BEVERLY WOODS

Multi-instrumentalist **Shana Aisenberg** plays ukulele, acoustic guitar, lap steel guitar, mandolin, fiddle, banjo, fretted dulcimer, and more. She specializes in American roots styles including fingerpicking blues, slide guitar, bluegrass, old-time flatpicking, swing, and New England contra dance—as well as European folk music styles such as Celtic, klezmer, Balkan, and Scandinavian.

In addition to being a respected author, Shana has recorded, produced, and played on over 50 albums. She has also composed music for films. In 1981, Shana was a triple winner at the prestigious Walnut Valley National Flatpicking Championships, held in Winfield, Kansas, where she placed in the categories of fingerstyle guitar, mandolin, and fretted dulcimer. Shana performs regularly with duo partner Beverly Woods and teaches private lessons and group classes in New Hampshire and online. You can visit Shana on the Web at: www.shanasongs.com

MP3 CD

00

Track 00

An MP3 CD is included with this book to make learning easier and more enjoyable. The symbol shown at bottom left appears next to every example in the book that features an MP3 track. Use the MP3s to ensure you're capturing the feel of the examples and interpreting the rhythms correctly. The track number below the symbol corresponds directly to the example you want to hear (example numbers are above the icon). All the track numbers are unique to each "book" within this volume, meaning every book has its own Track 1, Track 2, and so on. (For example, *Beginning Ukulele* starts with Track 1, as does *Intermediate Ukulele* and *Mastering Ukulele*.)

To access the MP3s on the CD, place the CD in your computer's CD-ROM drive. In Windows, double-click on My Computer, then right-click on the CD icon labeled "MP3 CD" and select Explore to view the files and copy them to your hard drive. For Mac, double-click on the CD icon on your desktop labeled "MP3 CD" to view the files and copy them to your hard drive.

INTRODUCTION

Aloha! Welcome to *Ukulele: Complete Edition,* a method designed for ukulele students who are either teaching themselves or working with teachers. This book consists of three separate volumes, now available in this one edition. The three volumes (*Beginning Ukulele, Intermediate Ukulele,* and *Mastering Ukulele*) cover the styles, techniques, and musicianship you need to take your playing as far as you want to go. You have chosen a fun and unique instrument that is becoming more popular than ever. The ukulele is accessible, portable, and sounds great whether you play it simply or with dazzling virtuosity. This book is written to help you have fun and play real music you will love as quickly as possible.

WHO SHOULD USE *BEGINNING UKULELE?*
The first section of this book, *Beginning Ukulele,* is written to get you started playing ukulele even if you've never touched an instrument before. The intermediate player can also benefit from this section, using it to brush up on fundamental skills and lay a solid foundation for further development. Players of other fretted instruments will be able to use *Beginning Ukulele* to add the uke to their musical bag of tricks.

WHAT IS IN *BEGINNING UKULELE?*
This section covers basic musical skills that apply to all styles. Some of the skills and concepts you will learn include:
- How to choose, tune, hold, and strum your ukulele
- A bit about uke history and the players that have inspired its popularity
- Strumming basic open chords to accompany songs
- Reading standard music notation and tablature (TAB)
- Strumming styles to accompany old-time fiddle music, traditional jazz, and swing
- The basics of scales and improvising
- The structure of major scales, keys, and chords
- Moveable chord shapes that allow you to play every major, minor, and dominant 7th chord
- Specialized techniques that apply to Hawaiian music, swing, blues, fingerstyle, and rock ukulele

HOW TO USE *BEGINNING UKULELE*
Each chapter in this section contains a group of lessons that are related by a theme or set of skills. The chapters are progressive, meaning each lesson within a chapter builds on the previous lesson. This section is designed so that you can work from the beginning to the end, but it is also possible to skip around and work on multiple chapters simultaneously once you master the basic skills found in Chapters 1 and 2.

WATCH FOR SUPER UKE TIPS!
These highlighted tips will give you secrets to help you practice and acquire new skills.

WHERE DO I GO FROM HERE?
Beginning Ukulele is designed to progress directly to *Intermediate Ukulele,* the second part of this book. The skills and techniques you learn here will be developed and expanded in that section. You will learn more tunes, styles, scales, chords, and improvisation techniques. Happy picking!

CHAPTER 1

Getting Started

LESSON 1: KNOW YOUR UKE

ABOUT THE UKULELE

'Ukulele is a Hawaiian word meaning "jumping flea," alternately translated as "gift that came here." The Hawaiian spelling begins with the *'okina*, which looks like a single quotation mark and signifies a glottal stop (a type of sound used in many spoken languages produced by momentary closure of the glottis followed by a quick release). The Hawaiian pronunciation is "ook-oo-LEH-leh." Many players outside Hawaii pronounce it "you-kuh-LAY-lee," or *uke* for short. The authors of this method acknowledge and respect the ukulele's Hawaiian heritage, but have chosen to use the Anglicized spelling without the *'okina*.

There are a few theories on how the ukulele got its name, including that the player's hand leaps like a "jumping flea" across the strings. The uke began its journey in the Portuguese archipelago of Madeira. The construction of the ukulele is based on the Portuguese *machete*, a relative of the *cavaquinho* and guitar. The *machete* was enormously popular in 19th-century Madeira. Madeirans were recruited for work in Hawaii in the late 1800s. Three luthier/cabinet makers, Manuel Nunes (1843–1922), Jose do Espirito Santo (1850–1905), and Augusto Dias (1842–1915) arrived in 1879. In the 1880s, they began building instruments in Honolulu. Soon, the tiny *machete* acquired the tuning of its larger sibling, the *rajão* (which would evolve into the Hawaiian *taropatch*), and became the ukulele.

A renaissance of traditional Hawaiian music, poetry, and dance was blossoming under King Kalakaua (1836–1891) and his sister Queen Liliuokalani (1838–1917) at that time. They both loved the ukulele and helped create the repertoire and popularity that made it synonymous with Hawaiian culture. The best ukuleles were built of koa (*Acacia koa*), a native Hawaiian wood.

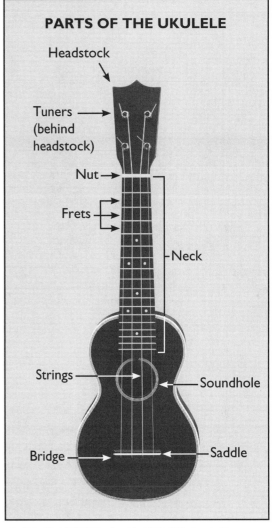

PARTS OF THE UKULELE

Headstock

Tuners (behind headstock)

Nut

Frets

Neck

Strings

Soundhole

Bridge

Saddle

The ukulele had been heard on the mainland but it really became a hit at the 1915 Panama Pacific International Exhibition in San Francisco. This sparked a uke craze that plowed through the 1920s with musical shows, traveling bands, sheet music, and thousands of ukes sold by catalogs and top builders like Martin. Virtuoso performers like Roy Smeck, Cliff "Ukulele Ike" Edwards, and later England's George Formby kept the uke visible through films and records.

The popularity and "cool factor" of the uke has waxed and waned several times since then. There was a boom in the '50s when TV star Arthur Godfrey inspired the sales of millions of mass-produced plastic ukes. The late '60s saw a revival of Tin Pan Alley uke songs from artists like Tiny Tim and Ian Whitcomb. From the '70s onward, the uke has enjoyed unparalleled diversity through players like Herb "Ohta-San" Ohta, Gordon Mark, Lyle Ritz, and many others.

Now, nearly 100 years after the "Frisco Exhibition," the ukulele is in a new golden age thanks to school programs, internet videos, and virtuosos like Jake Shimabukuro and James Hill. You could be next! For more about the players of the past and present, look for their pictures in this book. Also, see page 97 for excellent reference sources on uke history.

TYPES OF UKULELES

There are four basic types of four-string ukuleles, from smallest to largest: *soprano*, *concert* (sometimes called *alto*), *tenor*, and *baritone*. The soprano, concert, and tenor sizes can be tuned identically (see *Tuning* on page 10), and any of these three sizes can be used with all three sections of this book. (Note: The baritone uke is tuned differently, like the first four strings of a guitar, and should not be used with this method.)

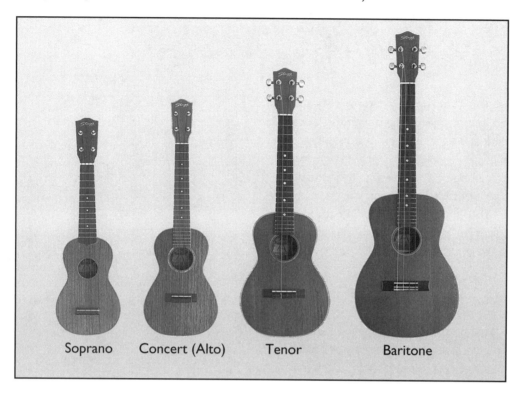

| Soprano | Concert (Alto) | Tenor | Baritone |

THE BANJO UKE

The *banjo uke* has a four-string ukulele neck (usually around concert size) on a banjo body. These can be tuned and played just like the other uke types. There are also many multi-string variations of the ukulele, including instruments such as the *taropatch ukulele*, the *tiple*, and the *liliu*. Much of the material in this method can be adapted to these instruments, but it's best to start with a four-string uke or banjo uke.

Banjo Ukulele.

WHICH SIZE?

Which ukulele should you start with? It's purely a matter of preference and comfort. If there is a good selection available to you, pick up several and see how they feel. The most common, and least expensive, is the soprano size. You can do everything in this book with a soprano uke. Ukulele virtuosos often play concert and tenor sizes because they afford more room for intricate fingerwork and a fuller tone. At any rate, try to buy your first uke from a seller that has experience and can point you to a quality instrument. Some inexpensive ukes are great, and others have tuning or stability problems that make for later headaches. The uke from the gift shop on the beach may not give you the lifetime of enjoyment you seek!

HOLDING THE UKULELE

Most ukuleles are so small and light they can easily be played sitting or standing without a strap. The most stable position is seated, with the lower bout of the uke resting on the right leg. Use the right forearm to gently hold the uke to the body. Another variation is to hold the uke farther up on the stomach, cradled in the crook of the right arm. Players who are using their thumb exclusively will often support the upper bout of the uke with their right-hand fingers. For unrestricted access to the most advanced techniques, you may find a strap helpful. A strap supports the instrument without restricting the placement of the hands, and also allows you to rock out on stage without fear. Many ukes do not come with strap buttons to attach the strap, but you can get them installed easily and cheaply at a repair shop.

Correct sitting position.

Correct standing position.

PLAYING THE OPEN STRINGS

When you hold the uke with the soundhole facing forward, the string closest to the floor is called the *1st string*. Without touching the strings with your left-hand fingers, try plucking the 1st string with your right-hand thumb or index finger. You don't have to dig deeply into the strings or pull hard on them. Just go for a "medium gentle" level of sound. Move to the next string (away from the floor)—this is the *2nd string*. Then try the *3rd string*. The string closest to your head is the *4th string*. If you're not out of strings yet, you may not have the right instrument for this book!

ABOUT THE 4TH STRING
In the standard tuning used in this book (see *TUNING, next page*), the 1st string is the highest-sounding open note (an A). The 2nd string is lower, an E. The 3rd string is lower, a C. So, the pattern is that the notes get lower as you go from the 1st to 3rd strings. The 4th string breaks the pattern. It is higher in pitch, sounding a G note between the A of the 1st string and the E of the 2nd string. This type of tuning is called a *reentrant tuning* (pronounced "re-entrant"). The 4th string in this tuning is sometimes called the *reentrant string*.

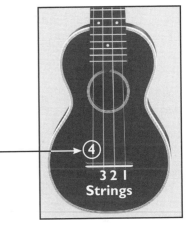

"LOW-G" TUNING
There is another popular and useful tuning called "Low-G" tuning, in which the 4th string is tuned an octave lower than the reentrant tuning, to a G below the C of the 3rd string. This tuning expands the range of the instrument and increases the options for scales and melodies. This tuning can be easier for guitar players to adapt to, as it is similar to the tuning of the first four strings of a guitar capoed at the 5th fret. For more information, see the Appendix about Low-G tuning on page 95.

Take a few minutes to play on the different open strings. Take the uke down the hall and show your pets and relatives what you can do. The big time is just around the corner!

TUNING

Ukulele: Complete Edition uses the most common standard tuning for the soprano, concert, and tenor ukulele: the G–C–E–A tuning with a high (or "reentrant") G. This will allow you to work through most of the examples in this series with one uke. This tuning is also called "C" or "C6" tuning, because the open notes form a C6 chord (you'll learn what this means later). The first step in tuning is to memorize the names of the open-string notes in standard tuning. The names come from letters in the *music alphabet* (coming up in a few pages). For now, just memorize the letters and which strings they go to (see above).

Tuning a stringed instrument for the first time is not easy. You might prefer to enlist an experienced helper at first. Tuning is a skill that involves listening closely and learning to match pitches exactly. The strings can be tuned by matching them to the tuning notes in the video. An electronic tuner or tuning app on your mobile device can also be very handy. Following are a few other methods you can use to tune.

THE "MATCHING FRETS" METHOD

Step 1: Tune the 1st string to exactly match an A note (also known as A440) on a reference device like a tuner, piano, or pitch pipe.

Step 2: Play your newly tuned A string and listen to the note. Now play the 5th fret on the 2nd string and compare it to the open 1st string. Tune the 2nd string so that the pitch of the 5th fret exactly matches the pitch of the open 1st string. It's okay to play a string and let it ring while you turn the tuning machine. This can help you judge how far to go.

Step 3: Play your newly tuned E string (2nd string) open and listen to the note. You will then tune the 3rd string (C string) so that the 4th fret note exactly matches the open 2nd string.

Step 4: To tune the 4th string, play the 3rd fret on the 2nd string. This step is a little different because you're going to use the fretted note as the reference. Tune the 4th string (G) so that it exactly matches the 3rd fret of the 2nd string.

FOR GUITAR PLAYERS ONLY
The tuning of the uke is very similar in interval structure to the tuning of the guitar. Imagine the first four strings of the guitar (D–G–B–E, from low to high) capoed or barred at the 5th fret, giving the notes G–C–E–A (low to high). Now, imagine the 4th string replaced with a thinner string and tuned up an octave. This is uke tuning. If you're a guitar player, you'll recognize many chord shapes and scale formations, but they will have different names due to the different tuning.

THE PIANO OR KEYBOARD METHOD

You can tune to a piano by matching the strings to the keys shown.

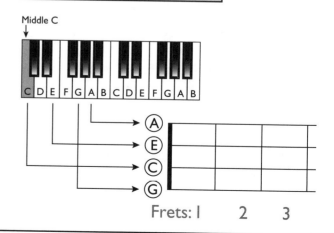

THE LEFT-HAND POSITION

The key to a good left-hand position is to keep your thumb behind the neck, resting lightly and allowing the palm to be open. The position that affords the most agility with the least strain is a guitar-style grip with the pad of the thumb near the center of the back of the neck and the palm completely open. Your fingers should be curved. If you are coming to the uke from playing violin or mandolin, you can modify a position that cradles the neck between the thumb and the side of the lowest joint of the index finger. In this position, the fingers may be angled slightly to reach higher frets. Try not to hold up the weight of the neck with your left hand. Use a strap or sit so the uke is supported.

Guitar-style grip.

Mandolin-style grip.

FRETTING AND PLAYING NOTES

To fret a note, place your finger just to the left of the fret you want to play, and press the string down so that it makes solid contact with the fret. Pluck the string with your right-hand index finger or thumb. Do not press down directly on top of the fret, as your finger will mute the string. Keep the pressure steady for as long as you want the note to ring. It helps to remember: *the fret makes the note, the finger gets the string to the fret.*

LEFT-HAND FINGERS

Your left-hand fingers are numbered as follows:

Index = 1
Middle = 2
Ring = 3
Pinky = 4

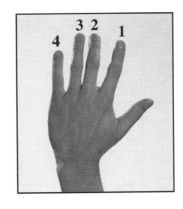

A HIDDEN SOURCE OF DIFFICULTY

The most important factors for a long life of playing are to keep the fingers curved and the hand muscles as relaxed as possible. A spot to watch out for is the muscle group at the joint of the thumb and the hand. Often, these muscles will become tense and squeeze together when you are concentrating while practicing—you may not even know it's happening! It may also happen if you are holding up the neck with your hand. This is a source of tension in your hand that can cause fatigue and difficulty. Check on it often and consciously relax this muscle group until it learns to stay that way.

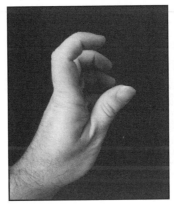
Bad, tense, ouch!

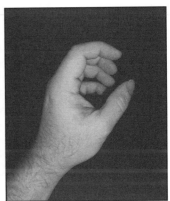
Good, open, relaxed.

READING WHATLATURE?

Tablature, called *TAB* for short, is a system of writing music for fretted string instruments. It tells you what fret to play and what string to play it on.

The long horizontal lines represent the strings. The top line is the 1st string (A), and the bottom line is the 4th string (G). The numbers indicate which fret to play. Underneath the TAB you'll see a row of numbers that indicate which left-hand finger to use for each note. Try fingering the notes indicated below.

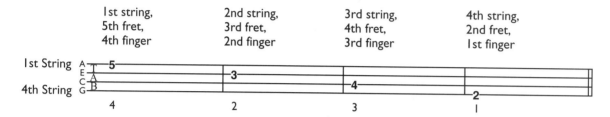

1st string,
5th fret,
4th finger

2nd string,
3rd fret,
2nd finger

3rd string,
4th fret,
3rd finger

4th string,
2nd fret,
1st finger

SUPER UKE TIP

The dots, or fret markers, on your ukulele neck will help you keep track of the frets (especially as you get up high on the neck). Dots are commonly found marking frets 5, 7, 10, and 12. Soprano ukes often have necks that join the body at the 12th fret, so this fret may not be marked. There are variations in the position markers used on ukes, so be sure to familiarize yourself with your own uke!

TAB is often attached to written music known as *standard music notation*, so the player will know how long the notes last and when they occur. Standard music notation is introduced in Chapter 3 (pages 31–42), and as you become accustomed to reading it, it will become more and more helpful. The following tune shows TAB and standard music notation. If you do not read music yet, do not panic. Just play the frets and strings indicated in a slow, steady rhythm, giving each note an equal amount of time. You may recognize the tune.

 ## MARY HAD A BORDER COLLIE

Track
1

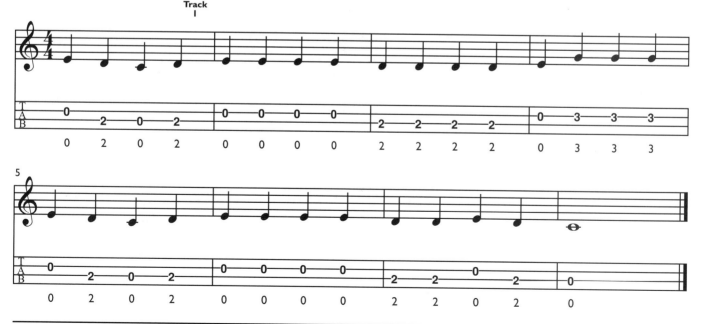

LESSON 3: THE NOTES ON THE FRETBOARD

The trick to learning the notes on the fretboard is understanding the musical alphabet. You only need to remember four things to master the musical alphabet:

1. The musical alphabet goes from A to G, then starts over again with A:

A B C D E F G A B C and so on

This series of seven notes, called *natural notes,* repeats in a continuous cycle. As you move forward through the alphabet, the notes get higher in pitch. When moving through the series, each note can be called a *step.*

2. Steps come in two sizes: *half steps* (1 fret) and *whole steps* (2 frets).

The closest one note can be to another on the ukulele is the distance of one fret. This one-fret distance is called a *half step.* The distance of two frets (or two half steps) is called a *whole step.* For example, from the 1st fret to the 2nd fret is a half step, while the distance from the 1st to the 3rd fret is a whole step.

Half step = One fret
Whole step = Two frets

3. In the musical alphabet, all letters are a whole step apart except B to C and E to F (which are each a half step apart.)

B to C is a half step
E to F is a half step

Below is the musical alphabet from A to A with each block representing a half step, or one fret.

Musical Alphabet (Showing Natural Notes Only)

A		B	C		D		E	F		G		A

4. Special symbols called *accidentals* are used to name the notes between the natural notes. Remember, there are no notes between B and C or E and F.

MEET THE ACCIDENTALS		
Symbol	Name	Description
♯	Sharp	A *sharp* raises a natural note by one half step (one fret). For example, the note one half step above A is called "A sharp" (A♯).
♭	Flat	A *flat* lowers a natural note by one half step (one fret). For example, the note one half step below B is called "B flat" (B♭).
♮	Natural	A *natural* returns a sharp or flat note to its original, natural position. Notes are assumed to be natural unless a flat or sharp is indicated. You can call the A note "A natural," or just "A."

All sharp notes can have a flat name, and all flat notes can have a sharp name. In other words, each note that is in-between two natural notes has two names, a sharp name and a flat name. The note between A and B can be called A♯ or B♭, and both names fall on the same fret. Two notes that have different names but the same sound are called *enharmonic equivalents*.

THE CHROMATIC SCALE

The music alphabet, with all the half steps included, is called the *chromatic scale*. It has 12 half steps. In other words, if you start on A, the 13th note you reach will be A again. Each repetition of the same note in the cycle is called an *octave*. This is because the cycle contains only seven distinct letters, so the eighth letter you reach will be the one you started with.

Here is the music alphabet, or chromatic scale, again. Can you fill in the missing note names? Check the 1st string on the chart at the bottom of the page to see how you did.

A	A♯ B♭	B	C	___ ___	D	___	E	F	___	G	___	A

Practice naming the notes of the chromatic scale forward *and* backward (using both sharp and flat names) until you can do it perfectly every time.

REVIEWING THE OPEN STRINGS
The strings of your ukulele are tuned to the following pitches:

Note:	G	C	E	A
String:	4	3	2	1

If you haven't yet, memorize the notes of the open strings: **G**rizzly **C**owboys **E**at **A**lone!

Now that you know the music alphabet and the open strings, pick any string and try to name the notes starting from open. Below are all the notes on the ukulele from the open string to the 12th fret. Note that the 12th fret brings you back to the note name you started with for that string. The 12th fret marks the octave of the open string, so we say that the neck "starts over" at the 12th fret.

All the Notes on the Ukulele Fretboard

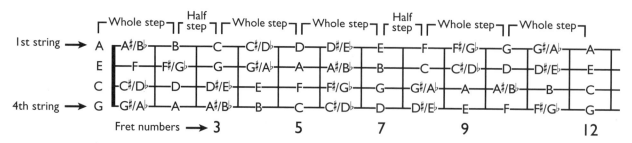

CHAPTER 2

Strum, Strum, Strum

LESSON 1: YOUR FIRST CHORDS

With just a few chords and a bit of know-how, you can make some real music right away. A *chord* is three or more notes sounded simultaneously. The way to remember that is a *note* is one sound at a time (like one person singing), and a *chord* is a bunch of notes played or sung together. Your first chords are called *open chords* because they involve a mixture of *open* (unfingered) strings and fretted notes.

> **SUPER UKE TIP**
> *During this phase of your learning, it is more important to practice often than to practice for long periods of time. Play for a while, then put the uke down and come back to it again later (but not days and days later!).*

Muscle memory is what gives us the ability to perform a complex action (like walking) without having to plan it out every time. Muscle memory builds through cycles of repetition, then rest, then returning to repeat the motion again. Give yourself the patience, persistence, and time to let your fingers learn how to master each new skill.

STRUMMING

One of the most common ways to play a chord is to *strum*. You can strum with a pick, fingers, or thumb. Many uke players do most of their strumming using the index, middle, or ring finger—all of which carry the added bonus of being hard to misplace or send through the clothes dryer (unlike a pick).

Strum setup.

To strum with a finger (of your strumming hand), start with your hand held near the place where the neck joins the body, with your finger above the 4th string. In one motion, rapidly move your finger across all the strings, striking them all (see photos to the right). It should sound like you hit them all at the same time. It may feel like flicking the back of your fingernail across the strings, or like flicking your hand from the wrist, or a bit of both. Stay very loose and relaxed and practice this several times on the open strings.

Strumming symbols:

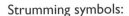 *Downstroke* (strum toward the floor)

V *Upstroke* (strum toward the ceiling)

Strum follow-through.

> **SUPER UKE TIP**
> *The best basic uke tone is produced by strumming the strings somewhere between the soundhole and the neck joint (where the neck meets the body). Find the spot that is comfortable and sounds good to you, and use this spot as "home base" most of the time. Next, try moving toward the headstock where the sound gets softer and sweeter, and then toward the bridge where the sound gets louder, brighter, and, eventually, more nasal or metallic. It's your uke. Go nuts.*

READING CHORD DIAGRAMS

Chords, like notes, are named after letters in the music alphabet, sometimes with additional words or numbers to describe the chord better. The chords you will learn first are called *major* chords, which denotes a special sound and structure you'll learn about soon. Usually, a chord is assumed to be major unless stated otherwise, so it's not necessary to indicate it verbally or in the music. For instance, a "C" chord is understood as C Major, a "G" chord as G Major, etc.

The tuning of the uke produces a very nice chord using just the open strings, called C6 ("C six.") To play other chords, you'll need the fingers of your fretting hand. Chords are most often shown using *chord diagrams*. A chord diagram is like a picture of the fretboard that shows which strings, fingers, and frets are used to make the chord. To the right is a diagram for a C chord, with a little tour to show you around.

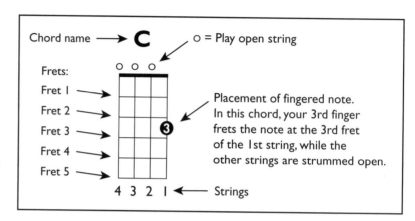

READING A CHORD CHART

You can learn songs using *chord charts* written in *slash notation*. The chord chart shows which chords to play and when to change them. Each slash indicates one beat in a steady rhythm. The *beat* is the steady pulse of the music. Imagine marching military style, counting steps 1, 2, 3, 4, with each step in the same rhythm. That's the same as keeping a beat in music. The beats in the example below are grouped in *measures* (or *bars*) of four beats. Vertical *bar lines* mark the measures. The *final double bar line* at the end indicates that the song is over and it's time to get a drink. Try strumming this example using your C chord. Keep a steady beat by counting out loud and strumming at the same time.

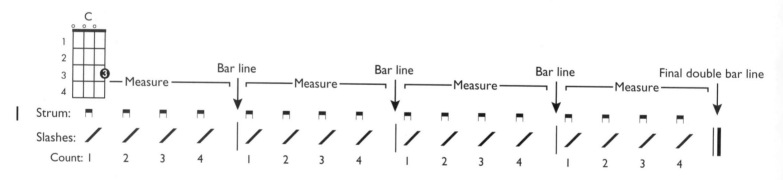

Here's another one that lets you switch between your C chord and the C6 chord made by the open strings. Switch to C6 in measure 3. The two dots before the double bar tell you to repeat the song.

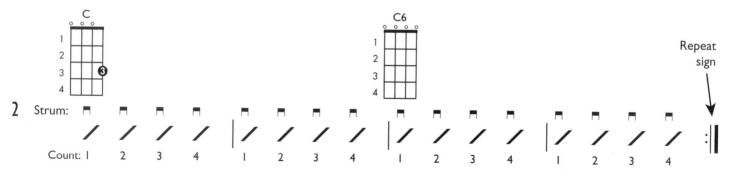

NEW CHORDS: F AND G7

Below is a reminder for C and C6, and, also, two new chords to try: F and G7. The F chord uses two fingers, and the G7 uses three. Practice making them over and over, and switching between them. Strum them normally, but also remember to pick each string individually to make sure all the notes in the chord ring out. Sometimes, you'll find one of your fingers is touching an open string, or that a bad note is hiding among the good ones. (Bad notes are sneaky.)

C 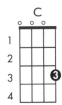   C6 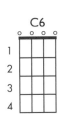   F 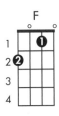   G7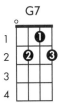

It might help to talk through each chord diagram out loud, one string at a time. For instance:

For the G7 chord, you have:
1st string, 3rd finger, 2nd fret
2nd string, 1st finger, 1st fret
3rd string, 2nd finger, 2nd fret
4th string, open

TOTALLY AWESOME PRACTICE STRATEGIES FOR LEARNING NEW CHORDS

The "Squeeze and Relax" Trick

A great way to help get a new chord shape into your muscle memory is to try these steps.

1. Form the chord as perfectly as you can, making sure all the notes ring out.
2. Instead of moving on to another chord, just relax the pressure of your fingers *without lifting them off the string.* This gives you a rest from squeezing but lets you stay on the same chord.
3. After relaxing the pressure for a second or two, press the notes back down ("squeeze") and strum the chord again. Beware that fingers may have shifted slightly between squeezings and you may have to correct their positions.
4. Repeat the squeeze/strum and relax steps several times before changing chords. You won't notice a big difference right away, but each time you revisit the chord with this process, it will get easier and easier.

Switching Chords in Pairs and the Two-Pronged Strategy

Once the individual chords start to get easier, you can begin to work on switching them in pairs. Start with C and F. A good strategy is to use two different types of practicing:

- *Slow Motion Practicing:* Play the first chord, then figure out where each finger needs to go for the second chord. Practice going back and forth slowly, without rhythm, teaching your fingers to move together to the new chord.
- *Practicing in Rhythm:* After you've done the slow motion practice for a few minutes, try counting a slow, steady beat and play two measures of each chord as shown on the next page. Repeat the progression over and over so that you practice switching both to and from the new chord.
- *Use both approaches each time you practice!* Even though it won't be smooth at first, you'll see improvement over a few practice sessions with this two-pronged approach and a bit of patience. You can work on several pairs of chords in each practice session. It will keep you from getting bored with just two chords, and before long, you'll be switching like a pro.

Following are three pairs of chords you can practice. Usually, a repeat sign means "repeat just once," but you should repeat these examples several times. Treat each example like it is a longer song made of just two chords. Count out loud so you know exactly when to change chords.

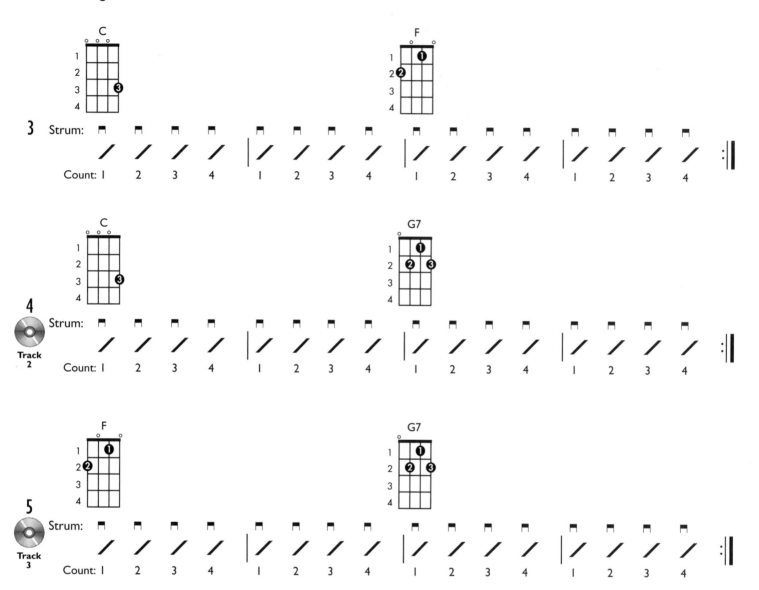

When you have the two-chord examples above going fairly smoothly, try this progression using all four chords.

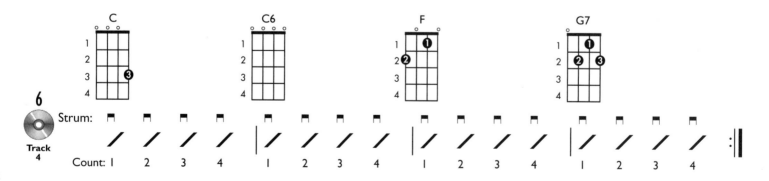

Here are a couple of full-sized songs you can use to practice your C, F, and G7 chords and your strumming. It might help to count the beats out loud the first few times through. Then, later, you can try adding the words. In these songs, the words can be sung on the same beats you strum, though not every strum is going to have a word. Soon you'll be able to loosen up the phrasing of the words, while still keeping a steady beat with the strums.

OH! SUSANNA

Track 5
Track 6: Chords Only
Track 7: Melody Only

Stephen Foster
(1826–1864)

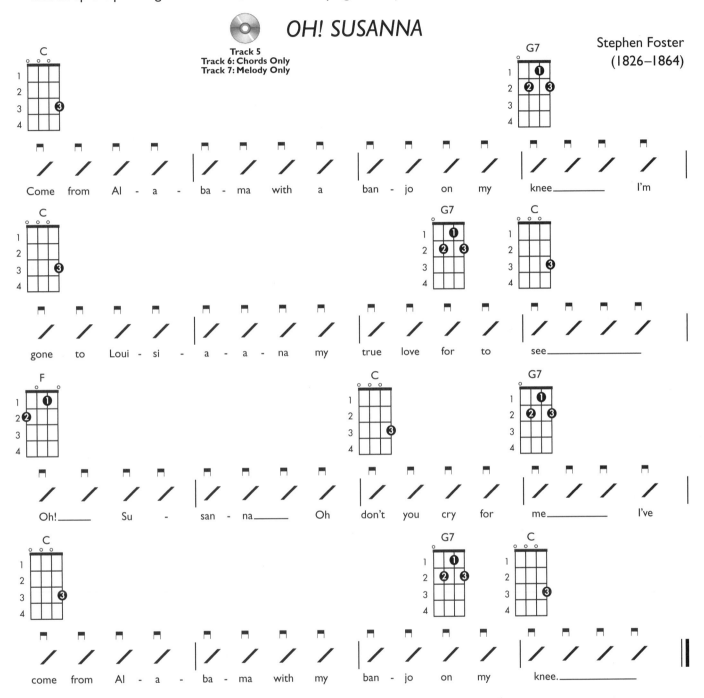

WHAT KEY ARE WE IN?

Both of the songs in this lesson are in the key of C. The *key* of a song is named after the note or chord upon which the music *resolves,* or comes to rest, called the *tonic note* or *tonic chord.* Songs don't always begin on the tonic chord, but they often end on it. Imagine that a passage of music is like going on a walk and a key is like a neighborhood. The tonic note or chord is like "home." You may go away from home and come back many times, but eventually you are likely to return home and stay. In these songs, "home" is the C chord. You can test this by playing the song, and then trying one of the other chords at the end. In the key of C, only the C chord will make the song sound finished or complete.

WHEN THE SAINTS GO MARCHING IN

Track 8
Track 9: Chords Only

Key: C

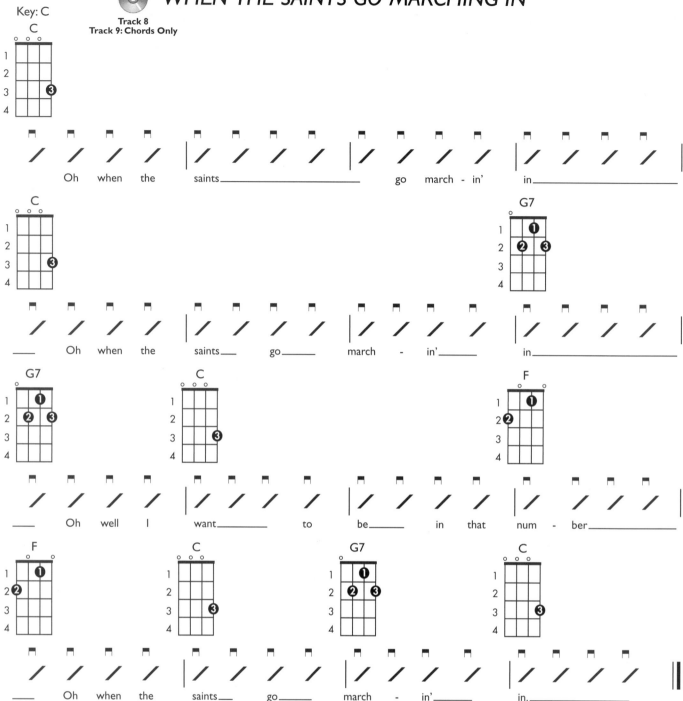

Oh when the saints _____ go march - in' in _____

Oh when the saints ___ go ___ march - in' ___ in _____

Oh well I want ___ to be ___ in that num - ber _____

Oh when the saints ___ go ___ march - in' ___ in. _____

TIPS FOR PLAYING AND SINGING

Notice in this song that the first word is on beat 2 of the bar. This is true for each of the four lines. When you play and sing, sometimes you'll play and sing together; other times you'll be strumming without words to keep the beat. If you count out the measures and study the music, you'll always know what beat to come in on.

In recent years, the ukulele has become an instrument of choice for songwriters and performers who share their music through Internet video sites like YouTube. **Julia Nunes** *(b. 1989) began posting songs from her room at home in 2007. Her originals and distinctive covers have generated millions of views.*

PHOTO BY GAGE SKIDMORE

20   Beginning Ukulele

Now that you are comfortable with at least a few basic chords and can keep a steady beat, you can shift your attention from your left hand to your right hand and begin refining your strumming technique.

Here are some things to keep in mind when working on your strumming:

• Keep your wrist loose and your arm and fingers relaxed. This is a hallmark of ukulele style!

• Resist the urge to tighten up your muscles as you play faster. Slow the beat down so you can stay relaxed.

SUPER UKE TIP

To become a truly good uke player, you must develop an internal sense of rhythm that is steady and predictable. The best way to do this is to tap your foot on the beats and count out loud. Practice slowly and synchronize the movements of your right hand with the tapping and counting. As you get better, work with a metronome (see page 97) to further solidify your beat.

RHYTHMIC NOTATION

The following examples introduce *rhythmic notation*. This is a common way to show strumming rhythms when a specific rhythm is called for, without having to show every note of the chord. Rhythmic notation differs from standard notation (see Chapter 3) in that the note values are indicated with slashes or diamond shapes instead of circles.

QUARTER NOTES

You've already learned that the beat is the steady pulse that remains constant throughout a passage of music, and that beats are grouped into measures. You've been playing in measures of four beats, which is such a common division of beats that it is known as *common time*. In common time, each beat of the four beats is one quarter of the whole measure, so we call all notes that last one beat *quarter notes* (even when they're not in common time).

Quarter Note

SIGNS OF THE TIMES: THE TIME SIGNATURE

At the beginning of a piece of music, you will see what looks like a fraction. This is a *time signature*. The top number 4 indicates four beats per measure. The bottom number 4, like a fraction, can be understood as "fourths" or "quarters." The $\frac{4}{4}$ time signature means "four quarter note beats in every measure." Sometimes, $\frac{4}{4}$ is shown as $\mathbf{C}$ for "common time."

Time Signature

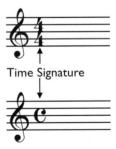

PLAYING QUARTER NOTES

Below are two bars of quarter notes in rhythmic notation. Play a C chord just as if the quarter notes were slashes.

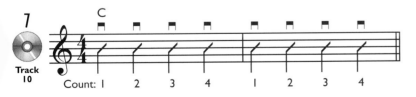

EIGHTH NOTES

If you divide a quarter note into two equal pieces, you get *eighth notes*. In notation, a single eighth note looks like a quarter note with a flag attached to the stem. When eighth notes appear in groups (often in groups of two or four), they can be *beamed* together. In counting, we want to preserve the same beat and counts we used for quarter notes, so we insert the word "and" in between the numbers to indicate the second possible eighth note of each beat. ("One and two and three and four and," or "1 & 2 & 3 & 4 &.")

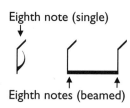

Eighth note (single)

Eighth notes (beamed)

STRUMMING EIGHTH NOTES

When strumming eighth notes, strum down on all numbered beats and up (away from the floor) on all the "&'s." This will get you moving in a steady, alternating down-up motion that you will use to learn new strums. It will probably work best to use your right-hand index finger to strum both down and up. Here are two measures of eighth notes for you to count and strum. Note the repeat sign!

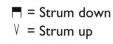

⊓ = Strum down
V = Strum up

8

Track 11

SUPER UKE TIP

Repeat this sentence to yourself and make it your rule for strumming:

   "Down on the numbers, up on the 'ands!'"

Use this rule even if you are playing quarter notes and not hitting the strings on the "&." You can tap your foot the same way. Tap down on the number and move the foot up on the "&."

MIXING IT UP

Below is a great sounding strum for lots of songs. You'll want to practice this one over and over with all of your chords until it feels natural. Make sure you keep the eighth notes equal in length; it's easy for them to become uneven.

9

Track 12

Note that it helps to count the "&'s" that are part of the quarter notes even though you're not playing them. This will keep your rhythm more steady and will remind you to move your hand up on the "&" so you will be ready for the next down.

When you're comfortable with the example above, go back to the songs in the previous lesson and apply this strum pattern to each measure.

INTRODUCING G, D, D7, A, AND A7

You've already learned G7—now you can learn G, which, coincidentally, looks like G7 upside down on the fretboard. G is a simpler sounding major chord and can be used in place of G7 in many circumstances.

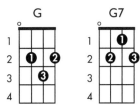

The D chord is shown with two fingerings. Many chords can be played in different ways depending on the needs of the situation. Start with a fingering that works for you, then learn other fingerings later. The second fingering of D uses the 1st finger across three strings to make a *barre* (see page 67). To make a barre, you have to use the flat underside of your finger instead of the tip. D7 is also shown with two fingerings.

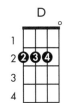 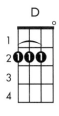 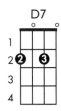 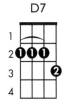

To the right are the A and A7 chords. A7 has two fingerings. As with D7 above, the two fingerings actually produce different arrangements of the notes in an A7 chord, so they are referred to as different *voicings*.

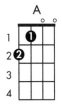 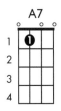 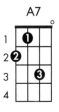

Here's a practice song you can use to work on your new chords. This song uses D, G, A, and A7, and is in the key of D. Notice how the music comes to rest on the tonic chord of D at the end. You can also try using the alternate fingerings for D or A7 shown above.

 MY DEAR, DEAR MAMA FROM MADEIRA

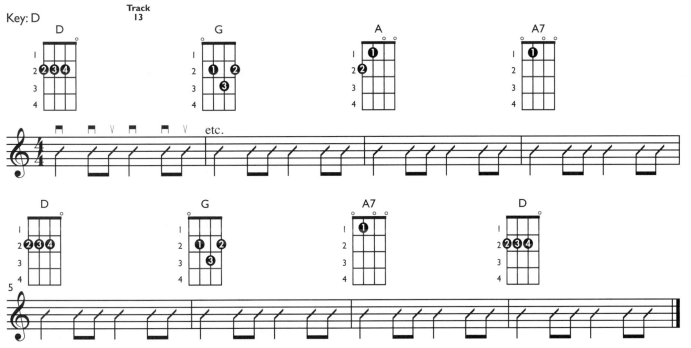

Below are the chords for the traditional Hawaiian song "Wai O Ke Aniani (Crystal Water)." This song is in the key of G. It is popular with players of the *Hawaiian slack-key guitar style*, which involves special tunings and fingerstyle techniques and is sometimes accompanied by ukulele. Slack-key master Gabby Pahinui recorded this song in the 1940s, and many other artists have recorded it since then. "Wai O Ke Aniani" has different melodies for the verse and chorus but the chord progression is the same.

To get even more out of practicing this song, you can also try it with the alternate fingering of D7, or you can play either fingering of the D chord in place of the D7.

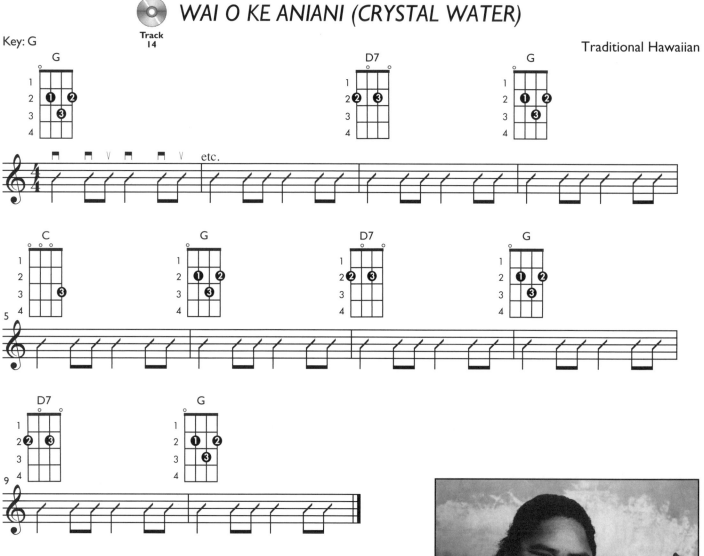

WAI O KE ANIANI (CRYSTAL WATER)

Key: G

Track 14

Traditional Hawaiian

Israel "IZ" Kamakawiwo'ole (1959–1997) was known to his fans as "Bruddah Iz." He inspired new interest in ukulele music with his 1993 interpretation of "Over the Rainbow/ What a Wonderful World," which became a worldwide hit in the 2000s. In 1976, Iz co-founded the Makaha Sons of Ni'ihau, a band focused on bringing traditional Hawaiian music to a modern audience. Iz was much beloved for his tenor voice and tireless devotion to preserving Hawaiian cultural memory and independence through music.

LESSON 6: MINOR CHORDS

The chords you have learned so far are called "major" chords. They can be described as having a bright, happy sound because of the way the notes relate to each other. As you have seen, chord symbols for major chords are simply the letter name of the root. Any chord that is marked *min* is a *minor* chord. Minor chords have a darker or sadder emotional quality. You will learn more about the structures that create these sounds later.

Below are the minor chords that can be played in *open position* on the ukulele. (Open position refers to the open strings plus the first four frets.) In the case of Cmin, the first fingering is more common; the second fingering is shown if you have trouble barring your finger at first. To play the second fingering for Cmin, you have to mute the 2nd string (indicated by the "x"). You can do this by leaning your 2nd finger at a slight angle so that part of the finger touches the 2nd string to keep it from ringing. Use whichever Cmin works best for you.

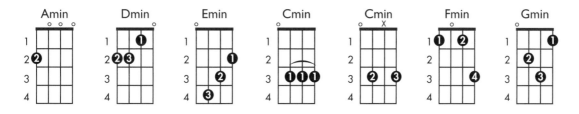

Try "It's Only a Minor Inconvenience" to get familiar with Amin, Dmin, and Emin. You'll notice a couple of new things.

- The chord diagrams are not shown. Many chord charts for songs only show the names of the chords. It's time to make sure you are memorizing new chords so that you know them whether or not the diagram is shown!

- There is a new strum pattern to try: three quarter notes and two eighths (down, down, down, down-up).

IT'S ONLY A MINOR INCONVENIENCE

Track
15

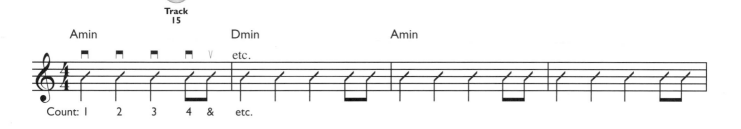

SUPER UKE TIP: IT'S OK TO LEAVE EARLY!

Have you noticed that when you're strumming, it's hard to change to a new chord on time? This is especially true if the strum pattern has an eighth note at the end (on the "&" of 4). Experienced strummers have a way to deal with this. You can lift your left-hand fingers up on the last upstroke in the strum pattern and move toward the new chord. That way you will be able to place your fingers on the new chord at the next downstroke. You will hear your upstroke striking the open strings as your fingers move. This may sound a little strange all by itself, but in the flow of the rhythm, it's so short that it becomes masked by the sound of the real chords. You may want to strum a little lighter on that last upstroke so that the open strings don't get as much emphasis.

Here's what it would look like if we added a diagram for the open chord in the strum you learned on page 25. Think of it not as a distinct chord (technically it's a C6) but as a transition chord.

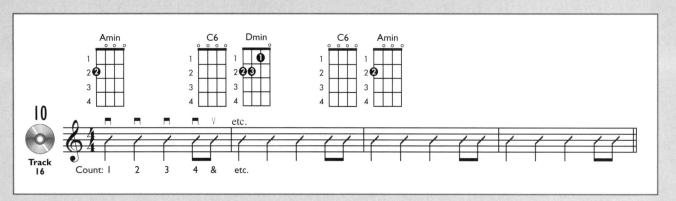

The rule to remember is this: It is more important to get to the next chord on time than it is to hold the current chord through the last eighth note. Of course, if you can do both, that's even better!

Here's one more progression to try using Cmin, Gmin, Dmin, and Fmin. Don't forget your new trick (above) for switching chords on time.

◊ = *Half-note strum.* One strum rings out for two beats.

LESSON 7: WALTZ TIME $\frac{3}{4}$

Waltz time is another name for $\frac{3}{4}$ time. This means there are three beats in every measure and the quarter note gets one beat. First, familiarize yourself with the feel of three beats per measure by counting and tapping your foot for a few bars.

12

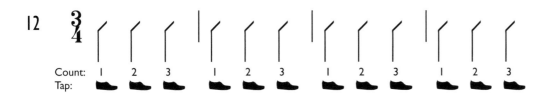

There are a variety of ways to strum in $\frac{3}{4}$ time.

13

Track 18

Waltz Strum No 1:

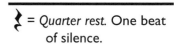

ξ = *Quarter rest.* One beat of silence.

14

Track 19

Waltz Strum No. 2:

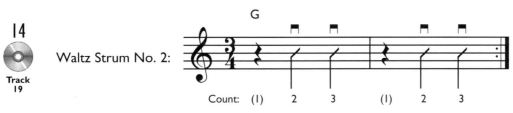

15

Track 20

Waltz Strum No. 3:

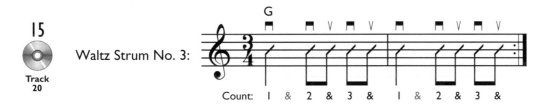

The gentle roll of waltz time can be particularly beautiful and lyrical. One of the most famous songs in $\frac{3}{4}$ is "Amazing Grace." Practice the chords using any of the strums on the previous page. You can also try the melody, which is shown in standard notation and TAB. You may have an easier time learning the melody if you come back to it after you've worked through Chapter 3. This arrangement of "Amazing Grace" is in the key of G. If you need to, you can simplify the chords by playing D instead of D7, and G instead of G7.

PICKUPS

The melody of "Amazing Grace" has two eighth notes before the first full measure. This is called a *pickup*. The two eighth notes that begin "Amazing Grace" are counted as beat 3 of an empty (or count-in) measure. The value of the pickup is then subtracted from the last measure. Sometimes it helps to count a waltz in with two measures. Count "1, 2, 3, 1, 2" and begin playing on beat 3. If you are strumming chords, wait until beat 1 of the first full measure (after the pickup notes) to come in with your strum pattern.

INTRODUCTION TO DOTTED HALF NOTES

Additionally, notice that the melody contains dotted half notes () in measures 7 and 15. These last for three beats. For more on dotted half notes, see page 35.

AMADING GRACE

Track 21
Track 22: Chords Only

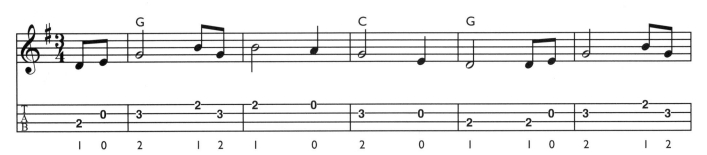

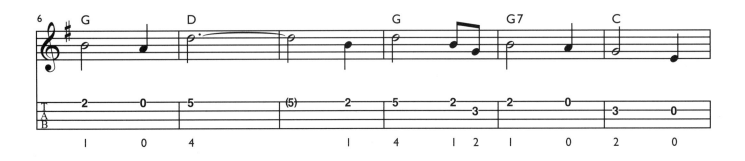

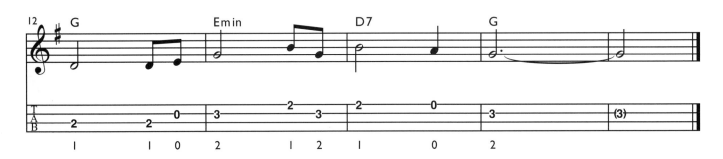

Check out the *Intermediate Ukulele* volume in this method. You'll revisit "Amazing Grace" with alternate chords and learn how to make a solo arrangement of it.

Now that you've had some experience playing the ukulele, it's time to look at the tools we can use to produce different sounds. Here are the main options used by most players:

- Index finger (usually labeled *i*)—using downstrokes and upstrokes
- Thumb (labeled *T*)—using downstrokes and upstrokes
- Combination of *i* and *T*.
- Fingerstyle—using thumb (*T*), index (*i*), middle (*m*), and ring (*a*) fingers.
- Pick—either a guitar-style plastic pick, or a hardened felt ukulele pick. Other materials are available, like wood and leather.
- Some fingerstyle players use a thumbpick and/or fingerpicks so they can achieve the brightness and volume of picks with the agility of fingerstyle.

Fingerstyle.

Thumbpick and fingerpicks.

Guitar-style pick.

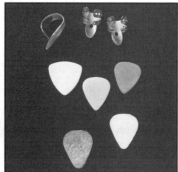
Thumbpick, fingerpicks, guitar picks, and felt ukulele picks.

HOW TO HOLD A PICK

Place your right-hand thumb across the top of the pick, with the point at a 90-degree angle from your thumb. Then, curve your index finger behind the pick, holding it between your thumb and the side of the first joint of your index finger. Your other fingers can curl into your palm or hang loosely. Just keep them relaxed. If the pick moves around too much when you play, hold it a little closer to the point.

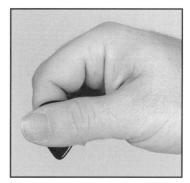
The correct way to hold a pick.

REST STROKES AND FREE STROKES

There are two main ways to strike a string with the thumb, fingers, or pick. Strumming is usually done with free strokes, while melodies can be played with either free or rest strokes.

Free strokes are the type of strokes you probably have already been using (whether you know it or not). The pick, thumb, or finger strikes the string (or strings) in an uninterrupted motion, either with a downstroke or upstroke. With a free stroke, the string vibrates in a more lateral motion*, roughly parallel to the top.

With a *rest stroke*, the thumb, finger, or pick strikes the string and then comes to rest on the next string that falls in its path (or simulates this motion if there is no string to rest on). Rest strokes cause the strings to vibrate in a motion that is more perpendicular to the top. This transmits more vibration to the bridge and creates a full, round, and sometimes louder tone. Rest strokes with the thumb are used by traditional Hawaiian thumb-style players to get an amazing tone out of the tiny ukulele.

* Technically, the string vibrates in an elliptical or oval pattern that is wider near the middle of the string.

Try any technique you are exposed to. You will find different techniques and tools have different applications in the music you play. Following are the pros and cons of some of the tools discussed in this lesson. Most of this section will work with most styles, though some techniques are more specific.

TOOL	PROS	CONS
Index finger only	• Easy to keep track of • The fingernail gives the downstroke brightness and definition • Can be easily blended with thumb techniques and fingerpicking • Bright sound that projects well	• Can get fatiguing in long, loud jam sessions if you're not careful • Downstroke and upstroke have different tonal qualities due to the fingernail
Thumb only	• Gives a softer, mellower sound with a big, round tone • Thumbnail can add brightness • Easily blended with finger techniques	• Downstroke and upstroke have different tonal qualities due to the thumbnail
Index finger and thumb, or fingerstyle: thumb, index, middle, and ring	• Provides a variety of tonal combinations • Experienced players are able to play with a great deal of speed using the combination of index and thumb • New techniques like triple strums and rolls become possible • See page 89 for more info	• Takes more practice and coordination to get used to • Sacrifices some of the volume and projection that is possible with a pick (in order to gain more tonal color and nuance)
Pick (see below for specific types)	• Easy to strum for long periods of time with a steady, even tone • Upstrokes and downstrokes have very similar tone and projection • Ample volume and bright tone	• More difficult to integrate with finger techniques • Some specialized uke techniques are not possible with a pick
Guitar-style pick (hard plastic or similar)	• Brightest and loudest tone • Readily available • Many shapes, sizes, varieties, and thicknesses • Thin picks make a softer, brighter tone; thick picks make a fuller, louder tone	• Tone may be more brittle or thin sounding than finger/ thumb techniques, especially on single notes
Felt "uke" picks	• Made of thick, rigid felt • Softer tone than guitar picks • Over time, the felt becomes more flexible and develops a sound that is similar to strumming with the index finger	• Harder to find in music stores, though still widely available • New picks need some break-in time (keep track of your "good one!")
Thumbpick and/or fingerpicks	• Adds the volume, crisp tone and agility of a pick to the thumb technique • Thumbpick with bare fingers is a good compromise between the pick style and fingerstyle	• Requires quite a bit of practice to become proficient • Fingerpicks, especially the more common metal ones, can sound too bright and harsh on nylon strings

CHAPTER 3

Reading Standard Music Notation

This chapter will provide a quick introduction to reading standard music notation in the 1st position of the ukulele fretboard. You may want to work with this chapter at the same time as you are learning to strum the chords and melodies in Chapters 2 and 5. This will add variety to your practice and keep things interesting. Also, you will be improving in several areas at once, instead of one at a time. Most examples in this chapter do not have tablature, but TAB is used throughout the rest of the book. You do not have to master reading standard music notation in order to work on the other chapters, since TAB is always present.

Reading standard music notation is a rewarding skill that is easier to develop than most people think. It enhances tablature and chord charts by allowing you to read exact rhythms, vocal melodies, and music for other instruments. Even the most basic understanding of the notes of the staff (Lesson 1, below) will give you a point of departure for the concepts introduced later in this book.

LESSON 1: THE NOTES AND THE STAFF

We use five horizontal lines as a sort of playing field for our notes. This is called the *staff*. The *natural notes* (notes without sharps or flats) are placed on the lines and spaces of the staff. Lower notes are near the bottom of the staff, higher notes are near the top. A *clef* sign at the beginning of the staff indicates which notes are represented by which lines and spaces. When the *G Clef* (𝄞) sits on the second line from the bottom of the staff it is called *treble clef*. The line it encircles in the large, lower part of the symbol is called G.

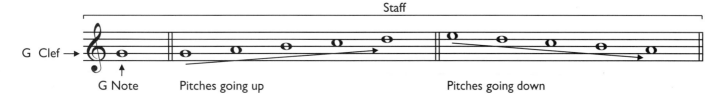

Now that you know the second line from the bottom is G, all the other notes can be related to that line. For example, the space under it is F, the note before G in the musical alphabet. The space above the G line is A, the next note in the musical alphabet.

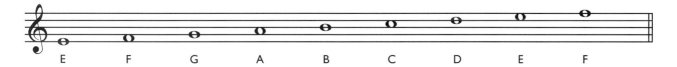

LEARNING THE NOTES ON THE STAFF

If you forget everything else, remember that the G clef encircles the line used for the G note. There are other memory devices you can use to quickly learn all the notes on the staff. One is to separate the notes on the lines from the notes in the spaces. The notes on the lines give you the first letter of each word of this sentence: "**E**very **G**ood **B**eginner **D**oes **F**ine." The notes in the spaces themselves spell the word "FACE." Memorize these and you won't get lost on the staff.

Every Good Beginner Does Fine   F   A   C   E

LESSON 2: THE NATURAL NOTES ON THE 3RD AND 2ND STRINGS

Reading notes on the staff is easier when you learn just a few at a time. Your first notes are on the 3rd and 2nd strings, using your 1st, 2nd, and 3rd fingers. The example below shows where the notes are located on the staff and ukulele. Notice that the C note appears on a *ledger line*. Ledger lines are additional lines that allow us to extend the range of the staff. The D note is in the space below the bottom line of the staff.

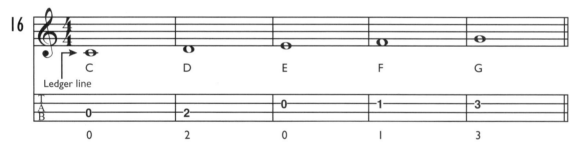

You can play melody notes by plucking them with your thumb or index finger, using either downstrokes or upstrokes. If you are using a pick, play these notes with downstrokes.

As mentioned on the previous page, this chapter will focus on reading notes only on strings 1, 2, and 3. The 4th string is tuned to a high-G note, one whole step below the open A of the 1st string (see About the 4th String on page 9). At first, the 4th string can add a lot of confusion to reading music, since it provides new options for fingering notes found on the first three strings. It is easier if you put off incorporating the 4th string until you can read fluently on the other three. Try the following exercises.

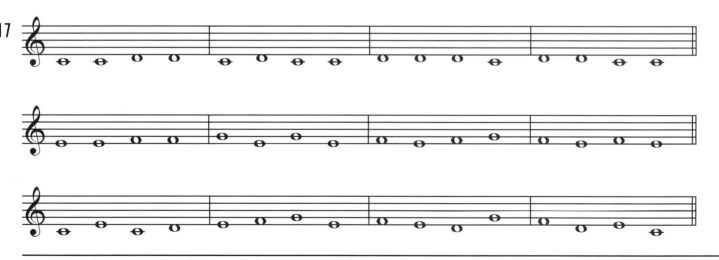

LESSON 3: TIME

In Chapter 2, you learned a bit about how rhythm is counted and notated. This lesson will review that information as it applies to reading melodies.

BEATS AND MEASURES

The *beat* is the steady, even pulse that remains constant throughout a passage of music. Musicians count beats and divide them into small groups. As you know, a group of beats is called a *measure*. Measures can consist of any number of beats. It is most common to have four beats in a measure. Measures are marked on the staff using *bar lines*. For this reason, measures are also called *bars*. A *double bar* indicates the end of a piece or section.

SIGNS OF THE TIMES

The *time signature* tells you how many beats are in a measure and which type of note will be used to count the pulse of the beat. It is found at the beginning of the piece, or wherever there is a change in time signature within the piece. The upper number indicates the number of beats per measure. The lower number shows what type of note is one beat. The lower number will very often be a 4, indicating that the quarter note (as in the fraction "one fourth") gets one beat.

THE LONG AND SHORT OF IT

The *value* of a note is its duration (in beats). The appearance of a note tells you its value. Following are three note values and their durations.

The *whole note* gets four beats. In a measure of four beats, the whole note lasts for the whole measure. When you play a whole note, make sure it rings for the whole four beats. Counting out loud and tapping your foot to the beat will help. Try these whole notes.

Whole note

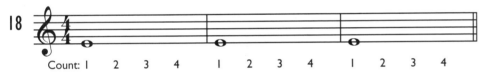

The *half note* lasts for two beats, or, half of a measure of four beats. In a four-beat measure, the half notes start on beats 1 and 3. The half note looks like a whole note with a stem. Normally, notes on or above the middle line of the staff have their stems going down, and notes below the middle line have their stems going up.

Half notes

The *quarter note* lasts for one beat. It looks like a half note that has been filled in.

Quarter notes

Try these half-note and quarter-note combinations. Don't forget to count!

NOTE ABOUT TEMPO
Division of the measure into whole, half, and quarter notes does not affect the speed of the beat itself. The rate of the beat is called tempo and is expressed in beats-per-minute (bpm). For example, a tempo of ♩ = 60 indicates 60 quarter-note beats per minute, or one beat per second.

Here is a tune to play using the notes you have learned. Start with a slow tempo and read the rhythm along with the notes. Don't wait until you've learned the notes to figure out the rhythm! By the time you learn just the notes, you may have accidentally made up a new rhythm that you'll have to unlearn. A good approach is to clap or tap out the rhythm of the tune before you even start on the notes.

GO TELL AUNT RHODY

Track 23

LESSON 4: RESTS

Silence is as important a part of music as sound. The symbols that represent silence are called *rests*, and just like notes, they are divided into wholes, halves, and quarters.

A *whole rest* is four beats of silence. It looks like a small rectangle that hangs like a full suitcase from the fourth line of the staff.

A *half rest* is two beats of silence. It is a small rectangle that sits like a hat on the third line of the staff.

A *quarter rest* is one beat of silence. It looks a bit like a bird flying sideways, if you use your imagination.

Whole rest

Half rest

Quarter rest

SUPER UKE TIP
Rests must be "played" with the same precision and intention as pitches. To play a rest, you must stop the string or strings from ringing, either by using your right-hand picking finger or thumb, or by lifting up a fretted note with your left-hand finger to stop the sound.

The following example uses some of the notes and rests you've learned. Can you play them perfectly?

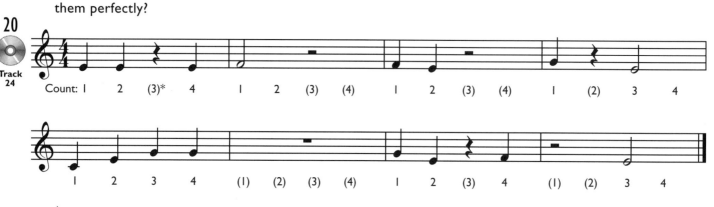

Track 24

* The counts in parentheses indicate rests.

LESSON 5: DOTTED HALF NOTES

A *dot* placed after a note head increases its duration by half of the note value. For example, a normal half note lasts for two beats. Half of that value is one beat, so if we add a dot to a half note, it will last for three beats (2 + 1 = 3).

Dotted half note

The traditional song "When the Saints Go Marching In" will give you a chance to work on your notes and rhythms, including quarter rests and dotted half notes. Chords are also shown so you can strum.

 WHEN THE SAINTS GO MARCHING IN

Track 25
Track 26: Chords Only

MORE ABOUT DOTTED NOTES
On page 38, you will learn about dotted quarter notes. Every type of note can be dotted to increase its duration by half of its original value. Even rests can be dotted!

LEGATO AND STACCATO
When you play melodies, each note should last for its full duration. The sound should not stop until the next note (or rest) sounds. This type of note articulation is called legato, *which comes from the Italian for "linked together." Legato is not usually indicated in the music, it is assumed. The alternative to legato is* staccato, *which means that the notes are detached. Staccato is indicated by dots that appear above or below the note head, opposite the stem. Do not confuse staccato dots with rhythmic dots, which appear to the right of the note head.*

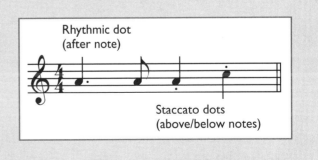

Rhythmic dot (after note)

Staccato dots (above/below notes)

LESSON 6: NATURAL NOTES ON THE 1ST STRING

Below are the notes on the 1st string followed by an exercise. (In the exercise, watch out for a note that snuck in from the 2nd string.) Memorize these notes and add them to your collection. You'll be using them all soon!

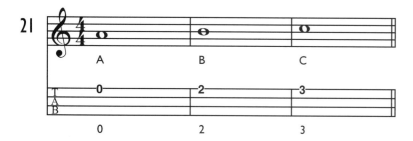

LESSON 7: THE C MAJOR SCALE

A *scale* is a collection of notes used to make melodies and chords. Each scale derives its sound and character from the interval relationships (distances measured in steps) between the tonic note and the other scale notes (for more on intervals, see page 45). The *major scale* has a familiar sound often heard as "Do Re Mi Fa Sol La Ti Do," or in the song "Do-Re-Mi" from *The Sound of Music*.

The major scale has seven notes (eight if you include the return to the tonic note at the end of the scale). It begins on the tonic note, then follows this step pattern to generate the other notes: whole–whole–half–whole–whole–whole–half. By always using this pattern, the major scale can be played in all the keys made possible by the 12 notes of the chromatic scale. In the key of C (using C as the tonic note), the major scale consists of the natural notes—the same notes you have learned in the 1st position of the first three strings. Below is the C Major scale, shown both ascending (going up) and descending (going down), also with the note names and steps.

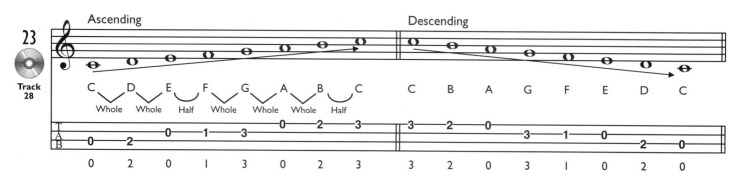

Take some time to practice and memorize the C Major scale. Say the note names out loud, both ascending and descending. What goes up must come down! You should also memorize the formula of steps to make major scales: whole–whole–half–whole–whole–whole–half.

LESSON 8: EIGHTH NOTES (OF COURSE)

As you learned on page 22, the quarter note can be divided into two *eighth notes*, each lasting half of a beat. Single eighth notes have a *flag* attached to the end of the stem opposite the note head. Groups of eighth notes are often *beamed* together. An eighth rest looks like a slash with a small flag waving from it and lasts for half a beat.

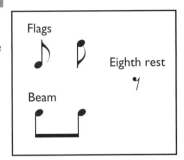

We can organize our note and rest values into a "tree" to help visualize the relationships.

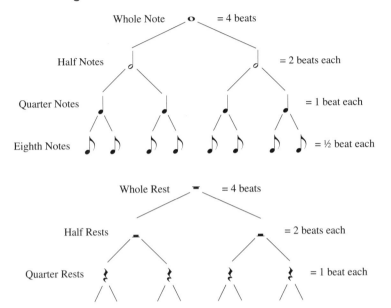

COUNTING EIGHTH NOTES

As you learned on page 22, eighth notes are counted "1 & 2 & 3 & 4 &." The numbered beats are often called *onbeats* or *downbeats,* and the "&'s" are often called *offbeats* or *upbeats.* While counting and playing eighth notes, tap your foot down on the downbeats and move it up on the upbeats.

PLAYING EIGHTH NOTES

When strumming all (or most) of the strings on the uke, it helps to stick with the alternating down-up rhythm you learned on page 22. Remember the Super Uke Tip: "Down on the numbers, up on the &'s!" The way you play eighth notes in single-note melodies depends on the right-hand technique you have chosen.

- If you are used to strumming chords with your index finger or a pick, follow the same "down on the numbers, up on the &'s" motion you would use for strumming chords.

- If you are playing thumb-style, use your thumb (*T*) for downstrokes on the downbeats. Use the index finger (*i*) to play the &'s with upstrokes. If the tempo isn't too fast, you can also use thumb downstrokes on the &'s.

- If you are using your index finger (*i*) in an upstroke, or plucking/fingerpicking motion to play the downbeats, then try using your middle finger (*m*) to play the &'s. This resembles the technique used by classical guitarists and electric bass players.

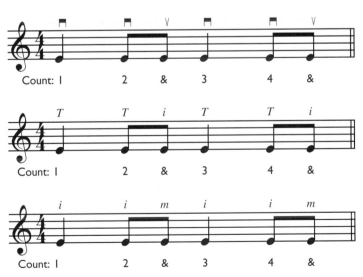

Here's a little exercise to practice your eighth notes. Most of the time, the pieces in this book won't indicate how to play the eighth notes in melodies since there are several good approaches. Choose the technique that works best for you and try to keep it consistent.

LESSON 9: DOTTED QUARTER NOTES

In Dotted Half Notes on page 35, you learned that a dot placed after a note head increases the duration by half of the original note value. A quarter note equals one beat. Half of that value is half a beat (equal to an eighth note), so a *dotted quarter note* equals one and one half beats (1½ beats). Dotted quarter notes very often are paired with an eighth note or eighth rest, either before or after the dotted quarter. This creates a grouping of notes that adds up to two beats.

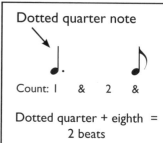

Here is the familiar Beethoven melody "Ode to Joy." Look at each line before you start, and look for the dotted quarter and eighth-note rhythms. Each line creates a four-measure *phrase*, which is like a musical sentence. (For more on phrasing, see page 93.) Four-measure (as well as two-measure and eight-measure) phrases are very common and can help you identify patterns in the music. This melody is easier to learn if you practice the C Major scale (page 36) before you start. All of the notes in this piece are in the C Major scale.

Track
30

ODE TO JOY
Theme to the Ninth Symphony (Opus 125)

Ludwig van Beethoven
(1770–1827)

ACCIDENTALS DO HAPPEN

Once you have become familiar with reading the natural notes, adding the accidentals
(sharps and flats, see page 13) is simple. Here's a quick review:

Symbol	Name	Description
♯	Sharp	Raises a natural note by one half step (one fret).
♭	Flat	Lowers a natural note by one half step (one fret).
♮	Natural	Cancels a sharp or flat—play the natural note.

In written music, a sharp, flat, or natural will appear just to the left of the note it affects.
When you say the note name out loud, say the letter first.

Say: "A-sharp   G-flat   A-natural"

ACCIDENTALS LAST FOR THE REST OF THE MEASURE
*When a sharp or flat appears on a note, that note remains affected by the sharp or flat until
the end of the measure. In other words, a sharp or flat can be canceled only by a natural or
a bar line.*

Here's a tune that will give you a chance to practice reading accidentals. You may need a
little help finding the new notes at first so the TAB is also shown.

RAISED BY GYPSIES

Track
31

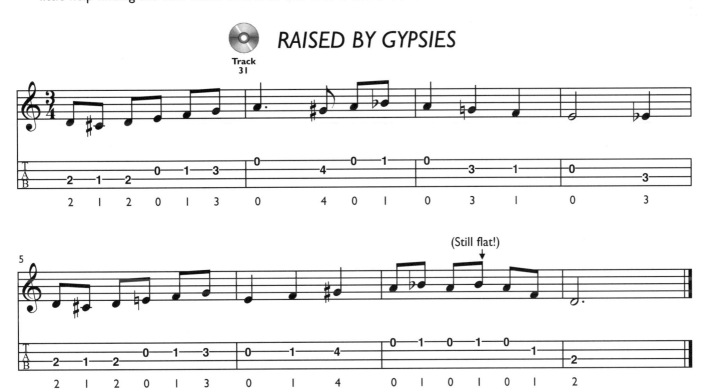

(Still flat!)

LESSON 11: ACCIDENTALS IN A KEY SIGNATURE

Most pieces of music have a *key* (see page 19). The key is named after the *tonal center* or *tonic* note. The tonic note is the first note of the scale for the key and the note that gives the strongest feeling of resolution or completion. Every major scale has its own unique set of notes, some of which may be sharp or flat. The *key signature* allows us to easily show which sharps or flats are in the key without cluttering the piece with accidentals.

A key signature appears just after the clef sign at the beginning of each line of music. It is a set of sharps or flats (never both). You will learn more in Chapter 4 about where key signatures come from and which keys they represent. If you see no key signature, it just means that the notes of the piece will all be natural notes, as in the key of C Major.

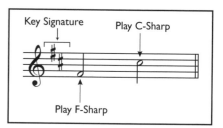

Reading a key signature is very simple. Look just to the right of the clef sign. Any sharps or flats that appear will affect that pitch throughout the entire piece of music. For instance, the key signature in the example to the right has an F♯ (F-sharp) and a C♯ (C-sharp). This means that *all* of the F notes and *all* of the C notes will be sharped unless marked with other accidentals.

IMPORTANT NOTE
Accidentals in key signatures affect the notes in every octave, not just the line or space on which the accidental appears.

Try reading through the classic cowboy song "Red River Valley," below. The key signature contains one flat, B♭ (B-flat), which is the signature of F Major. The notes affected by the key signature have been circled to remind you that they are flatted, but this is just to help you out this one time! TAB is also included.

 RED RIVER VALLEY

Track 32

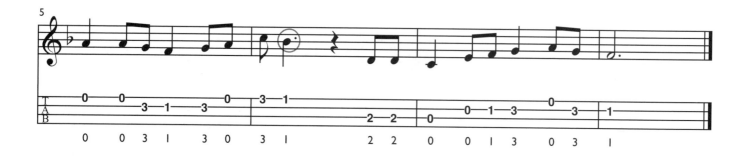

LESSON 12: TIES

A *tie* combines two note values (on the same pitch) so that they are expressed as one note lasting for the combined duration of the two values. For example, in the example to the right, the third note is tied to the fourth note. You would play the third note, but not the fourth note, since it is *tied to* (and therefore part of) the third note. Hold the third note through its own value *and* the value of the note it's tied to.

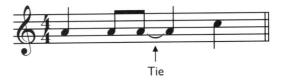

Tie

One way to remember how to handle ties is "play the first note and hold through the second note." Ties can bind together two note values within a measure, or they can cross the bar line so that a note that begins in one measure can last into the next measure.

Below is an exercise to work on reading ties and a new key signature. "King on the Beach" is in D Major, which contains F♯ and C♯. This time, you're on your own to make sure to find all the notes affected by the key signature. The TAB will help you catch any mistakes.

KING ON THE BEACH

Track 33

MORE ABOUT TIES

Ties connect notes of the same pitch. If you see an arc shape that looks like a tie but the connected notes are different, it's called a *slur*. Slurs do not change the rhythm, they affect the way you articulate the notes on the instrument. You'll learn about slurs on the ukulele later. An arc shape above the staff is a *phrase mark* (page 93).

Ties are sometimes used in situations where a simpler note value might make the rhythm harder to read. For example, a dotted quarter (1½ beats) might be followed by a note that lasts for one beat. It would seem sensible to write a quarter note for the second note, but it is more clear to write the second note as two eighths tied together (see right). This preserves the convention of each dotted quarter pairing with an eighth, making it easier to quickly understand the rhythm.

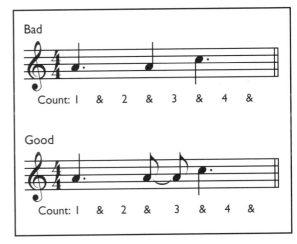

The following short piece contains some devices that allow a longer musical idea to fit into a shorter space on the page. The repeat sign at the end of the fourth bar tells you to repeat from the beginning. The *first ending* (measures 3 and 4) indicates the music you should play on the first time through. The *second ending* indicates that on the second time through, you should play the second ending instead of the first ending.

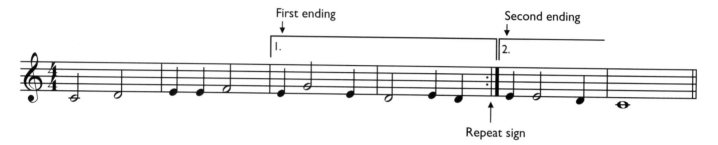

The markings above tell you to follow these steps:

1. Play measures 1 through 4 as normal.
2. Repeat from the beginning, playing measures 1 and 2.
3. At measure 3, skip over both measures 3 and 4 (the first ending), and, instead, play the second ending (the last two measures of the tune).

Following are a few other markings you might see as you become more advanced. They are provided as a reference. Like many musical markings, they originate in Italian terms.

D.C.	D.C. stands for *Da Capo*, Italian for "from the head." It tells you to repeat the whole piece of music from the beginning.
D.S. 𝄋	D.S. stands for *Dal Segno* (pronounced "sane-yo"), meaning "from the sign." D.S. tells you to look for the special sign (shown at left) earlier in the music and repeat the music from that point.
al Fine	*Fine* (pronounced "fee-nay") means "the end." *Al Fine* can be added to D.C. or D.S. Repeat the piece as indicated by D.C. or D.S., but end your second pass through the piece at the end of the measure marked "*Fine*."
al Coda 𝄌	A *coda* (meaning "tail") is new music added to the end of a piece. *Al Coda* can be added to D.C. or D.S. Repeat the piece as indicated by D.C. or D.S. up until you see the first coda symbol (shown at left). At this point, jump to a later point in the music marked with the second coda symbol and continue from there.

The markings above all require you to jump from one section of the written music to another without interrupting the flow of the music. Always check out a piece of music before you start playing it, looking for repeats, endings, and other similar directions. You may need to plan out where the "jumps" are, and even highlight them on the music so you know where to go ahead of time.

CHAPTER 4

Theory Without Fear, or A Little Knowledge Can Get You Jamming

THEORY IS GIVING NAMES TO SOUNDS

This chapter will give you some basic theory tools to accelerate your learning, jamming, and improvising. In music, *theory* is the collection of terms and concepts used to describe musical sounds and how they interact. Learning theory will not ruin the spontaneity and creativity of your playing—theory doesn't tell you how to play, it just tells you how to describe it.

LESSON 1: THE MAJOR SCALE IS YOUR MEASURING STICK

TWO FOUNDATIONS: THE CHROMATIC SCALE AND THE MAJOR SCALE

The foundations of music theory in the Western, or European, tradition are the chromatic scale and major scale. The chromatic scale, or music alphabet (see page 13), gives us the 12 tones in each octave on our instrument. If you're still shaky on the chromatic scale, go back and learn it by heart before proceeding.

The major scale gives us a very common set of notes and relationships we can use to make music. We also use the major scale as a "standard of measurement" to compare all the other scales to, much like we would compare a prize-winning giant cucumber to a ruler to see how long it was. Below is the C Major scale you learned on page 36. The notes can be numbered 1–7, with the 8th note being the same as note number 1 in the next octave. These numbers are called *scale degrees*.

25

Note:	C	D	E	F	G	A	B	C
Scale Degree:	1	2	3	4	5	6	7	8(1)

```
T
A                                      0    2    3
B           0    2    0    1    3
        0   2   0   1   3   0   2   3
```

THE SECRET FORMULA

The C Major scale is made by playing the natural notes C–D–E–F–G–A–B–C. You know from the music alphabet that there is a half step between B and C, and also between E and F. All of the other letters are a whole step apart. In terms of scale degrees, the half steps are between notes 3 and 4, and between notes 7 and 8 (which could also be called note 1). This gives us the series of whole steps and half steps that make every major scale. To the right is the C Major scale with the intervals and scale degrees shown.

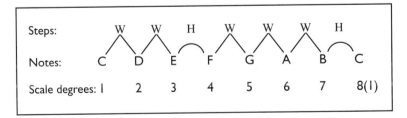

Steps:	W	W	H	W	W	W	H
Notes:	C	D	E	F	G	A	B	C
Scale degrees:	1	2	3	4	5	6	7	8(1)

W⋀ = Whole step

H⌒ = Half step

With careful use of the formula, you can *spell* (apply the formula of whole steps and half steps) the major scale starting on any note. Just start with the key note (1st scale degree) and then follow the formula, using each letter only once. The D Major scale is shown below. Notice that to make E to F a whole step, as the formula requires, we must raise the F a half step to F♯. Try spelling the A and B♭ Major scales (the correct answers are underneath the Hot Tips box below).

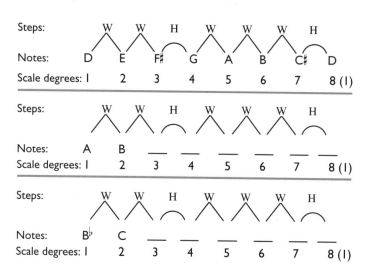

Steps:		W		W		H		W		W		W		H	
Notes:	D		E		F♯		G		A		B		C♯		D
Scale degrees:	1		2		3		4		5		6		7		8 (1)

Steps:		W		W		H		W		W		W		H	
Notes:	A		B		__		__		__		__		__		__
Scale degrees:	1		2		3		4		5		6		7		8 (1)

Steps:		W		W		H		W		W		W		H	
Notes:	B♭		C		__		__		__		__		__		__
Scale degrees:	1		2		3		4		5		6		7		8 (1)

HOT TIPS

1. Use every letter in the musical alphabet once, in alphabetical order.
2. The last note is the same as the first.
3. You will need to use either sharps or flats (never both) to make the notes fit the formula.

Answers:

Scale degrees:	1	2	3	4	5	6	7	8 (1)
Notes:	B♭	C	D	E♭	F	G	A	B♭

Scale degrees:	1	2	3	4	5	6	7	8 (1)
Notes:	A	B	C♯	D	E	F♯	G♯	A

Try playing the A Major scale by going up the 1st string. Playing the scale on a single string makes it easy to see the whole steps and half steps. When you get comfortable with it, try going backwards! You will learn other fingerings for major scales in different keys later in this book.

26
Track 34

Note:	A	B	C♯	D	E	F♯	G♯	A
Scale Degree:	1	2	3	4	5	6	7	8(1)

```
T|--0-----2-----4-----5-----7-----9-----11----12--
A|------------------------------------------------
B|------------------------------------------------

   0     1     3     4     1     3     4     4
```

LESSON 2: THE CIRCLE OF 5THS

The *circle of 5ths* is like the "secret agent decoder ring" of music theory. (And you don't have to send in any cereal box tops to get it!) A *5th* is the distance between the 1st and 5th degrees of a scale. To make a circle of 5ths, just take the keys and arrange them in a circle so that the next keynote (going clockwise) is the 5th degree of the last scale. For example, the 5th degree of a D Major scale is A, so the next key in the circle is A.

The circle of 5ths makes it easy to learn the key signature for each key. The "sharp keys" (clockwise on the circle) add one sharp for each new key. The new sharp is always the 7th scale degree of that key. The "flat keys" (counterclockwise) add one new flat for each key. That new flat is always the 4th scale degree of the key.

Notice that the keys of G♭ and F♯ are in the same position in the circle. The two scales are played on exactly the same strings and frets and sound exactly the same. Remember, when two notes have the same sound but different names, they are *enharmonic equivalents*.

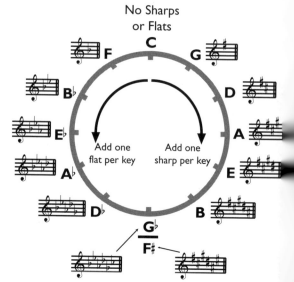

No Sharps or Flats

Add one flat per key   Add one sharp per key

44   Beginning Ukulele

LESSON 3: INTERVALS ARE YOUR BUILDING BLOCKS

Along with the music alphabet and the major scale, *intervals* are a fundamental element of music theory. An interval is the distance between two notes, measured in steps. You've already worked with a couple of intervals: the half step (known in interval lingo as a *minor 2nd*) and the whole step (*major 2nd*).

HOW INTERVALS ARE NAMED

Interval names include a number (like 2nd or 3rd) and a word that describes the interval's *quality* (major, minor, augmented, diminished, or perfect). The number describes how many steps, or letters in the music alphabet, are spanned by the interval. The quality helps describe the interval more precisely. The distance in an interval is always calculated from the lower of the two pitches to the higher.

THE INTERVALS IN ONE OCTAVE AND HOW TO PLAY THEM

Because of its unique reentrant tuning, there are many ways to play the various intervals on the ukulele. You will encounter many of them as your learning progresses. The important thing right now is that you become familiar with the naming system for intervals and their sounds. A simple way to do this is to use the 4th string (G) as a constant root note and making the intervals above G on the 2nd and 1st strings. Here are all the intervals in one octave using G as the lowest note (or root). The note names are shown above the music. You can play the intervals *harmonically* (together, as shown) or *melodically* (one note after the other). After you have tried them out, you will learn about the different types.

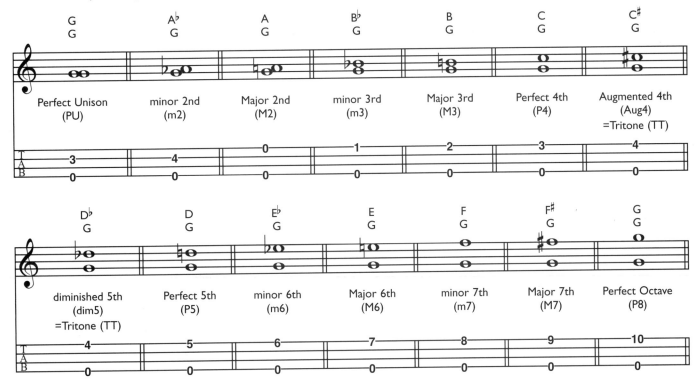

THEORY TIP

The intervals shown above are arranged from the smallest to the largest, with the augmented 4th and diminished 5th producing the enharmonic names of the same note (C♯ and D♭). It's a great idea to memorize the names of the intervals in ascending order as well as their half steps. The chart on the next page shows the intervals and half steps.

The chart to the right shows the intervals and their abbreviations from smallest to largest by half steps.

PERFECT INTERVALS

There are only four intervals in an octave that are described as *perfect*. They are the unison, the 4th, the 5th, and the octave (or PU, P4, P5, and P8). These intervals do not come in major and minor versions (see below). When the two notes of a perfect interval are played together on a well tuned instrument, they resonate with great clarity, like a camera lens that is in perfect focus.

MAJOR AND MINOR INTERVALS

The following intervals come in major or minor versions: 2nds, 3rds, 6ths, and 7ths. In the case of any one of these intervals, the *major* interval is larger, or farther apart, by one half step. The *minor* interval is smaller, or closer together, by one half step. The abbreviations for major intervals use an uppercase "M," while the minor intervals use a lowercase "m." The major and perfect intervals correspond to the steps in the major scale (see below).

Interval	Abbreviation	Half Steps
Perfect Unison	PU	0
minor 2nd	m2	1
Major 2nd	M2	2
minor 3rd	m3	3
Major 3rd	M3	4
Perfect 4th	P4	5
Augmented 4th (or Tritone)	Aug4 or TT	6
Diminished 5th (or Tritone)	dim5 or TT	6
Perfect 5th	P5	7
minor 6th	m6	8
Major 6th	M6	9
minor 7th	m7	10
Major 7th	M7	11
Perfect Octave	P8	12

AUGMENTED AND DIMINISHED INTERVALS

All types of intervals can be augmented or diminished. To augment means to add to or make bigger. An *augmented* interval is one half step larger than a major or perfect interval. To diminish means to make smaller. A *diminished* interval is one half step smaller than a minor or perfect interval.

THE TRITONE (AUGMENTED 4TH/DIMINISHED 5TH)

Between the perfect 4th and perfect 5th is an interval called a *tritone* (abbreviated TT). "Tone" is another word for whole step, so, a tritone equals three whole steps (equivalent to six half steps). In the interval naming system, a tritone is either an augmented 4th (one half step larger than a perfect 4th) or a diminished 5th (one half step smaller than a perfect 5th). Both the augmented 4th and the diminished 5th refer to the same distance of six half steps.

INTERVALS OF THE MAJOR SCALE

You can use the major scale as a reference for your intervals. To make a major scale, use only the perfect and major intervals. You can then find the minor intervals by lowering any major interval by one half step. Below are the intervals of the G Major scale. The upper notes show the scale, while the lower note remains G throughout to show the interval distances from the tonic.

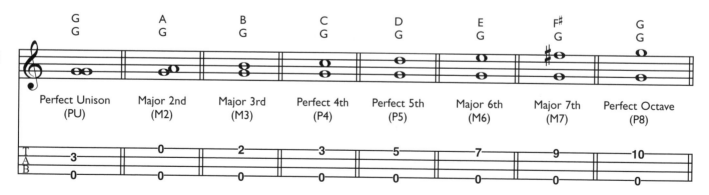

28

Remember, a chord is any three or more notes played together. The subject of chords and how they behave is called *harmony*. The most basic kind of chord is called a *triad*. A triad is a three-note chord, generally made by stacking one interval of a 3rd on top of another. You have already learned several major and minor chords, and some 6th and 7th chords. The major and minor chords are triads (sometimes with a note repeated if you are strumming all four strings). The 6th and 7th chords have four notes.

Below is a C Major scale that has been *harmonized*. This means that 3rds have been stacked above each note of the scale to form triads. The harmony notes are all within the scale—no sharps or flats have been added or changed. This is called *diatonic harmony,* or harmony within the key. TAB has been included so it will be easy for you to hear what the harmonized scale sounds like. You can also play the chords using any other familiar fingerings. You will find three types of triads: major, minor, and diminished, which are all discussed below.

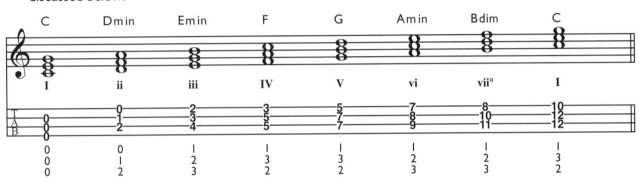

Notice that the chords have been designated with Roman numerals. This allows for a distinction between scale degrees and chord numbers. The Roman numerals also show the quality of the chord (uppercase for major chords, and lowercase for minor and diminished chords). Diminished chords are also labeled with a small superscript circle (as in B°).

Roman Numeral Review

I or i.............. 1	V or v............ 5
II or ii............ 2	VI or vi.......... 6
III or iii.......... 3	VII or vii....... 7
IV or iv.......... 4	

THREE KINDS OF TRIADS
The three types of triads that result from harmonizing the major scale are all made with different combinations of major and minor 3rds.

- A *major triad* is a major 3rd with a minor 3rd on top. Its structure is root–3rd–5th.

- A *minor triad* is a minor 3rd with a major 3rd on top. Its structure is root–♭3rd–5th.

- A *diminished triad* is a minor 3rd with another minor 3rd on top. Its structure is root–♭3rd–♭5th.

For comparison, this example shows the three types of triads, all built on a C root.

TRIAD STRUCTURE
The bottom note of the triad is the *root*. The root is always the note the chord is named for. The middle note, which is a 3rd above the root, is called the *3rd*. The top note, which is a 3rd above the 3rd and a 5th above the root, is called the *5th*.

5th
3rd
Root

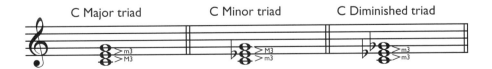

THREE PRIMARY CHORDS

The *primary chords* in every major key are the I, IV, and V (one, four, and five) chords.

Here is a C Major scale with the roots of the I, IV, and V chords circled.

Below is a chord progression using I, IV, and V. The key of C Major is indicated. Also try it in D and G. Use any chord fingerings or strum patterns you like.

Key of C Major

Key of D Major
Fill in the blanks. The answers are at the bottom of the page.

Key of G Major
Fill in the blanks. The answers are at the bottom of the page.

THE TRIUMPHANT RETURN OF THE CIRCLE OF 5THS

The circle of 5ths can be used to show basic harmonic movement. Instead of keys, these are major chords. Box or circle any three adjacent chords. The one in the middle is I. The one going clockwise is V. The one going counterclockwise is IV.

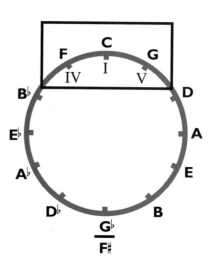

Answers:

Key of D: D G A
         I IV V

Key of G: G C D
         I IV V

CHAPTER 5

Old-Time Ukulele and Backing Up Fiddle Tunes

Old-time music is an American traditional style based on fiddle tunes and songs that were played for dances and parties in the late 1800s and early 1900s. The roots of the music are in tunes that have been played for hundreds of years in Europe and the British Isles, mixed with influences from Africa, Native Americans, and immigrant cultures. Old-time music is one of the roots of more recent styles like bluegrass and Americana.

Old-time music is a community music and lots of fun to play along with. Sometimes a picking session is just a few people, but some jams can get very large with many fiddles, banjos, and guitars. The portability and unique voice of the uke have made it an adopted member of the old-time family. The banjo uke (see page 8) is a particular favorite in old-time jams because it is louder and more percussive than wooden ukes, but you can play with any type of uke.

The role of the uke in an old-time jam is generally as part of the rhythm section (along with guitars and upright basses). Since the uke is high pitched and has little sustain, it projects best when strumming chords in a steady rhythm. The constant, repetitive groove made by the rhythm section provides a foundation for the fiddles, banjos, and mandolins to play syncopated melodies against.

THE COMMON FIDDLE KEYS

The fiddle is a central instrument in old-time music. The keys of C, G, D, and A allow the fiddle to make use of its open strings for extra harmony notes, and so these keys have become the most common keys for tunes. This chapter will focus on playing in D, G, and A, since you've already played several songs in C. It's a good idea to memorize the primary chords (I, IV, and V) for these common keys. That way, when someone tells you the key for a tune, you'll have at least an idea of what some of the chords might be. The chart to the right shows what you need to know.

KEY	I	IV	V
C	C	F	G or G7
G	G	C	D or D7
D	D	G	A or A7
A	A	D	E or E7

PHOTO BY JOE DEL TUFO

Jeff Claus—of the Ithaca, New York band The Horse Flies—helped spark new interest in using the banjo uke to accompany old-time music starting in the mid-1980s. The Horse Flies play traditional acoustic fiddle tunes with drive and momentum, but they are also known for using echo and wah effects to create minimalist soundscapes reminiscent of composer Steve Reich, and for their influences of punk, indie, and new wave.

You can use your index finger to strum old-time music. Let your strumming motion come from a loose, relaxed wrist and fingers. Many uke players who play old-time music like to use a pick instead. A long high-energy jam can really wear down your fingernail if you're not careful. See page 29 for more on picks. Here are a couple of strums that work well for old-time uke. The first one ought to be pretty familiar by now! Try each one many times over using different chords.

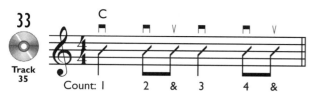

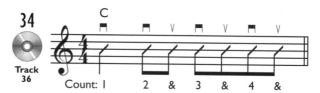

Below are the chords to a classic old-time and bluegrass song also known as "Nine Pound Hammer" or "Roll On, Buddy." Try it with the second strum shown above, or mix up the strum patterns. Stay loose, because these tunes can get pretty fast in jam situations! This tune is in the key of G. The chords are G (I), C (IV), and D (V).

 ## THIS HAMMER'S TOO HEAVY

Track 37

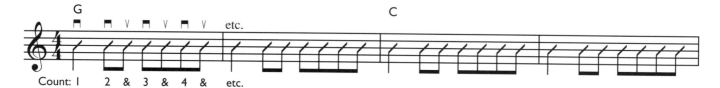

C TUNING OR D TUNING?

You can ignore this box and lead a happy uke life, but if you're curious about tunings, read on. This book is written for ukuleles tuned G–C–E–A, also known as C or C6 tuning. Some players like to tune a whole step higher to A–D–F♯–B. This is known as D or D6 tuning. Here's where it helps to know the I, IV, and V chords in common keys. In D tuning, just transpose the chord shapes for each key down a whole step from what you normally use in C tuning.

For example, if you were playing in the key of D in standard C tuning, your chord shapes would be D (I), G (IV), and A (V). If you were playing in the key of D in D tuning, your chord shapes would be fingered like C, F, and G in C tuning. The D tuning is a whole step higher, so the corresponding chord shapes are a whole step lower.

You can simulate this on a standard tuned uke by placing a capo (a device that clamps the strings down to a fret) at the 2nd fret. Some players also like the D tuning because it puts more tension on the strings, giving the uke an even brighter, snappier tone when strummed.

LESSON 2: ACCENTING THE BACKBEAT, THE E AND E7 CHORDS, AND *SALLY ANN* IN A

One way to inject more propulsion into the old-time groove is to accent the backbeat.
An *accent* (>) is a musical symbol that tells you to play a note or chord louder than the
surrounding notes. Many grooves in blues, jazz, rock, bluegrass, and old-time are based on
a four-beat rhythm pattern: bass note or kick drum on beats 1 and 3, and a high-pitched
sound like a snare drum or guitar chord on 2 and 4. Beats 2 and 4 in this rhythm are called
the *backbeat*. This rhythm has its roots in the basic foot-stomp and handclap rhythm that
accompanied spirituals and work songs sung by Africans in America during the era of slavery.
The backbeat rhythm became the heartbeat of many styles of music.

Try the following strum using a medium volume for most of the strokes and a louder strum
on beats 2 and 4. You can achieve this with a stronger snap of the wrist, or by flicking your
finger a little more forcefully. If you're using a pick, hold the pick a little tighter on the
accent beats and you'll hear them pop out.

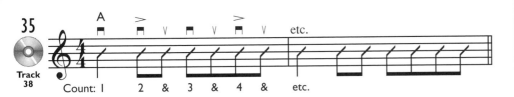

Here are the chords to "Sally Ann" in the key of A, using the accented
backbeat strum. "Sally Ann" has two sections, the A part and the B part.
Each part is repeated, and the whole tune can be played many times.
Note the *right-facing repeat* at the start of the B part; it tells you that the
repeat at the end of the B part (*left-facing*) begins here.

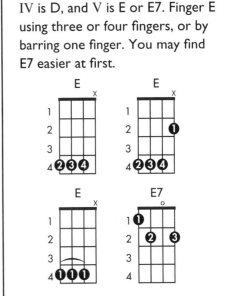

In the key of A, I is an A chord,
IV is D, and V is E or E7. Finger E
using three or four fingers, or by
barring one finger. You may find
E7 easier at first.

SALLY ANN

Track 39

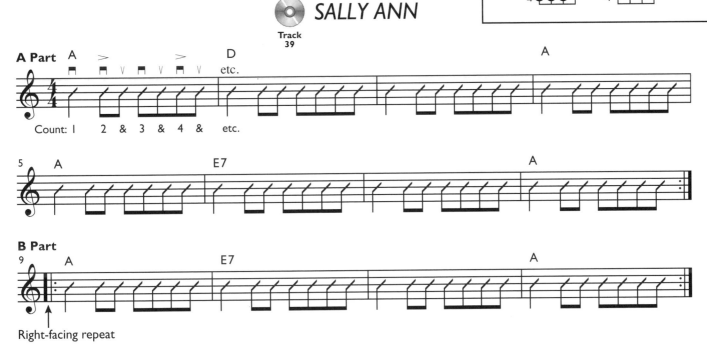

Right-facing repeat

LESSON 3: FIDDLE TUNE FORM AND *SOLDIER'S JOY* IN D

Form is the internal structure that repeats (or cycles through a series of sections) to make up a piece of music. One of the most common forms in old-time music is the *two-part fiddle tune*. This form is known in classical theory as a *binary form*. The two main sections of the tune are labeled the A part and the B part. Each part is repeated before moving on. The basic form of the tune can be described as "A A B B." This form is then repeated over and over for as long as the group wants to jam on it.

One of the oldest and most popular tunes in the repertoire is "Soldier's Joy" in the key of D. The I, IV, and V chords are D, G, and A respectively. Don't forget to repeat both the A part and the B part. The melody is a little tricky to play on the uke, but a simplified version is shown with TAB if you want to try it (pay close attention to the fingering shown below the TAB!). On the video, you'll hear the melody played by the fiddle, as well as a bass line to give you the feel of a real jam. Use any of the patterns from this chapter to strum.

SOLDIER'S JOY

Track 40
Track 41: Backing Track

CHAPTER 6

Old School: The Swingin' Ukulele

The first big wave of international popularity for the ukulele came in the early decades of the 1900s. During this same period, various streams of popular music—including parlor songs of the 1800s, ragtime, marching band music, and blues—were combining and evolving into jazz. The jazz and swing band music heard on the radio and in dance halls was sophisticated and virtuosic, requiring experienced musicians and a lot of practice. When the ukulele came along, it offered the average person an accessible way to capture some of the energy and rhythm of a swing band. The uke was relatively inexpensive and you could carry it to the college pep rally in the pocket of your oversize fur coat (an essential fashion item of the time).

TIN PAN ALLEY AND HAPA HAOLE

The fad of the ukulele and Hawaiian music (or semi-Hawaiian music) took over the 1920s, and many modern uke enthusiasts still play the songs and styles that evolved during this era. A major source of material in this period were the writers and publishers of sheet music for popular songs. This industry was based in New York City and is referred to as "Tin Pan Alley." The Tin Pan Alley writers worked night and day to create new songs that could be sold to a public that was hungry to join whatever fad was hot at the moment. They created hundreds of songs that combined Hawaiian words, fake Hawaiian-sounding language, and humorous or romantic themes in English set to the popular swing rhythms of the day. These mixed-language songs became known as *hapa haole* songs, where *hapa* (pronounced HAH-pah) means half, and *haole* (pronounced HOW-leh) means non-native or Caucasian.

LESSON 1: HOW TO SWING

The basis of swing and jazz music is a way of counting and feeling the underlying beat of the music. You have already played music with eighth notes, so you know that eighth notes divide the beat into two equal pieces. This type of eighth notes is called *straight eighths*.

There is another way to count eighth notes called *swing eighths*. In swing eighths, the onbeat is given longer emphasis while the offbeat ("&") is made shorter. In straight eighths the beat is divided into two equal pieces. In the swing feel, the pulse of the beat is divided into three pieces, or eighth-note triplets. To count triplets, try saying this aloud to a steady beat: "Tri-pul-let, tri-pul-let."

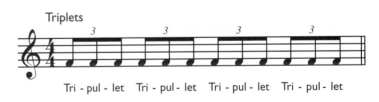

In swing eighths, the first two notes of the triplet are tied together, so that you don't hear an individual note on the second eighth. In the swing feel, this rhythm happens so much that it becomes unwieldy to write and count full triplets all the time. Instead, the swing-eighths rhythm is counted as if it were eighth notes with an onbeat that is twice as long as the offbeat.

Swing eighths are designated at the beginning of a piece of music in one of two ways (see right). If you see either designation, it means all eighth notes in the piece are to be "swung."

Grab a C chord on your ukulele and try strumming and counting some swing eighths. This next example introduces a new symbol called the *simile mark*. It looks like a slash with a dot on either side. The simile mark tells you to duplicate whatever you were doing in the previous measure. In the following examples, it tells you to continue the same strumming pattern.

Now try your trusty quarter-and-two-eighths strum using the swing-eighths feel. This makes a great strum for swing tunes. Try it with different chords or make up some progressions.

I SEE YOU'VE GONE STACCATO

Here's a nifty way to put a little jump in your swing strum. You have already learned a bit about legato and staccato (page 35). Remember, legato means the notes are held for their full duration, which is the normal, or "default," way that we play notes and chords. Staccato means the sustain of the note or chord is cut off early, resulting in a "clipped" sound for that beat. You can play a staccato chord by relaxing the pressure of the fretting fingers just after you strum the chord. Don't take them all the way off the strings. Technically, this is not full staccato, because the open strings in the chord will still be ringing, but it is enough to give a nice texture to the groove.

Try the following strum on a G chord with staccato chords on beats 1, 2, and 3. Staccato is indicated with a dot above or below the note head, opposite the stem. Use the squeezing and relaxing pressure of your left-hand fingers to create the staccato. You can also throw in staccato notes to other strum patterns.

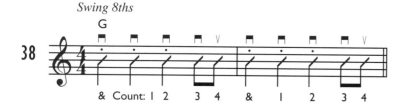

JAZZY PROGRESSIONS NEED JAZZY CHORDS

One of the most recognizable characteristics of jazz and swing is the use of chords that move beyond the three notes of the triad. As soon as a fourth note is added to a chord, it becomes more colorful and complex.

6TH CHORDS

As you have learned, a major triad consists of a root, 3rd, and 5th, corresponding to the first, third, and fifth notes of a major scale. If you add the sixth note of the major scale to the triad, you get a *major 6th chord*. An example (shown on the right) is the C6 chord, which contains the notes C, E, G, and A (root, 3rd, 5th, and 6th).

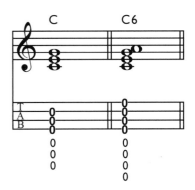

Below are fingerings for 6th chords based on the major chords you have learned. As you learn each one, try alternating the 6th chord with the corresponding major chord. This will help you see the similarity and hear the difference between them.

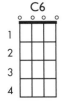 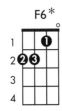 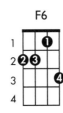 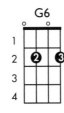 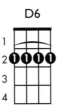 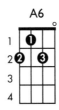 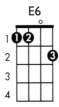

Try the progression below. It may look difficult to switch chords every two beats, but if you look carefully you will notice that you only have to move one or two fingers in each bar to make the change. It's very common to use 6th chords alternating with major or 7th chords to give melodic motion within one basic chord. Remember that you can lift on the last upstroke of the bar in order to move to the next chord in time.

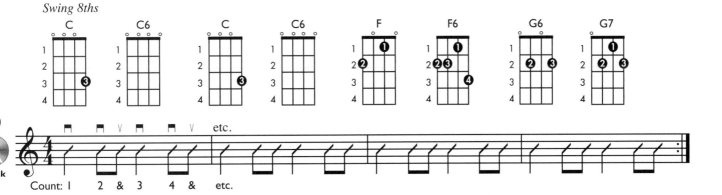

* This F6 should remind you of Dmin, because it has the same notes! A full F6 chord contains F, A, C, and D. This fingering only contains F, A, and D, which also make up a Dmin chord. This fingering for F6 is shown here because it is easy to get to from the familiar two-finger F chord. On the uke, it is not uncommon to have chord voicings that leave out a note or two from the full versions of the chords. The next F6 contains all of the notes in the chord.

The next progression gives you a chance to try out D6, A6, and E6 from the previous page. If D6 gives you trouble as a one-finger barre chord (see page 67 for tips), you can try fingering the normal three-finger D chord you've been using and add the 4th finger on the 2nd fret of the 1st string to make it D6. This progression uses the staccato strum you learned in the previous lesson. It works well here because these chords have few open strings, making it easier to hear the staccato notes cut off as you relax the pressure of your fingers.

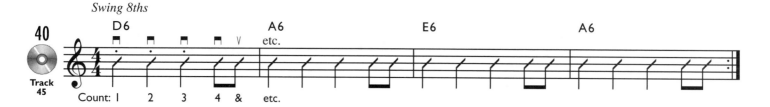

DOMINANT 7TH CHORDS

A *7th chord* is made by stacking another 3rd on top of a triad (root–3rd–5th–7th). There are several types of 7th chords. The type you are going to learn first is called a *dominant 7th chord*. The dominant 7th chord is a major triad with a minor 7th (♭7) added. The chord symbol for a dominant 7th chord consists of a root note followed by the number 7 (as in G7). For example, the G7 chord contains the notes G–B–D–F (root–3rd–5th–♭7th).

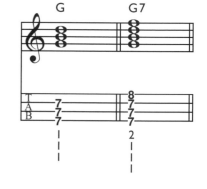

You have learned many of these dominant 7th chords already, but here they are for review. A few have multiple fingering/voicing options. You'll be using some of these dominant 7ths in the next lesson, so make sure you can do at least one fingering for each.

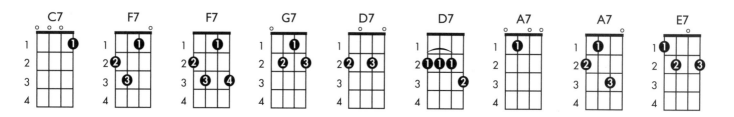

"DOMINANT" IS ANOTHER WORD FOR THE V CHORD

The name *dominant* refers to the 5th note (or V chord) of a major scale. The dominant 7th chord is the type of 7th chord that occurs on the V chord in a major key. For example, the G7 chord discussed above is the V chord of the key of C Major, and all of its notes are found in the C Major scale.

Dominant 7th chords can be used as the V chord of a major key, but they can also be used to add additional color to major triads. Sometimes it sounds great, other times it adds too much color to the chord. The best approach is to try it and see if you like it. Here's a tip if you're overwhelmed by learning lots of chords at once: In any situation that calls for a 6th chord or dominant 7th chord, you can play the plain major chord instead. The major triad is part of each of these chords, so all you would be doing is leaving a note out. No problem!

LESSON 3: THE CIRCLE OF 5THS PROGRESSION

The roots of jazz are in *ragtime*, a popular form of music in the late 1800s and early 1900s. Ragtime was known for its syncopated rhythms, catchy tunes, and virtuosic performers. One of the most common progressions to come out of ragtime is the *circle of 5ths progression*. This progression creates an unusual sound because it does not follow all of the diatonic chord qualities of the major scale.

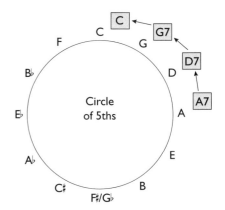

Imagine that the circle of 5ths shown on the right represents major chords. If you follow the circle counterclockwise, each chord is the V chord of the next chord in the circle. When we use V chords that belong to chords other than the I chord of the key, they are called *secondary dominants*.

A circle of 5ths progression usually follows four chords around the circle (going counterclockwise), with the last chord being the I chord of the key. The other three chords can be played as dominant 7ths to increase the sense of each chord being a V chord to the next; for example, the progression shown in the highlighted chords in the illustration above goes A7–D7–G7–C. This is a circle of 5ths progression in C Major.

You can play circle of 5ths progressions by following any set of four adjacent chords counterclockwise around the circle. Try it with major chords and with dominant 7ths. To get you started, here's a progression in C that begins on C (the I chord), then jumps to A7 and follows the circle of 5ths counterclockwise back to C. There are probably thousands of songs that include this progression or something like it!

Cliff Edwards (1895–1971), known by his nickname "Ukulele Ike," was a prolific recording artist and performer during the uke heyday of the '20s and '30s. The massive popularity of his records, including a #1 hit recording of "Singin' in the Rain," helped inspire the sale of vast numbers of ukuleles and Tin Pan Alley songs in sheet music. Edwards appeared in movies as an actor/singer and as a voice actor for animated films. His most known role was as the voice of Jiminy Cricket in the 1940 Disney movie Pinnochio.

PHOTO BY WILLIAM P. GOTTLIEB

Here, we move the same progression to the key of F. Can you find the chords on the circle of 5ths?

The next example moves the progression to the key of G, then follows with a typical ragtime treatment. The strums are shown to give you some rhythm ideas. The third line has a new *syncopated* rhythm like the horn section might play in a big band. In syncopated rhythms, emphasis is placed on the offbeats rather than the onbeats (for more on syncopation, see page 63).

HOW WILL I EVER LEARN TO CHARLESTON
IF I CAN'T EVEN TIE MY OWN SHOES?

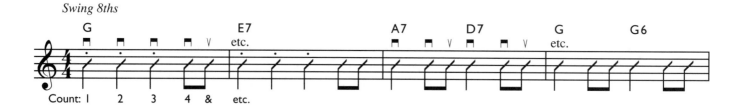

LESSON 4: THE TRIPLE STRUM

The ukulele is one of the easiest instruments to play for simple song accompaniment. It is also capable of fun and somewhat acrobatic special effects, especially in the form of unique strums. So far, your strums have involved just two strokes: the downstroke and upstroke. The *triple strum* (also called a *triple stroke* or just a *triple*) adds an extra stroke to the mix, creating a three-stroke pattern that can be placed in the rhythm in various ways.

The triple strum works best using a combination of thumb and fingers. You can simulate the motion with a pick, but you may have a hard time getting as much speed as you can with the thumb and finger. There are several ways to execute a triple. Here, you will learn the "down-down-up" technique.

The triple strum is not synonymous with a rhythmic triplet. Though triple strums can be played in a triplet rhythm, they can also be adapted to a variety of other rhythms.

TRIPLE STRUM: DOWN-DOWN-UP

The following photos show the unused fingers curled up into the palm. This is just so you can see the motion of the active fingers better. In reality, you can either curl your unused fingers under or let them hang out extended. Stay relaxed and loose!

1. Downstroke with index finger (or with a combination of middle and ring fingers).

2. Downstroke with thumb.

3. Upstroke with index finger.

Below are several bars of the triple strum in $\frac{3}{4}$ time so you can practice giving each stroke equal time and emphasis. Try the triple strum on lots of different chords.

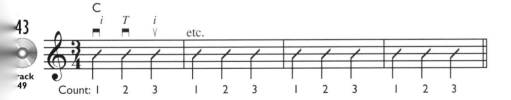

TWO TRIPLES AND A DOUBLE IN ONE BAR, OR, 3+3+2

While this may sound like a lovely evening out after a hard day at work, it's actually just a way to include triples into a measure of eighth notes.

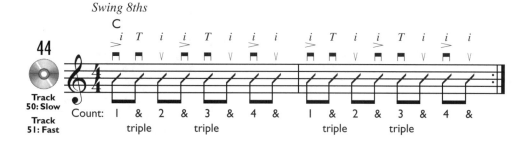

THE TRIPLE AS A TRIPLET

Here, the triple strum is used to play triplet eighth notes on the last beat of the measure. Remember, the eighth notes are swung, so the triplet feel is already present in the rhythm. All you have to do is insert the thumb downstroke between the normal downstroke and upstroke on the fourth beat.

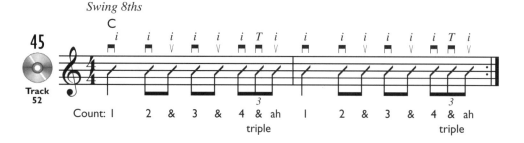

On the next page, you'll put these patterns into practice. You can also use them to strum through the progressions earlier in this chapter, or just sprinkle them into another pattern to spice things up.

The following exercise uses the 3+3+2 strum in the first four measures, then the triplet triple strum in the next three measures. The triple strums have been highlighted. This exercise also contains a four-finger version of F7 in measure four that you might not have tried yet. If you're having trouble getting the triple strums together, try strumming through this progression a few times with simple swing eighths using the regular down-up alternating motion. Practice the triple strum patterns separately and then try plugging them into the progression as they get easier.

THE SECRET HANDSHAKE RAG

LESSON 5: THE TRIPLE BURST STRUM

You have learned how to incorporate the triple strum into regular eighth-note strumming. You can also learn to do triples very fast and use them as a flourish to accentuate a normal rhythm. These types of flourishes are sometimes called *bursts, rolls,* or *shakes* after both the sound and the quick movement of the hand.

INTRODUCING THE SIXTEENTH-NOTE TRIPLET
The triple burst is shown as a *sixteenth-note triplet. Sixteenth notes* look like eighth notes, but with a double beam, or a double flag for single sixteenths. Normal sixteenth notes divide a quarter note into four pieces, counted "1-e-&-a."

Triplet sixteenths, like all triplets, allow you to fit three notes where there are normally two. Normal sixteenths are *two* equal notes in the space of an eighth note. Triplet sixteenths are *three* equal notes in the space of one eighth note. One common way to count two sets of sixteenth-note triplets (one full beat's worth) is "1-la-li-&-la-li." This can be a tongue twister if the tempos are fast, so an alternative is "1-a-la-&-a-la."

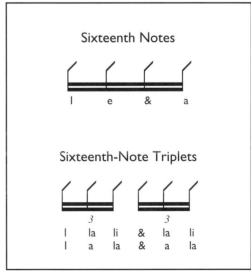

A *triple burst* is a sixteenth-note triplet followed by an accented downstroke. The triplet falls on the "&" of the beat before the accented downbeat. The end result should sound like a burst of four strums (kind of like a machine-gun burst), with the last strum falling on a strong downbeat. To get an idea of how it fits in the rhythm, try saying this out loud "gimme a BEAT!" In that phrase, "gimme a" is the triplet, and "BEAT!" is the accented downbeat.

Here is a triple burst consisting of a down-down-up (*i-T-i*) triple strum immediately followed by an accented downstroke of the *i* finger.

Triple Burst

You can also do triple bursts using just downstrokes and upstrokes of the index finger or pick. The tricky thing is that the final accented beat will fall on an upstroke instead of a normal downstroke.

Alternating-Stroke Burst

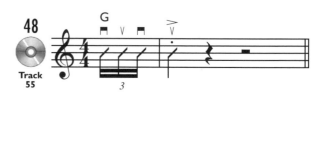

When you practice this, try holding your index finger and thumb in a "U" shape as you start the triple motion. This will help the thumb follow right behind the index in a single hand motion.

The example below contains a lot of information, but it's not too difficult if you think it through. The basic strum is a staccato quarter note followed by eighth notes. On the last eighth of the measure (the "&" of 4), do a triplet sixteenth-note burst into the accented first beat of the next bar. Don't forget to swing the eighths!

HITCH IN MY GIT-ALONG RAG

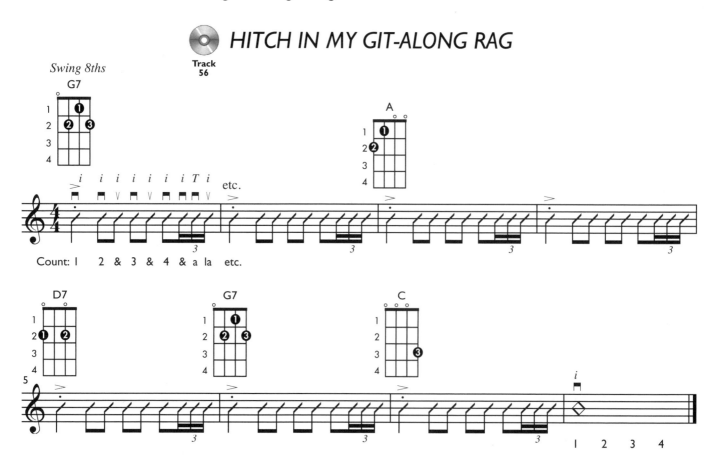

CHAPTER 7

Rocking Out the Uke

In recent years, the uke has come to be a symbol for musicians who are a little different, who don't travel the well-worn path. The uke has snuck into punk clubs, songwriter listening rooms, and major pop hits like "Hey, Soul Sister" by Train. Nowhere has the uke blossomed more than on Internet video sites like YouTube. It fits easily in a Webcam close-up, sounds okay through a cheap computer mic and speakers, and is simple enough to allow just about anyone to share their own song with the whole world. This chapter will help you learn some new strums and chords so you can join the new pop ukulele revolution.

LESSON 1: THE SYNCOPATED STRUM

Syncopation means to shift the emphasis to the offbeat. To show syncopation in written music, dotted rhythms, rests, and ties are sometimes used.

The strum shown below is the Swiss Army knife of strum patterns. It is the universal folk-rock-alternative-swing-funk-punk-campfire strum. This one is good at any speed, fast or slow, swinging or straight. Note the tie that connects the "&" of beat 2 to beat 3, creating a syncopation. Be sure to tap your foot and count out loud.

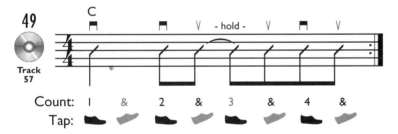

If you find this rhythm a little confusing, break it down into one- or two-beat segments:

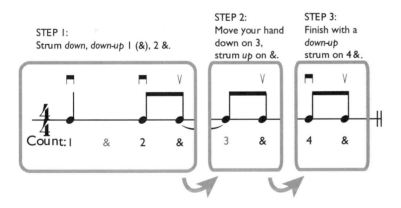

To practice the syncopated strum, here are some exercises that follow the same progression as parts of Train's "Hey, Soul Sister." This progression of diatonic chords goes I-V-vi-IV, a progression that can be heard in countless songs. Remember that in a major key, I, IV, and V are major, while vi is minor. Here it is in the key of C.

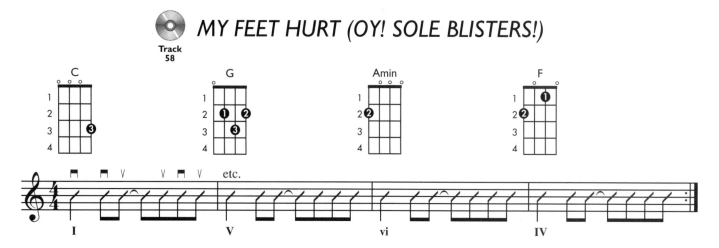

MY FEET HURT (OY! SOLE BLISTERS!)
Track 58

Now try it in G. The vi chord is Emin, which you haven't had a chance to play very much.

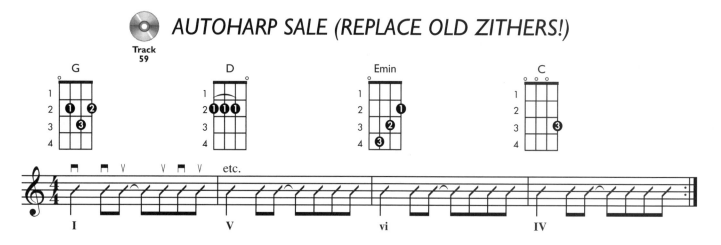

AUTOHARP SALE (REPLACE OLD ZITHERS!)
Track 59

Here's one more I-V-vi-IV progression. This time, the rhythm is in swing eighths and the strum has a slight variation (leaving out the upstroke on the "&" of beat 2). The key is F. This progression introduces the B♭ chord. If the 1st-finger barre gives you trouble, play strings 4, 3, and 2, and let the side of your 1st finger mute the 1st string.

DREAMS OF SUMMER ON A GLOOMY DAY (HAZE, COLD, MISTERS)
Track 60   *Swing 8ths*

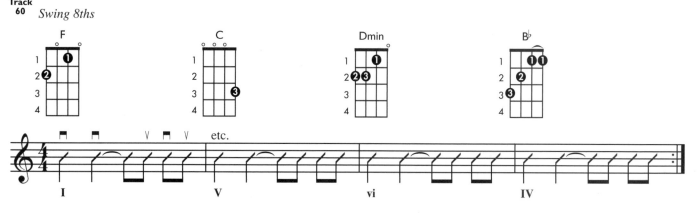

A *mute stroke* is a downstroke where the strings have been muted or damped. All you hear is the percussive snap of the downstroke, but none of the notes of the chord. You can mute the strings with either the right or left hand. Mute strokes allow you to introduce a new texture into your strumming so that you can play more sophisticated grooves. You can even create the impression of more than one instrument playing!

THE RIGHT-HAND MUTE STROKE

By muting the strings with the right hand as you strum down, you can create the loudest form of mute stroke. The right-hand mute stroke works great even if you are strumming chords with open strings. These steps will show you how to do it.

1. First, make sure your left hand is not fingering a chord or touching the strings while you learn how to do the stroke.

2. Now, holding your uke in playing position, place your right-hand palm on the strings, fingers stretched out, covering up the soundhole. Keep your wrist fairly straight so that your hand falls across the strings at a natural angle. (See photo to the right.)

Step 2.

3. Rock your hand backward on the strings so that your thumb sticks up at about a 45 degree angle to the top. The other side of your hand should still be touching the strings. Think of this as the "karate chop" part of your hand. This is the part that mutes the strings. (See photo.)

Step 3.

4. Now that your fingers have some room to move, you should be able to perform a downstroke with your index finger while keeping the strings muted with the "karate chop" part of your hand (see photo). You should hear just a percussive sound. If you hear notes, the muting part of your hand is not doing its job!

5. Repeat the downstroke several times so that you get used to the sound and feel of it. You're not done yet, though!

Step 4.

6. The tricky part is that you need to execute the mute at the same time you are performing a normal downstroke. First, lift your hand off the strings and perform a normal downstroke. Now try it again in slow motion, but this time turn your hand to the right so that the "karate chop" part contacts the strings a fraction of a moment before the index finger does the downstroke. It will take some practice to get the timing just right. Repeat it over and over so that you can do it in one fluid motion.

7. You can do the right-hand mute stroke with the index finger downstroke or with a pick. The motion and basic sound is the same.

MUTE STROKES ON THE BACKBEAT

Remember the backbeat? The backbeat is beats 2 and 4 of a measure of 4 beats (see page 51). In a rock or blues drum pattern, these are the beats where the loud crack of the snare drum is heard. You can use mute strokes (shown with an X on the note head) to simulate the snare drum in a rock beat. Remember, on the mute stroke, you should hear *no notes, only percussion!*

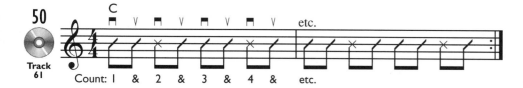

The strum pattern shown above is reminiscent of the guitar grooves used by John Fogerty of Creedence Clearwater Revival. This groove has its roots in Tex-Mex, a Texas hybrid of Mexican traditional music and Texas blues and rock. Following is a progression to practice using your new strum. You can change chords on the beats as written, or you can *anticipate* them by changing chords a half a beat sooner. For example, in the first measure, change to the F chord on the "&" of beat 4. (Note: In the video, Examples 51 and 52 are played using this anticipation technique.)

TRY IT WITH A SWING

If you use the mute stroke with a swing-eighths feel, you get a Jamaican reggae kind of groove. Try the above progression with swing eighths. Then try the one below. It has an additional challenge of switching chords within the measure on bars 2 and 4. You may need to practice these separately before trying the whole progression.

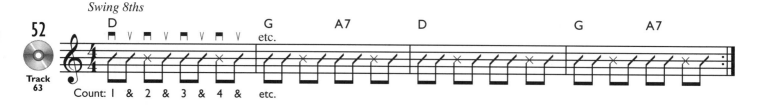

THE LEFT-HAND MUTE STROKE

You can also use your left-hand fingers to create mute strokes. To do this, strum normally and relax the pressure of your fretting fingers on the beats you want muted. This works best on chords that have few open strings, like D and G. You'll be able to use this approach a lot more with the moveable chord forms in the next lesson. Try it with the progressions on this page to hear which chords work better.

LESSON 3: MOVEABLE CHORD FORMS, OR HOW I LEARNED TO BE MY OWN CHORD DICTIONARY IN MY SPARE TIME WITH NO MONEY DOWN!

When you learned your first chords, you were told "here's how to play a C chord; any time you see a C chord in the music, play it like this." You can play a ton of great music just using simple open position major and minor chords. But if you really want to take the lid off of your capabilities, you need *moveable chord forms*.

Moveable chord forms are based on the interval structures and shapes of open-position chords. As these structures move up the neck, they no longer have open strings. When you take open strings out of the equation, you can move any shape to any fret position and get the same type of chord and sound on a new root note.

PASSING THE BARRE EXAM

To take advantage of moveable chord forms, you're going to need to be able to play multiple strings with one finger (usually your 1st finger). This is called a *barre*. You may have to barre two, three, or four strings.

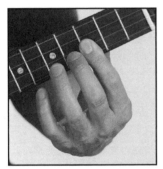
2-string barre.

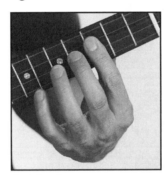
3-string barre.

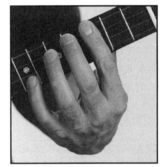
4-string barre.

You have had opportunities to try barres and partial barres throughout this book. If you've been avoiding them or felt like you couldn't make them work, now is the time to prevail! Here are a few tips:

- **The goal of the barre is to get the strings down to the fret!** It doesn't matter how hard you press or how much you grit your teeth if the strings aren't getting to the fret. It shouldn't take too much physical effort, but you need to be aware of what is happening with the strings.

- A barre requires a different finger placement than a normal note. Don't use the tip of your finger, instead use the flat part where your fingerprint is.

- You may need to straighten out your finger and use two joints to cover the strings. Be careful that the little dip at the finger joint doesn't get placed on a string, or that string might not get pressed down.

- You may also need to shift your finger up or down, or roll your finger slightly to one side or another to get the notes to sound.

- Above all, be patient and persistent. Try practicing barres for a few minutes every day. It's amazing what you can do if you give things time to develop!

THE A FORM MOVEABLE CHORDS

Let's start your exploration of moveable forms with forms based on open A chords. Below are the variations of A chords you have worked with so far: A Major, A Minor, and two fingerings of A7. Underneath each diagram, the chord tones are labeled.

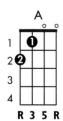
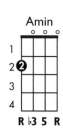
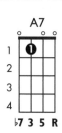
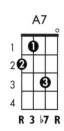

R	=	root
3	=	3rd (major 3rd)
♭3	=	minor 3rd
5	=	5th
♭7	=	minor 7th

Following are the same chord forms moved up one half step (one position) to form chords in B♭. Look at the first chord (B♭ Major) and compare it with A Major above. Each note on the 3rd and 4th string have been moved up one half step, with the fingering changed to the 3rd and 2nd finger. This frees up the 1st finger to barre strings 1 and 2 at the 1st fret. These notes were open in the A Major chord but need to be on the 1st fret in the B♭ chord. The structure of roots, 3rds, and 5ths is identical. Try learning and comparing all the fingerings.

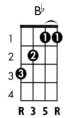
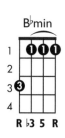
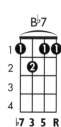
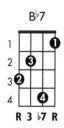

We'll call these fingerings the *A form* chords because they are based on the structures used for the open A chords. The fingerings for the B♭ chords can continue to be moved up the neck to make new chords based on the A forms. You can follow the root notes up the A string (1st string) to find all of the new chords (see chart below). For example, if you put your 1st finger at the 5th fret and build the minor chord fingering shown above, you'll have a D Minor chord.

The A Form Chords by Position (Root on String 1)

Here are the chords you get by moving the A form up the neck. The fret positions indicate the position of the barre finger. If you use the minor shape, you get minor chords. If you use the dominant 7th shapes, you get dominant 7th chords. Try starting at the 1st fret with any fingering, and name the chords as you move up one fret at a time.

Fret position:		1st	2nd	3rd	4th	5th	6th	7th	8th	9th	10th	11th
Chord:	A	A♯/B♭	B	C	C♯/D♭	D	D♯/E♭	E	F	F♯/G♭	G	G♯/A♭

Note: Depending on how many frets your uke has, you may not be able to move the position past the 9th or 10th fret.

THE C FORM MOVEABLE CHORDS

Below are the open C and C7 chords, with the chord tones shown underneath. Since the 3rd of the chord is on the open 2nd string, and therefore can't be lowered to a minor 3rd, we won't have a minor fingering in this set. To the right of the C chords are the corresponding D chords you get by moving the C chords up one whole step. The barred 1st finger replaces the notes that were open in the C chords.

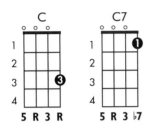

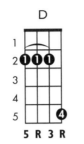

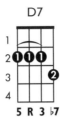

The C Form Chords by Position (Root on String 3)

Here are the chords you get by moving the C form up the neck. The root of this form is on the 3rd string.

Fret position:		1st	2nd	3rd	4th	5th	6th	7th	8th	9th	10th	11th
Chord:	C	C#/Db	D	D#/Eb	E	F	F#/Gb	G	G#/Ab	A	A#/Bb	B

THE F FORM MOVEABLE CHORDS

Now, let's look at the F forms. Below is the open F chord plus two fingerings of F7. F Minor can be played in open position but it requires a few changes to the structure so we'll leave it out for now. Compare the F chord fingerings to the G chords you get by moving the F chords up one whole step.

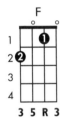

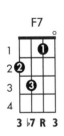

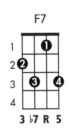

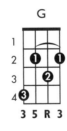

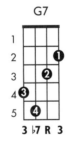

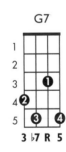

The F Form Chords by Position (Root on String 2)

Here are the chords you get by moving the F form up the neck. The fret positions indicate the position of the root note on the 2nd string. Note that this form has notes that are lower on the neck than the position of the root note, so *the root note position does not equal the position of the barre.*

Fret position:	1st	2nd	3rd	4th	5th	6th	7th	8th	9th	10th	11th	12th
Chord:	F	F#/Gb	G	G#/Ab	A	A#/Bb	B	C	C#/Db	D	D#/Eb	E

THE G FORM MOVEABLE CHORDS

Here are fingerings for G, G Minor, and G7, followed by the moveable fingerings you get if you move the G chords up one whole step.

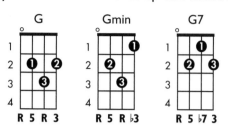

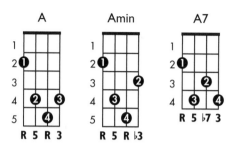

SUPER UKE TIP

Sometimes, we don't play or finger all of the available notes in a chord. For example, it would be very common (and easier) to finger and play only the first three strings of the A chords shown. You have to remember where your root is!

The G Form Chords by Position (Root on String 4)

Here are the chords you get by moving the G form up the neck. The root of these forms is on the 4th string.

Fret position:		1st	2nd	3rd	4th	5th	6th	7th	8th	9th	10th	11th
Chord:	G	G#/ Ab	A	A#/ Bb	B	C	C#/ Db	D	D#/ Eb	E	F	F#/ Gb

THE D FORM MOVEABLE CHORDS

The last form we'll look at is based on D chords. Here are D, D Minor, and D7, followed by E, E Minor, and E7 with the same structures moved up a whole step. You may remember another fingering for D7 that appeared with the C form chords. Some of the forms do overlap in parts of their shapes.

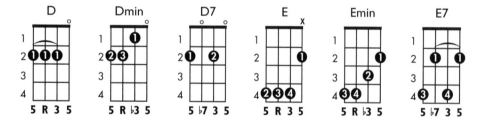

The D Form Chords by Position (Root on String 2)

Here are the chords you get by moving the D form up the neck. The root for the D and D Minor forms is on the 2nd string. The D7 form is tricky, because it doesn't have the root in this fingering. The best way to keep track is to visualize the D Major form to find the position of the chord you are looking for, then make the necessary fingering changes to get the dominant 7th form of that chord.

Fret position:	2nd	3rd	4th	5th	6th	7th	8th	9th	10th	11th	12th	13th
Chord:	D	D#/ Eb	E	F	F#/ Gb	G	G#/ Ab	A	A#/ Bb	B	C	C#/ Db

LESSON 4: USING MOVEABLE CHORDS, LEFT-HAND MUTE STROKES, REGGAE, AND SOUL

This lesson will make use of your new moveable chord shapes and recombine some of your strumming techniques to get new grooves.

THE REGGAE BEAT, SCRATCHING, AND SQUEEZING

Reggae music originated in Jamaica in the 1960s and became a worldwide phenomenon in the 1970s with artists like Bob Marley, Peter Tosh, and Jimmy Cliff. Reggae's influence continues both as a vehicle for political expression and in the laid-back grooves of artists like Jack Johnson and Jason Mraz.

The rhythm guitar of Bob Marley established one of the most imitated grooves of all time. The trick is to use moveable chord forms so there are no open strings. The mute strokes (indicated by an "X" on the note head) are made by relaxing the finger pressure of the left hand without lifting the fingers off the strings. The mute strokes are "scratching." The following groove scratches on beats 1 and 3, while squeezing the chord on beats 2 and 4. Think "scratch, squeeze, scratch, squeeze." Don't forget to swing the eighths!

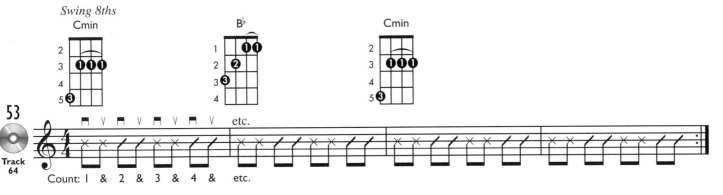

Here's another chance to work with the reggae groove. You'll be playing in the key of B♭, using chord shapes from the A form and D form. The E♭ and F chords shown might give you trouble depending on your particular fingers. It's perfectly okay to just play strings 2, 3, and 4 on these chords, leaving the 1st string muted so you can focus your effort on the 3rd-finger barre. Note that in measures 2, 4, and 6, you have to change chords within the measure—but you're just moving the same form up or down two frets.

WHO WANTS A COOL BEVERAGE?

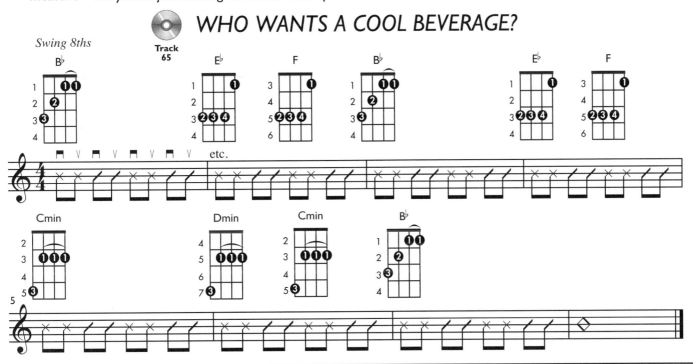

The next exercise uses scratch strokes in a different part of the groove. This strum pattern has more space in it, beginning with a half note followed by a staccato quarter note, then eighth-note mute strokes. The eighth notes are straight (not swung) and the groove has an old-school gospel/soul feel like the music of Curtis Mayfield. The groove changes up to a simple strum on the third line. "Uke Got Soul" is in the key of D Major and uses moveable chord shapes from the C form, A form, F form, and G form.

UKE GOT SOUL

CHAPTER 8

Taking It Home: Island Style

The Hawaiian style of ukulele is full of variety and continues to evolve in the present through young modern players like Herb Ohta, Jr. and Daniel Ho. Hawaiian music comes in many flavors and rhythms, from the swing-influenced Hapa Haole songs of the '20s and '30s to the rolling fingerpicked guitar style known as "slack-key." If you dig deep into the Hawaiian repertoire, you will find that songs are often presented in many different styles and tempos. Overall, the Hawaiian ukulele style prizes beautiful tone, delicately textured rhythms, and a sense of ebb and flow that recalls the natural beauty of the islands and the surrounding ocean.

If you were to only learn one Hawaiian song, a good choice is *Aloha 'Oe*, composed in 1878 by Queen Lili'uokalani, the last monarch of Hawaii. The melody shows the influence of Christian hymns brought to the islands by missionaries in the 1800s. The lyrics tell of a parting embrace, which has come to symbolize longing for loved ones and for homeland. There are countless recordings, from Hawaiian steel guitarists to Elvis.

The following arrangement in the key of F shows both the melody and the chords. Try strumming it first in a slow walking tempo with straight-eighth notes, using the rhythm you learned on page 22. Also, try it using swing eighths or with other strum patterns you have used. You can use the standard notation or the TAB to learn the melody, which consists of a 16-measure verse and a 16-measure chorus. The phrase marks (page 93) show that the verse and chorus each consist of four phrases of about 4 bars each. Here are the chord shapes you'll need:

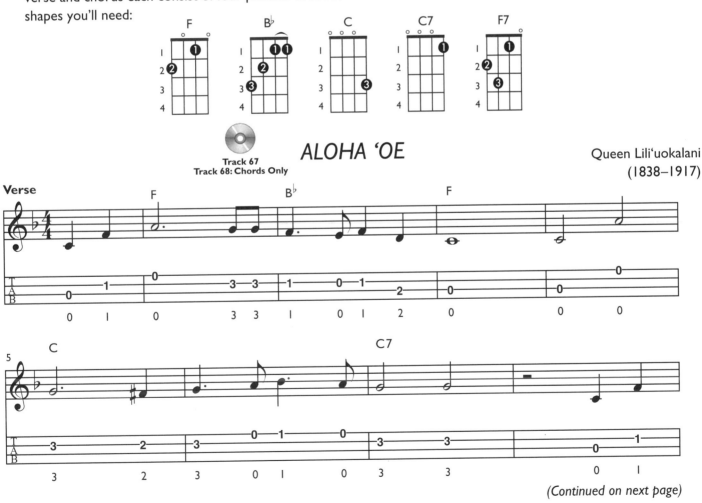

Track 67
Track 68: Chords Only

ALOHA 'OE

Queen Lili'uokalani
(1838–1917)

(Continued on next page)

Chorus

In this lesson, you will learn a few new strums that fit nicely with a swing-eighths groove for Hawaiian-style songs. First, start by strumming and counting basic swing eighths with the index finger. Take notice of the "&" of beats 2 and 4 (marked with *). You'll be doing something special with these soon.

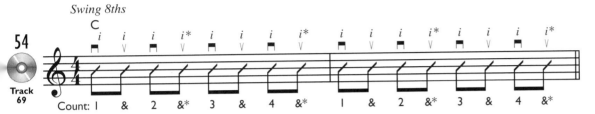

ROLLING WITH A RAKE

One technique that adds texture is to *roll* the chord on certain beats within the pattern. Each normal stroke should sound like all the strings are hit at once but a roll sounds like the notes of the chord come out very quickly one after the other. There are many ways to accomplish this effect. The simplest way to roll the chord is called a *rake*. This is done by dragging the finger through the strings so that they sound one at a time but still quickly enough that they ring together as a chord on the beat. A rake can be a downstroke or an upstroke depending on the beat on which it falls. Try adding a rake on the "&" of 2 and the "&" of 4 in your strum pattern. These will be upstroke rakes.

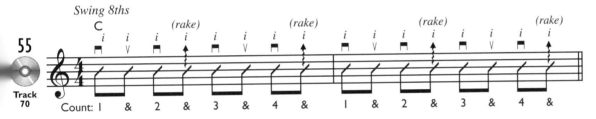

THE ALTERNATING TRIPLE STRUM

Another strumming groove for swing eighths incorporates one of the triple strums you learned on page 60. Here, the triple strum produces a triplet rhythm on beats 2 and 4. This triple strum is a downstroke with *i*, followed by another downstroke with the thumb (*T*), and then an upstroke with *i*.

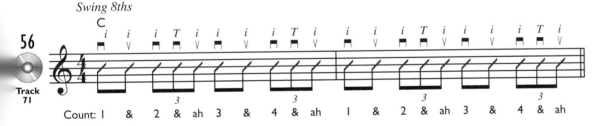

ALTERNATING TRIPLE WITH A RAKE

Once you're very comfortable with the above strums, try adding rakes to the alternating triple strum. Go slowly and count the beats. This strum was inspired by some advanced strums used by ukulele player and falsetto singing master Richard Hoʻopiʻi (pronounced Ho-OH-pee-ee) and other players.

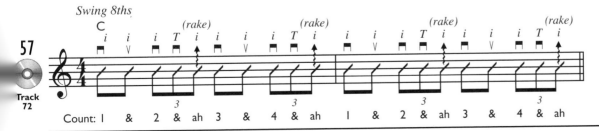

Here's a short strumming tune that pays tribute to the style of Richard Ho'opi'i. The song is in the key of C and begins with a two-bar vamp of D7, G7, and C. The *vamp* is a common introduction for songs that accompany traditional Hawaiian hula dancing. It can be repeated as many times as desired before the rest of the song starts. The eight beats of the vamp match up with the eight counts of the hula dance step called the *kaholo*, used at the introduction of hula dances.

This song will introduce you to some new chords, such as Csus4 (an abbreviation for the full name "C suspended fourth"), F Minor (Fmin), and new voicings for D7 and G7. You can try all of the new techniques as shown, or use simpler strums and familiar voicings of the chords.

HULA FOR HO'OPI'I

Track 73

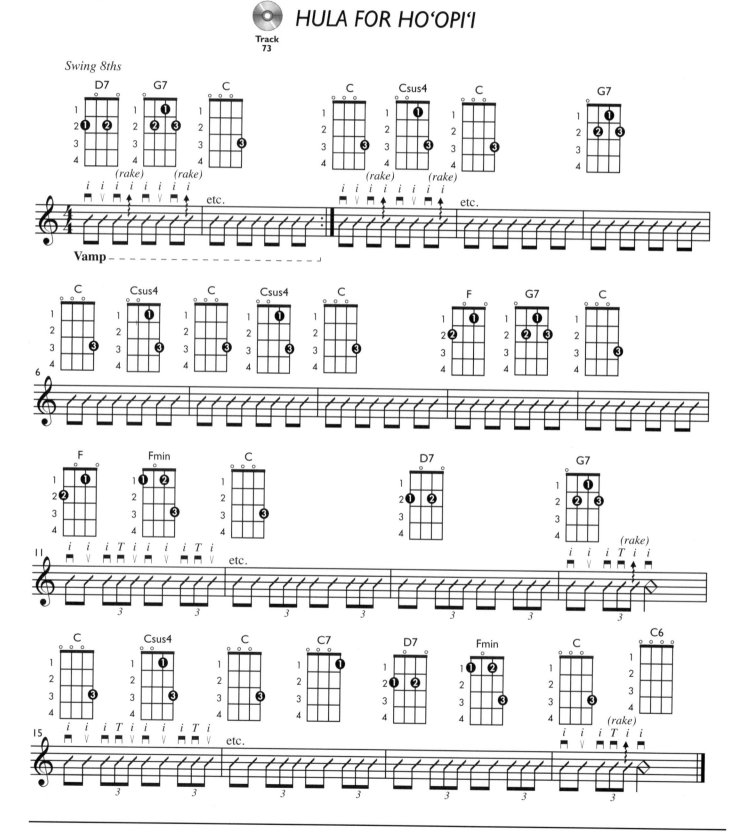

CHAPTER 9

Ukulele Blues

The blues is so much a part of American music that its influence is felt in nearly every style. Far more than just the feeling of "good times that done gone bad," the blues is:

- A musical style
- A form of poetry
- A type of scale
- An attitude
- A specific musical form and chord progression
- An incurable, infectious human condition that is both miserable and joyful at the same time

LESSON 1: THE 12-BAR BLUES

THE FORM

The *12-bar blues* is one of the most basic song *forms*. Remember, the form is the organization, or structure, of a piece. The 12-bar blues derives its name from the number of measures (bars) in the form. Below is a common version of the 12-bar blues in the key of A. Included are chord symbols and Roman numerals indicating the analysis of the harmony. Try it with either simple downstrokes or one of the swing-eighths strums you learned on page 54. You can play this progression using the simple major chords shown, or you can replace each chord with dominant 7ths (A7, D7, E7). The blues progression is unusual in that it sounds good to use dominant 7ths on all chords, not just the V chord. Fingerings for these chords are on page 56.

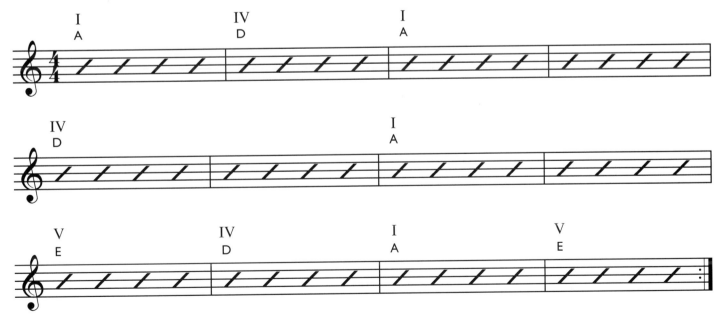

There may be times when you want to play with other people who don't know the same songs you do. The 12-bar blues is widely known by musicians at all levels of experience. A working knowledge of how to play through the progression, as well as improvising on it, can give you an "ace up your sleeve" in those difficult situations when you can't decide what to jam on.

BLUES POETRY

The 12-bar blues is organized in three lines of four measures each. This mirrors the poetic form of many blues lyrics. A common form of blues lyric consists of a statement (line 1), a repetition of the statement (line 2), and a sort of "clincher" (line 3). Check out these common blues verses:

> *My baby just left me, and man I feel so bad*
> *My baby just left me, and man I feel so bad*
> *Since my baby left me, I lost everything I had*

> *I'd rather drink muddy water, sleep in a hollow log*
> *I'd rather drink muddy water, sleep in a hollow log*
> *Than stay in this city, treated like a dirty dog*

PLAY BY NUMBERS

You may have noticed that the blues contains the three primary chords discussed on page 48. These are the I, IV, and V chords. In the key of A, these would be:

$$I = A \qquad IV = D \qquad V = E$$

Try to memorize the progression using these numbers. That way, you will learn its structure without being limited to the key of A. Soon, you will be able play the blues in any key, as long as you know what the I, IV, and V chords are for that key. To make it easier, memorize one line at a time.

PLAY IT IN YOUR SLEEP

To get the most out of learning the blues, try to memorize the progression. Be able to play it over and over without losing your place in the form. This will make it much easier to jam with other players. You will be able to enjoy the musical interaction of the moment without worrying about whether you brought your music or whether you are on bar 10 or bar 6.

In addition, you should know there are many possible variations on the 12-bar blues form. Some have more chords, some have fewer, and some have different chords substituted for the common ones. By burning a specific, basic version of the pattern into your brain through repetition and study, you will have an easier time compensating for slight variations from song to song.

LESSON 3: THE BLUES SHUFFLE RHYTHM

The blues progression can be played to just about any rhythm you can imagine. One of the classic rhythms, particularly associated with Chicago blues, is the *shuffle*. In music, the word shuffle can mean different things to different people. For example, to a fiddler, a shuffle is a particular type of bowing pattern. To a blues player, a shuffle is a type of groove played in the swing-eighths feel. There is, of course, an exception. A "straight shuffle" uses the same patterns you are learning here but with a straight-eighths (un-swung) feel.

PLAYING THE SHUFFLE

The following shuffle pattern is based on patterns you hear from rhythm guitar players or the left hand of a blues piano player. This type of shuffle starts with a major chord on the first two eighth notes, then moves the 5th of the chord up a whole step to the 6th for two eighth notes.

Below, the shuffle pattern is shown for each chord you will need in the key of A. Practice each pattern separately for several bars. In blues rhythm, chords can be played as full triads, or as just the root with the 5th (alternating with the 6th), as is shown for the D and E chords. To give it a more authoritative sound, use all downstrokes instead of alternating down-up.

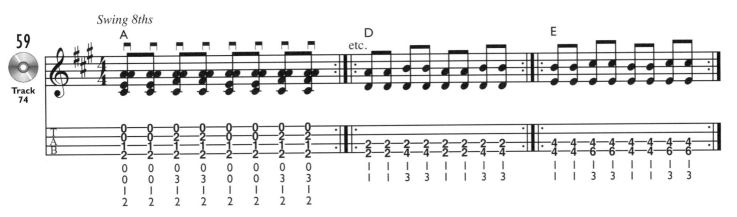

Here are a few more tidbits about playing the shuffle:

- These shuffle patterns above represent the concept of *playing a pattern that represents a single chord*. Even though, technically, you are alternating between, say, A and A6, the pattern functions in the same way as an unchanging A chord. Sometimes in the blues, single-note riffs or even tiny progressions are used to represent each chord.

- When you are playing the D and E shuffles, you have to press down both the 3rd and 4th strings with your 1st finger (barre). To do this, remember to use the flat part of your finger (where your fingerprint is) instead of the tip.

- On the D and E chords, you can use the 2nd finger instead of the 3rd if it works better for you.

Here is the whole 12-bar blues form in the key of A, using the shuffle patterns you just learned. The chord analysis (I, IV, V) is shown under the standard notation. Remember, if you get tired of the shuffle rhythm, you can play any versions of A, A7, D, D7, E, or E7 in place of the shuffle pattern for those chords.

> **WHY DOESN'T IT END ON THE I CHORD?**
> *This 12-bar blues progression ends on the E chord (the V). The V chord doesn't sound like a final resting place for the progression. Rather, the V chord makes it sound like it should repeat. When you have jammed through the form as many times as you want to, you can add one more simple A chord after the 12th measure to give your blues a sense of "coming home to the I chord."*

 ## SHUFFLIN' THROUGH THE BLUES IN A

Track 75

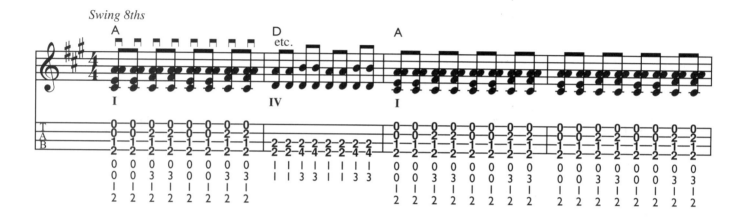

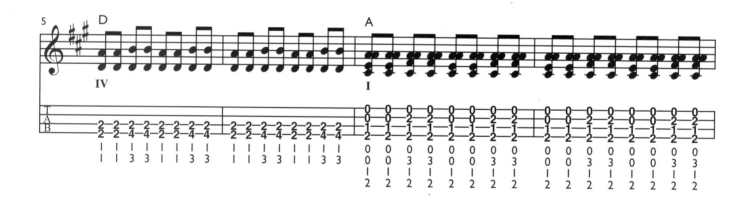

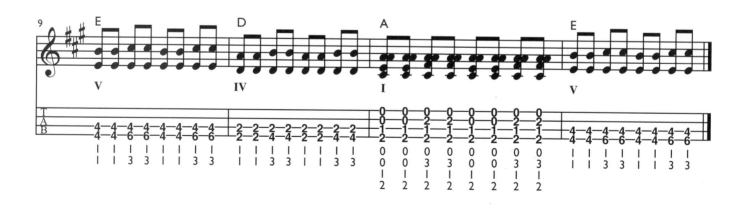

Many blues melodies and solos use the notes of the *minor pentatonic scale*. Unlike the major scale (page 43), which has seven different notes, the minor pentatonic scale has only five different notes (*penta* is the Greek word meaning "five"). Pentatonic scales are very common in folk and traditional music from many cultures around the world.

SCALE DEGREES OF THE MINOR PENTATONIC

Remember back on page 43 when you learned that the major scale can be used to help us understand other scales? Below is a comparison of the notes and scale degrees of an A Major scale and an A Minor Pentatonic scale. The notes and scale degrees show us the differences. The minor pentatonic scale leaves out scale degrees 2 and 6, and lowers the 3rd and 7th by one half step.

A Major Scale:	1 A	2 B	3 C#	4 D	5 E	6 F#	7 G#
A Minor Pentatonic Scale:	1 A		♭3 C	4 D	5 E		♭7 G

THE MINOR PENTATONIC SCALE IN THE KEY OF A ON ONE STRING

Below is the A Minor pentatonic scale shown on the 1st string. You can use any fingering you like. Once you have learned to go up and down the scale, try making up melodies and riffs. Play long and short notes, repeat notes and groups of notes, skip around—do anything to make it sound like music. For fun, try improvising with these notes while the recording of "Shufflin' Through the Blues in A" from page 80 plays in the background.

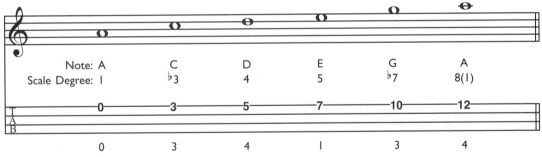

Note:	A	C	D	E	G	A
Scale Degree:	1	♭3	4	5	♭7	8(1)

BLUE NOTES

When a scale has a lowered 3rd degree (♭3), it is said to be a *minor scale*. The cool thing about the blues is that, while the chords are often major, the melody is often minor. This creates a funky, slightly *dissonant* (clashing) sound between the major chords and the minor melody, giving the blues its melancholy, expressive sound.

The minor pentatonic scale contains both the ♭3 and ♭7. These notes help us approximate the sound of old African scales that lie at the core of the blues. When these minor scale notes are played against major chords, they are called *blue notes*. Sometimes blue notes are "bent" out of tune a bit to make them even more expressive. You will learn about string bending in *Intermediate Ukulele*.

THE MINOR PENTATONIC SCALE IN A (OPEN POSITION)

The A Minor Pentatonic scale can also be played in open position. The only tricky thing is that our ukulele tuning only goes down to C, so we have to imagine the low A at the root of the scale. You can substitute the A an octave above (on the open 1st string, or 2nd fret, 4th string). Here are the notes and scale degrees, including an imaginary low A.

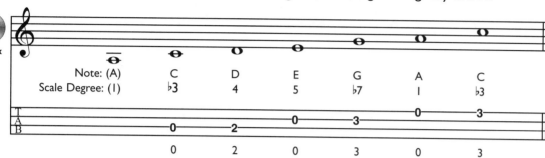

LEARNING TO IMPROVISE

The point of learning the minor pentatonic scale is to use it as a tool for improvising solos. Here are a few tips to get you going.

- When it's your time to solo, remember that you don't have to play a constant stream of notes. Leave some space and choose your moments.

- A *phrase* is like a musical sentence. It has a beginning, middle, and end. A phrase doesn't have to jump immediately into more notes. Imagine that you are inserting commas, periods, question marks, and exclamation points into your solo. This is called *phrasing* (for more, see page 93).

- Repetition is your friend. Repetition is your friend. Repetition creates something familiar for the listener so that when it changes, it has more meaning (like this sentence). You can repeat a note, a phrase, or a rhythmic idea.

- Your other best friend is the tonic note of the scale (note number 1). In the blues, the tonic note works with any of the chords. Even though it is not part of the V chord, it signals that the V chord is heading toward a chord with the tonic note in it. Any time you feel lost, go back and play the tonic note and let it hang for a moment. It's like a reset button for your solo. If you end phrases with a good strong tonic note, they will sound defined and resolved. Later on, you will learn how to creatively work with the other notes, but first, make friends with the tonic!

Here are a couple of short *licks* (mini-phrases) to get you started. Each one ends with the tonic note. Try these when you improvise over the blues progression. You can even try repeating licks like these over and over while the chords change underneath.

LESSON 5: TRANSPOSITION

Transposing means changing the key of a song.

WHY TRANSPOSE?

The most common reason for transposing a song to a new key is to better fit the vocal range of a singer. For example, imagine a song in the key of G Major. If this key is too low, you could transpose up to A or even B. Another reason to transpose is to make a melody or chord progression easier to play on the ukulele.

THE SUBSTITUTION METHOD

This method of transposition is the easiest to learn but not the most efficient. First, consider the following progression in G Major. Use simple downstrokes.

Transposing from G Major to D Major

First, you must know how far the new key is from the original key. The key of D is a perfect 5th (P5, seven half steps, seven frets) higher than the key of G. To transpose the song, substitute each of the original chords with the chord a perfect 5th higher:

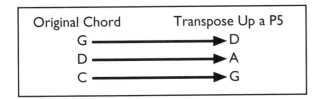

Here is the above progression transposed to D Major.

Transposing from G Major to A Major

Try using this method for yourself. Transpose the G Major progression above to the key of A and write in your answers. The answers are at the end of the lesson on page 84.

    1. How far above G is A?
    2. What is the new chord progression?

Transpose this example to the key of A (write in your answers):

THE CHORD ANALYSIS METHOD

At first, this method takes more practice and thought, but eventually you will be able to transpose songs without having to write out the new chords.

Here is an example progression in the key of D Major.

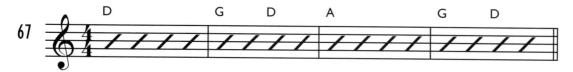

Transposing From D Major to G Major

First, analyze the chord progression with Roman numerals (page 47).

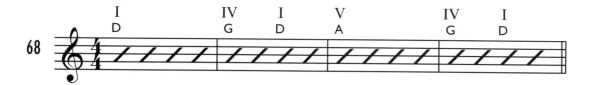

Now you are ready to transpose to any key. Try the key of G Major.

Key of G: I = G   IV = C   V = D

Track 82

Transposing from D Major to A Major

Try this one yourself (the correct answer is at the bottom of this page).

   1. What are the primary chords in the key of A Major?   I = ____   IV = ____   V = ___

Answers to Examples 66 and 70:

1. Key of A: I = A   IV = D   V = E

1. The key of A Major is one whole step higher than the key of G Major.

LESSON 6: TRANSPOSING THE BLUES AND THE MINOR PENTATONIC SCALE

Now that you have learned some of the basics of transposition, you can apply them to the blues. By now, you should have the blues progression memorized by chord number (I, IV, and V). This is useful because you never know what key someone might want to play in when you're in a jamming situation.

Let's say you want to play a 12-bar blues in C. First, you need the I, IV, and V chords in the key of C. You can either name them by memory or find them by counting up the C Major scale.

Key: C Major   I = C   IV = F V = G

You can plug those chords into the 12-bar blues formula you learned on page 77.

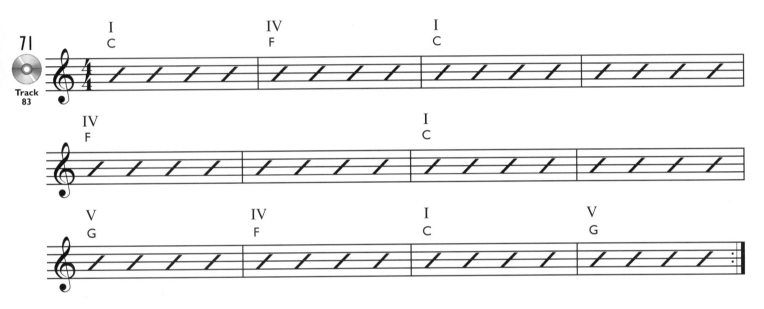

Now that you know what the chord progression is, you can choose the chord voicings and groove you might use to play it. Here are some options:

- The easiest option is to play the major chords in open position with simple downstrokes. Elegant and tasteful!

- You can use dominant 7th chords for each chord in the progression. Simply change C, F, and G to C7, F7, and G7.

- Try some of the different strum patterns, grooves, and swing-eighth/straight-eighth feels you have learned.

If you're up for a new challenge, try some moveable forms for dominant 7th chords. Give these fingerings a spin, then plug them into the 12-bar blues in C shown below with a staccato swing strum.

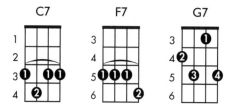

 ## 12-BAR BLUES IN C (A BOUNCY C!)

Track 84

Swing 8ths

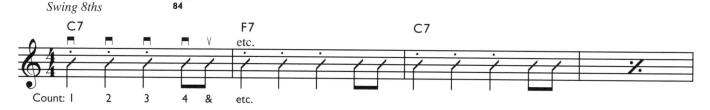

SUPER UKE TIP: MOVEABLE CHORDS MAKE FOR EASY TRANSPOSITION
If you learned the 12-bar blues in C using the moveable chords shown above, you can easily transpose to nearby keys by moving all the shapes up or down on the neck. For example, if you wanted to play the 12-bar blues in the key of D, just move the whole set of chords up one whole step (two frets).

You can also transpose the minor pentatonic scale to a new key. The easiest way to do this is to treat the scale fingering as a moveable shape. You learned the minor pentatonic scale in A. The key of C is a minor 3rd (three frets) higher than A. If you move all of the notes from the A Minor Pentatonic scale up three frets, you will have the C Minor Pentatonic scale. You get a bonus note in this key: the tonic note of C is available on the open 3rd string. Use this scale to improvise riffs and solos over "12-Bar Blues in C (A Bouncy C!)."

72

Track 85

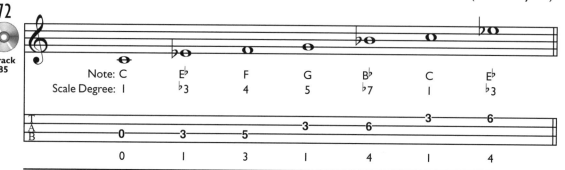

LESSON 7: BLUES IN A MINOR KEY

THE NATURAL MINOR SCALE IN A

Technically, any scale that has a minor 3rd (♭3) is considered minor. There is one particular scale that is called the *natural minor scale*. Here it is in the key of A on the 1st string.

73

Track 86

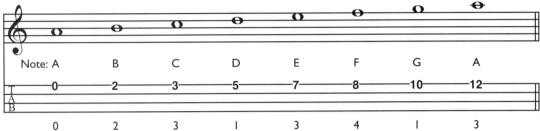

Following are a few things to notice about the natural minor scale.

Relative Minor (A Minor) and Relative Major (C Major)

In the key of A, the natural minor scale has no sharps and flats. It has the same notes and key signature as the key of C Major. We say that A Minor is the *relative minor* of C Major. The relative minor is always the scale whose root is the 6th note of the relative major.

Characteristic Notes: ♭3rd, ♭6th, and ♭7th

Let's compare the A Natural Minor scale with the A Major scale to see what is different. The 3rd, 6th, and 7th degrees are all a half step lower (♭3, ♭6, and ♭7).

A Major Scale:	A	B	C♯	D	E	F♯	G♯	A
Scale degrees:	1	2	3	4	5	6	7	8(1)
A Natural Minor Scale:	A	B	C	D	E	F	G	A
Scale degrees:	1	2	♭3	4	5	♭6	♭7	8(1)

The Primary Chords Are All Minor (i, iv, v)

If we build triads on the 1st, 4th, and 5th degrees using only the notes of the natural minor scale, we get i, iv, and v chords that are all minor. Fun fact: There are other minor scales that have different qualities on the IV and V chords, but those scales are also named differently.

74

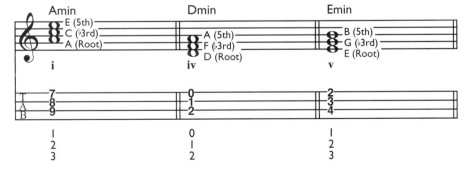

Here is a 12-bar blues progression in the key of A Minor. Note that the last measure stays on A Minor instead of going to the v chord of E Minor. Variations like this are common in blues progressions.

NUNMOOR BLUES:
A 12-BAR BLUES IN A MINOR

Track 87

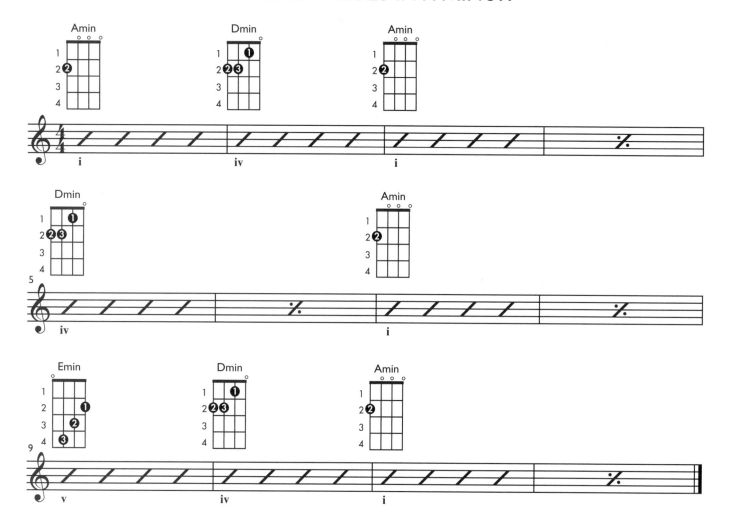

IMPROVISING ON A MINOR BLUES

The good news about playing in minor keys is that you can still use the minor pentatonic scale. In fact, it is more closely tied to the harmony of a minor key than it is to a major key. You can also fill in the missing 2nd and ♭6th degrees to make it a natural minor scale. Below is the A Minor pentatonic followed by the A Natural Minor in open position. Notice the imaginary low A and B notes that are needed to make the scale appear complete. These notes can be replaced with their counterparts an octave higher. Listen to the recording of the blues progression shown above and use it as a backing track to practice soloing.

	A Minor Pentatonic Scale							A Natural Minor Scale								
Note:	(A)	C	D	E	G	A	C	(A)	(B)	C	D	E	F	G	A	B	C
Scale Degree:	(1)	♭3	4	5	♭7	1	♭3	(1)	(2)	♭3	4	5	♭6	♭7	1	2	♭3

75

CHAPTER 10

Introduction to Fingerstyle

LESSON 1: THE RIGHT-HAND POSITION

Fingerstyle, or *fingerpicking*, means playing the ukulele with the right-hand fingers and thumb, using one digit per string. Many great ukulele players have incorporated fingerstyle into their playing. John King, for example, used classical techniques to bring the music of Bach to the uke. Others use fingerstyle to play folk, blues, or jazz.

RIGHT-HAND FINGERS

There are many stringed instruments played fingerstyle, so there are different systems for naming the right-hand fingers. Classical guitarists use abbreviations of the Spanish names for the fingers: *p, i, m, a* (*p* = thumb, *i* = index, *m* = middle, *a* = ring). The ukulele has many playing styles, including thumb style, which designates the thumb as *T*. Since we have already used *T* for the thumb, we will continue to use it throughout this method.

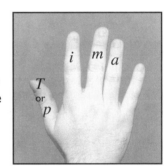

HOME POSITION

You will begin your exploration of fingerpicking by assigning each finger to one string. This may change later on, but it's a good place to start.

- *T* plays the 4th string.

- *i* plays the 3rd string.

- *m* plays the 2nd string.

- *a* plays the 1st string.

T	= Thumb
i	= index finger
m	= middle finger
a	= ring finger

Fingerstyle "home position."

THE RIGHT-HAND WRIST

To achieve the best technical fluency possible (to maximize tone and minimize stress), it is helpful to understand some basic terms regarding the wrist:

Arch
(up-and-down motion)

Rotation
(side-to-side motion)

Tilt
(Left-to-right motion from the elbow)

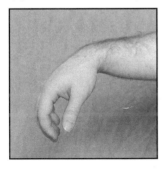
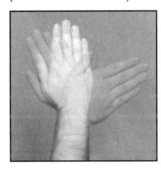
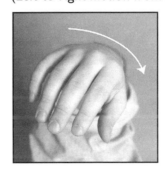

Your wrist should have a slight arch, little or no rotation, and perhaps a slight tilt in toward your thumb. Keep your fingers relaxed and avoid tension in your forearm. If you feel tension or tightness, stop and "shake it out."

A good way to start fingerpicking is to learn a few repetitive patterns. These can be used with any chords you know. By placing your fingers in "home position," you can concentrate on which finger to play without worrying about which string to play.

If you find yourself getting tripped up, remove your hand from the ukulele. Hold it up in the air and practice moving the fingers to the pattern while saying the right-hand pattern aloud a few times (for example: *T-i-m-a, T-i-m-a,* etc.). Then go back to the uke and try again.

The pattern on this page is called an *arpeggio*. An arpeggio is the notes of a chord sounded one at a time. They can be played ascending, descending, or in a more complex pattern. The reentrant 4th string of the uke adds complexity to the sound of the arpeggio pattern, even though the finger pattern is very simple. The pattern you will play goes "thumb-index-middle-ring," or *T-i-m-a*. The progression shown uses C, F, and G7 chords, but you can try this pattern with any chord progression. You may want to practice the pattern with each chord individually for a while before putting the song together.

This progression comes from a Hawaiian song named "Hiʻilawe" (pronounced "he-ee-LAH-vey"), written in the 1880s. This song is a standard among slack-key guitarists. Slack-key master Gabby Pahinui (1921–1980) made "Hiʻilawe" one of his signature songs.

HIʻILAWE

Track 88

Sam Liʻa Kalainaina, Sr.

LESSON 3: MIDDLE AND RING FINGERS TOGETHER

The pattern in this lesson goes "thumb-index-middle/ring-index," or *T-i-ma-i*. Your right-hand fingers will be in the same home position as the last lesson. The difference is that now your middle and ring fingers will play simultaneously. You can warm up for this pattern by tapping your fingers on a table. Try to get *m* and *a* to synchronize so they move as one. The following progression is in the key of G, but you can also try the pattern with other chords or the song from the previous lesson. The first iteration of the pattern has been highlighted to make it easier to see.

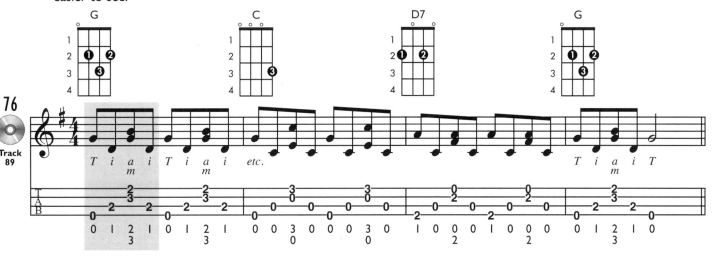

LESSON 4: FINGERPICKING IN 3/4

You can use a variation of the above pattern to fingerpick progressions in waltz time (3/4). Since the last pattern was actually two beats long, all you have to do is add two extra eighth notes to make the pattern three beats long.

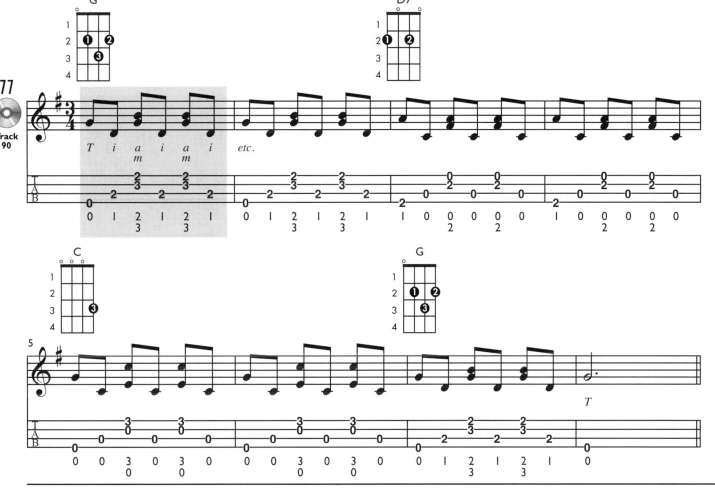

LESSON 5: ALTERNATING-THUMB PATTERN *T-i-T-m*

A CHANGE IN HOME POSITION

In alternating-thumb patterns, the thumb moves back and forth between two strings. You will have to change your home position so that the thumb can be in charge of both the 3rd and 4th strings. The index finger will play string 2, and the middle finger will play string 1. The ring finger can go for drinks.

Here is the pattern slowed down to quarter notes to make it easier to learn. The chords alternate between C and C6.

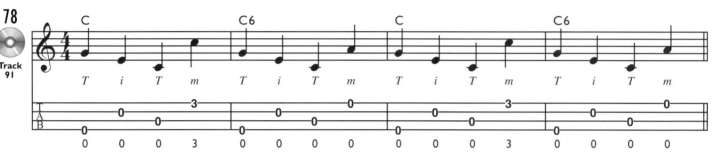

The fun thing about the alternating-thumb pattern is that when it combines with the reentrant tuning, it begins to play tricks on your ears. It's hard to tell where the pattern starts and stops. Try this solo fingerstyle piece. If you stay focused on the picking pattern, you won't get lost. There are a couple of new chords and voicings that give a sense of melody to the progression. Don't forget the repeats!

UKALEIDOSCOPE

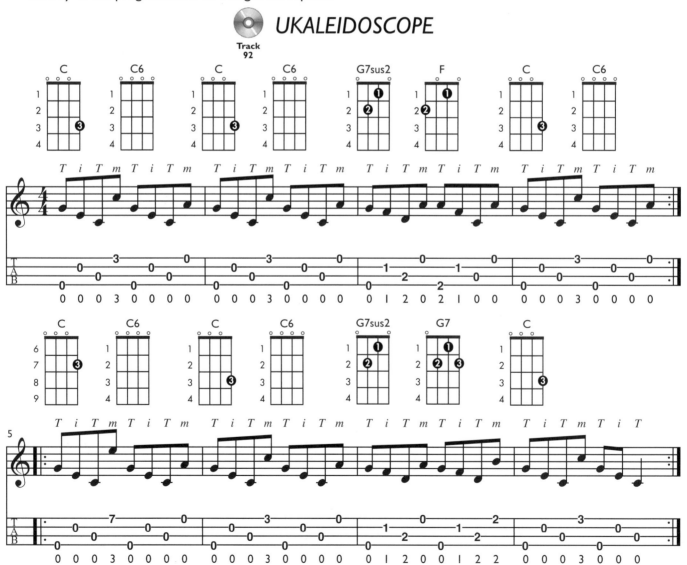

CHAPTER 11

Getting Ready for the Next Level

MUSICAL EXPRESSION

EXPRESSION
Music is not just about keeping time and playing the right notes or chords. In order for music to have an emotional effect, it needs a sense of *expression*. Two very important elements of musical expression are *phrasing* and *dynamics*.

PHRASING
Phrasing is the way that touch, volume, and tempo are used to imply a sense of direction, movement, and rest in a piece of music. If notes are like words, then phrasing is the way that the words are made to sound like sentences, or complete thoughts.

Phrase Markings
Written music uses a number of markings and terms to communicate phrasing and expression to the performer. Many of these terms are in Italian. A quick tour of a few commonly used terms should give you some ideas for your own music. First, the *phrase mark* is a curved line that loosely connects a passage of music. It can be confused with a slur or a tie, but the phrase mark is usually shown above the staff and may have slurs or ties beneath it.

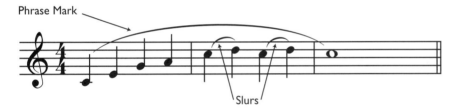

More About Phrases
- **Add your own phrase marks:** Phrase marks are sometimes shown in sheet music to give a detailed description of how the passage is to be expressed. You can also add your own phrase markings to help you break up a longer passage into smaller thoughts. This helps you learn it more quickly by working on smaller chunks of music at a time.

- **Common phrase lengths:** Musical phrases are very often two, four, or eight measures long. Four-bar phrases are probably the most common length, especially in vocal songs where four measures is the standard length for a line or two of lyrics.

- **Phrases don't always start on beat 1**: Sometimes phrases start on pickup notes before beat 1 (page 28). Often, if there are several phrases in a row, they may all have pickup notes.

- **Phrases create a sense of dialog:** Musical thoughts sometimes mirror the construction of speech. Two musical phrases might be paired together to form a musical "question and answer." Just as phrases are often two or four bars long, phrases themselves often appear in groups of two or four. Groups of phrases form larger sections of the form, like verses, choruses, and other types of sections.

OTHER PHRASING AND EXPRESSION TERMS		
TERM	DEFINITION	MARKING
Legato	Notes are to be played in a smooth, connected fashion.	The word "Legato" marked above the music.
Staccato	Short, detached, unconnected notes.	The word "*Staccato*" marked above the music, or small dots above or below individual note heads.
Accent	A note played louder than the surrounding notes.	This sign > above or below the note head.

DYNAMICS

Dynamics define how loud or soft the notes or passages of music will sound. Dynamic expression and contrast are very important to imparting a sense of emotion in a piece of music.

LOUD			SOFT		
Mark	Term	Definition	Mark	Term	Definition
mf	Mezzo Forte	Medium Loud	*mp*	Mezzo Piano	Medium soft
f	Forte	Loud	*p*	Piano	Soft
ff	Fortissimo	Very Loud	*pp*	Pianissimo	Very soft
fff	Fortississimo	Very, very loud	*ppp*	Pianississimo	Very, very soft
◁	Crescendo	Gradually becoming louder	▷	Decrescendo	Gradually becoming softer

THE DYNAMIC SCALE

Arranged from softest to loudest, the dynamic markings look like this:

Softest   *Loudest*

ppp   *pp*   *p*   *mp*   *mf*   *ff*   *fff*

THE "ARCH"

Often, a phrase or an entire piece of music will lend itself to a dynamic "arch" that begins at a softer dynamic, climaxes at a louder dynamic, then returns to a softer level. This is especially true if the melody moves from low notes up to high notes, then back down. Look for opportunities to place this kind of expression in your music. Also, look for spots where a "reverse arch" (loud to soft to loud) might work.

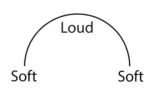

APPENDIX

LOW-G TUNING

The examples in this book have all utilized the reentrant tuning of G–C–E–A, where the 4th string, G, is tuned a whole step below the 1st string, A. This is also known as "high-G tuning." Another tuning is the "low-G" tuning, where the 4th string is tuned an octave lower than the standard tuning. This extends the range of the uke down a perfect 4th.

Low-G tuning can be used on any size ukulele. You will have to buy a special low-G set of strings, or a single low-G 4th string, as the string gauge of a high-G 4th string is too small to tune down a full octave without getting floppy. It's not very convenient to re-string the 4th string to switch back and forth. Many players keep a separate uke set up for low-G tuning all the time. Low-G tuning is popular for jazz improvisation and solo arrangements. A concert or tenor-size uke tuned to low-G will let you take advantage of the longer neck and greater fret access needed for more complex music.

HOW TO TUNE TO LOW-G TUNING
Below are the notes and matching frets (shown in parentheses) for both high-G tuning and low-G tuning, so you can see the difference.

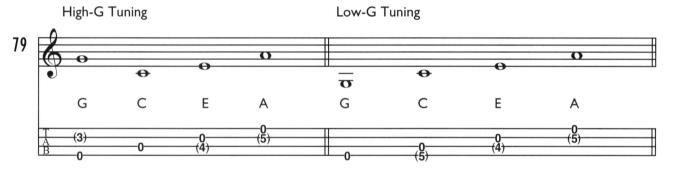

C MAJOR SCALE AND CHORDS
Following is a C Major scale in low-G tuning. In high-G tuning, the lowest note available is middle C. In low-G tuning, you get three extra scale steps below middle C. Not only does this improve the range of the C scale, but it makes it possible to play with greater range in all keys and positions. The C, F, and G chords are the I, IV, and V chords of the key of C. You can use the same fingerings you learned in standard tuning, but the notes produced are in a different voicing, giving more depth and range to each chord.

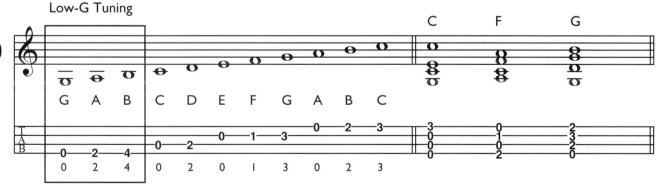

HOW TO PRACTICE

It is important from the beginning to play with the best, most relaxed technique you can. Though you will see and learn many variations of technique, this will become the "home base" to which your body will always return. Building these good habits requires two elements:

1. Technique Exercises
These allow you to concentrate on technique without worrying about keeping your place in the music.

2. Mental Focus
When you work on new songs or skills, be aware of your hand positions, body posture, rhythm, and touch.

WHEN TO PRACTICE

When you are first beginning, or when you are learning new skills, it is best to practice often. Five to ten minutes here and there on a new skill will work much better than an hour every three or four days. If you're lucky enough to be able to practice at the same time every day, you will see great improvement. You will also notice that you develop a better ability to focus on ukulele playing at that time. If it's not possible to practice at the same time every day, at least try to pick up the instrument for a few minutes every day, and then reinforce with longer sessions every couple of days.

WHAT TO PRACTICE

It is a great idea to have a small number of different "projects" going on in your practice sessions. This keeps you from feeling bored or bogged down and helps you improve several skills at once. Pick two or three things to work on every day for a week, then adjust your plan for the next week. Some of these projects might include reading music, learning to improvise, playing a new melody or learning a new chord progression. Be sure to spend time on each project every time you play.

ORGANIZING A PRACTICE SESSION

Here's a sample 30-minute practice session you may want to try for a few weeks. If you have more or less time, adjust the time on each item, while still visiting each item in every session.

1. Technical Exercises *5 minutes*
These include finger exercises, counting and foot-tapping practice, warm-ups, and scales.

2. Reading Music/Melody *10 minutes*
Try reading lots of new material in order to keep your reading skills in shape. If you are not working on reading music, work on melody playing and improvising.

3. Playing Melodies/Chords *10 minutes*
Spend some time every day working on new songs you are learning to strum, pick, or play melodies to. Give extra attention to new chord forms and rhythms that may need several successive practice sessions to improve.

4. Reviewing Old Material *5 minutes*
Always save a little time to go back and play songs you already play well. This keeps them "tuned up" and ready to go for times when you want to play for relaxation or with other people.

BUY A METRONOME

A *metronome* is an adjustable device that generates a beat pulse for you to play along with. Wind-up or battery-powered metronomes are available, as well as many downloadable apps. You can adjust the pulse from very slow to very fast. The speed is marked in beats-per-minute. A metronome speed of 60 is the same as one beat per second. The simplest metronomes make a ticking sound, while the more involved ones will make drum sounds and even mark measures for you.

When used regularly (and with a Zen-like patience), the metronome will help you learn to play with a steady rhythm. The only practice technique that is as valuable is to play with another person who has good rhythm—this can be difficult to do on a daily basis.

Don't let the metronome drive you crazy! At first, it may seem to be speeding up and slowing down while you play. Listen carefully—it's probably you. Pick a consistent, slow tempo to work with for the first few days and use the metronome while practicing one favorite song. See how many measures you can play before you and the metronome have a parting of the ways. Gradually increase your endurance before you increase the speed.

CONCLUSION AND RESOURCES FOR FURTHER STUDY

You can have years of fun with what you've learned in *Beginning Ukulele*, but there is also so much more. Check out the *Intermediate* and *Mastering* sections for more chords, rhythms, scales, techniques, theory, and styles to take you on toward ukulele virtuosity. Remember to play every chance you get, and happy picking!

Books on Ukulele History
The 'Ukulele: a history by Jim Tranquada and John King, University of Hawai'i Press. ©2012
The Ukulele: A Visual History by Jim Beloff, Backstreet Books. Published by Mel Bay. ©1997–2003
        United Entertainment Media

Websites
The Internet is always changing, but there are all kinds of resources available if you search around a bit. The Ukulele Underground, a world-wide community forum of ukulele enthusiasts discussing a wide range of topics, is a great place to start (link current at time of writing):
        http://www.ukuleleunderground.com/forum/forum.php

In addition to other players mentioned in this book, here are just a few more players to check out. Look for their Websites and videos, buy their recordings, and keep an eye out for the next generation of influences!

Ukulele Giants of the Past
Roy Smeck
Tessie O'Shea
Andy Cummings

Modern Players
Jason Arimoto	Brittni Paiva
Jim Beloff	Lyle Ritz
Benny Chong	Steven Sproat
Andy Eastwood	Brian Tolentino
Kimo Hussey	Byron Yasui
Eddie Kamae	The Sweet Hollywaiians
John King	The Ukulele Orchestra of Great Britain
Gordon Mark	The Wellington International Ukulele
Marcy Marxer	Orchestra

INTERMEDIATE UKULELE

CONTENTS

INTRODUCTION

Ukulele is an incredibly versatile instrument. While it can be very satisfying to strum chords and accompany songs, we can also play single-line melodies or combine chords and melodies into a single instrumental arrangement. There are no limitations on what kind of music you can play on the uke—songs from the early swing era to modern rock all sound great!

Intermediate Ukulele builds on what you have learned in *Beginning Ukulele*. In this section, we will cover:

- How to play more types of chords
- Major scales
- Major and minor pentatonic scales
- The blues scale
- How to work your way up the neck using moveable positions
- Music theory applied to the ukulele
- Playing techniques including hammer-ons, pull-offs, slides, muting, and bending
- Playing melodies in various keys
- Playing chord-melody style
- Improvisation

We will venture into various styles like blues, jazz, rock, folk, classical, and fingerpicking. As you work through this section, many songs and exercises can be combined to extend the range of possibilities. For example, you can try various rhythms learned in one chapter over a song or chord progression in another lesson.

Let's get started!

CHAPTER 1

The World A'Chording to Uke

LESSON 1: THEORY AND MAJOR TRIAD INVERSIONS

In this chapter, we'll explore playing chords up the neck. We do this by playing *moveable chord inversions*. As you learned in *Beginning Ukulele*, the term "moveable" refers to chords or scale shapes that do not use open strings. Because there are no open strings, you can move the shapes up and down the neck and retain the same chord qualities. (We'll learn about "inversions" below.) Once you learn these moveable shapes, you can use just a few chord shapes to play many different chords, moving each shape up the neck chromatically (or, the distance of one fret at a time). First, we'll review the theory of how these chords are constructed.

Let's start by taking a look at the harmonized major scale. Using only the notes of the C Major scale, we build triads on each note of the scale, skipping every other note. The chords built on I, IV, and V are *major triads* consisting of root, major 3rd, and 5th. These three major chords are the foundation of numerous songs in many styles. The chords built on ii, iii, and vi are *minor triads* consisting of root, ♭3rd, and 5th. And the chord built on vii is a *diminished triad* consisting of root, ♭3rd, and ♭5th. (Notice the "vii" underneath the staff below. The symbol beside it (○) means "diminished."

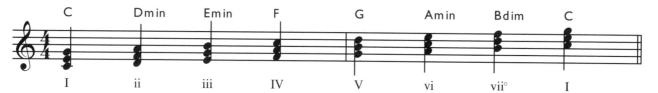

A chord inversion is created by placing any other note of the chord—beside the root—at the bottom. Below are three inversions of C, using one string for each note. The root-position chord is built root–3rd–5th; the *1st inversion* is 3rd–5th–root; and the *2nd inversion* is 5th–root–3rd. Notice in the example below we are going from the lowest position on the fretboard to the highest.

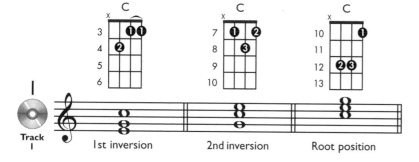

Track 1

1st inversion   2nd inversion   Root position

To the right are three moveable inversion shapes. Move any of the above C shapes up two frets and the chord becomes a D. Move it down two frets and it becomes a B♭. Each of these three shapes can be moved to become any of the 12 major chords. Practice finding the locations for all of the G chords, F chords, D chords, etc.

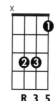
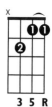
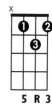

R 3 5   3 5 R   5 R 3

By doubling one note of each inversion, we can create moveable chord shapes using all four strings. These shapes are particularly usable for strumming any chord, as there are no open strings. Below are four moveable inversions of C.

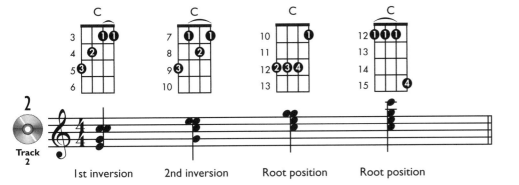

1st inversion   2nd inversion   Root position   Root position

Using any C shape above, move up one fret for D♭, another fret for D, and so on. Again, practice finding different chords using all four shapes below.

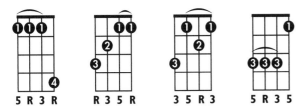

5 R 3 R   R 3 5 R   3 5 R 3   5 R 3 5

The moveable major shapes above are the basis for creating minor, diminished, and other types of chords, and will allow us to greatly expand our chord vocabularies.

LESSON 2: MINOR INVERSIONS

To build a moveable minor chord shape, simply flat the 3rd of the major chord.

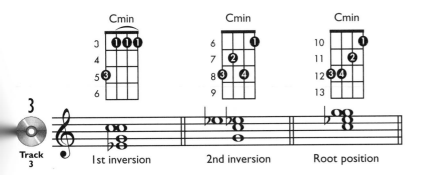

1st inversion   2nd inversion   Root position

Below are the moveable minor shapes. Practice finding the locations of different minor chords all over the fretboard.

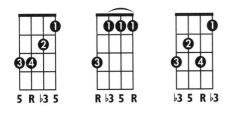

5 R ♭3 5   R ♭3 5 R   ♭3 5 R ♭3

LESSON 3: DIMINISHED AND AUGMENTED TRIADS

To build a diminished triad, flat the 5th degree of the minor chord. An interesting aspect of the diminished triad is that the interval from the root to the 3rd is a minor 3rd, and so is the interval from the 3rd to the 5th. So, it is perfectly symmetrical. We'll look at four-note inversions of the diminished chord on page 105.

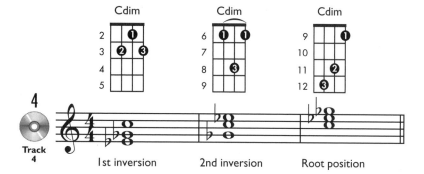

There is one more type of triad, which we didn't encounter in the harmonized major scale, and it is the *augmented triad*. The augmented triad is built by sharping the 5th of the major chord. As with the diminished triad, it is symmetrical; the interval from the root to the 3rd is a major 3rd, and so is the interval from the 3rd to the 5th. In addition, notice that all three augmented inversions are exactly the same shape. Three for the price of one!

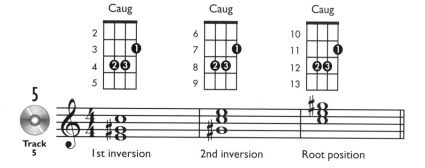

LESSON 4: DOMINANT 7TH CHORDS

Now, we'll take a look at the most commonly used four-note chord—the *dominant 7th*. It's constructed by adding a fourth note to the V (dominant) chord of any scale. In the key of C, the dominant (V) chord is G. The notes of the G Major triad are G–B–D. We'll add one more note from the C scale, F, which is an interval of seven scale tones from G. The resulting four-note chord, G–B–D–F, is the dominant 7th chord called G7.

Important Note: The dominant 7th chord is so commonly used that it isn't generally called by its full name. So, if a piece of music says to play G7, we assume that it's a dominant 7th chord. If you encounter a major 7th or minor 7th, those are different types of chords, and we'll be exploring them in depth later in this section.

Another way to look at the dominant 7th chord is by comparing it to a G Major scale: G–A–B–C–D–E–F#–G. If we take the seventh note of this scale and lower it by half a step, this note is considered a ♭7th. The formula for building any dominant 7th is root–3rd–5th–♭7th. We will now look at four moveable shapes of the dominant seventh chord containing all four of these notes. Below are the four moveable inversions in C. Notice there is a new inversion—3rd inversion—which has the 7th as the lowest note. Additionally, note that as we move up the neck, the melody note (on the 1st string) of the chord changes—from root to 3rd, then 5th, and then 7th. This will be the foundation of playing chord-melody style (see Chapter 8, pages 144–148).

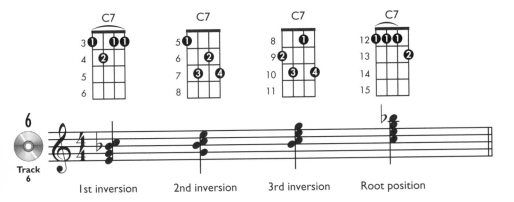

Try finding other 7th chords (G7, D7, A7, etc.) using these same shapes:

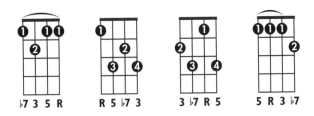

LESSON 5: DIMINISHED 7TH CHORDS

Another useful four-note chord is the diminished 7th chord. It is constructed by flatting (or *diminishing*) each note of a dominant 7th chord except the root. Its formula is root–♭3rd–♭5th–♭♭7th. The double-flatted 7th, which lowers a note by two half steps, can also be enharmonically considered a 6th. As an example, take a C7 chord, C–E–G–B♭, and flat each note to get C–E♭–G♭–B♭♭(A).

Another way to look at the diminished 7th chord is as consecutively stacked minor 3rds. It is a symmetrical chord, and each of the four notes in the chord can be its name. (Note: this is also true of the diminished triad.) So, Cdim7 is also E♭dim7, G♭dim7 (or F#dim7), and Adim7. To the right are the inversions of Cdim7. Notice that each new inversion is the exact same shape three frets higher.

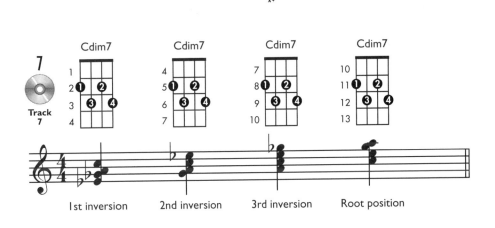

LESSON 6: I–IV–V PROGRESSIONS USING MOVEABLE SHAPES

Now, we'll examine some ways to use the moveable chord shapes we've been covering. Our first example is "Louie's Wild Thing," a common I–IV–V rock progression in the key of C, using major triads. You'll notice some melodic movement on the A string using these inversions—this will be the basis for creating chord-melody arrangements later on. Each two-measure fragment is a complete exercise that should be played a number of times before moving on to the next.

LOUIE'S WILD THING

Track 8

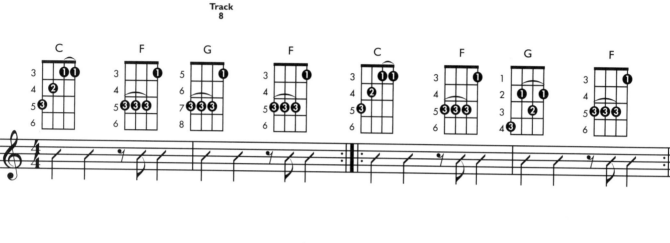

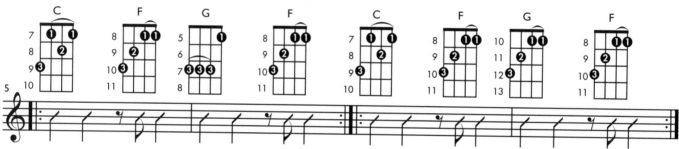

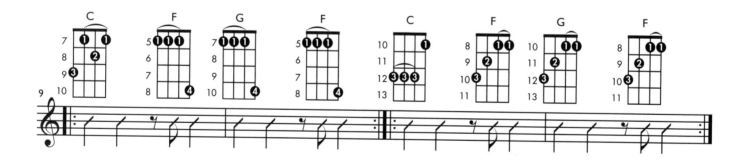

Now, we'll transpose a few of the examples from the preceding page into another key. Note that we're still using the same shapes but at different frets, since we're in a new key.

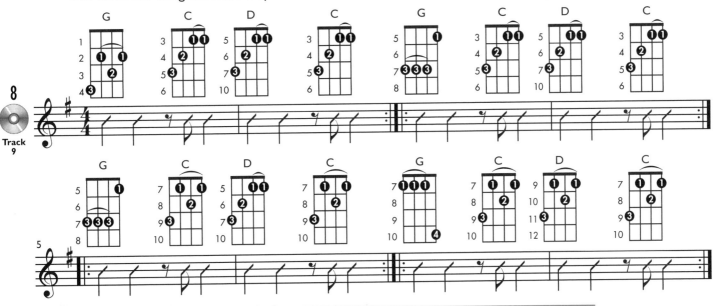

LESSON 7: I–vi–ii–V

Our next chord progression was common for 1950s ballads and uses moveable major, minor, and dominant 7th chord shapes. "There Must Be Fifty Ways (to Leave the Fifties)" is a I–vi–ii–V progression in the key of C. The time signature $\frac{6}{8}$ means there are six beats per measure with the eighth note getting one beat. In $\frac{6}{8}$ time, there are usually two accented beats, 1 and 4, so you would count: ONE-two-three, FOUR-five-six. (For more about $\frac{6}{8}$ time, see page 114.) As with the preceding examples, consider each four-measure segment a separate exercise to be practiced many times before moving on to the next.

THERE MUST BE FIFTY WAYS (TO LEAVE THE FIFTIES)

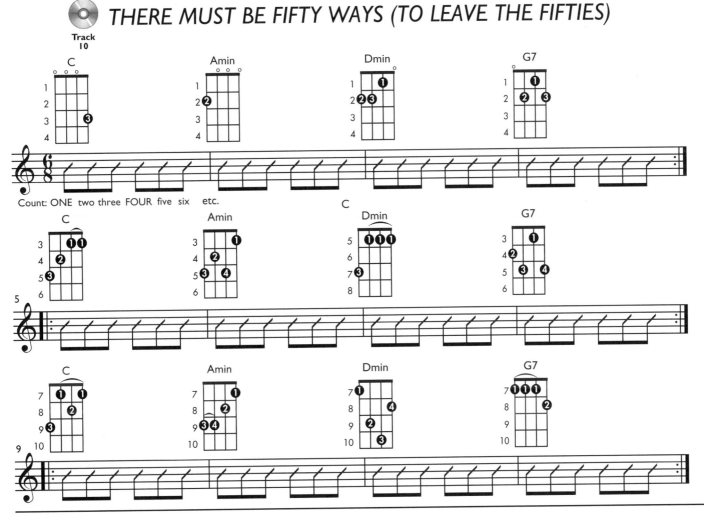

Now, let's transpose the tune from the preceding page into the key of F. Notice that we're still using many of the same chord shapes but at different frets. Try transposing this same progression into other keys as well.

 THERE MUST BE FIFTY WAYS (TO LEAVE THE FIFTIES) IN F

Track
11

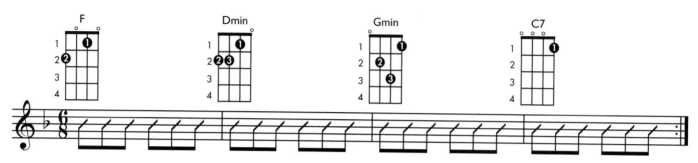

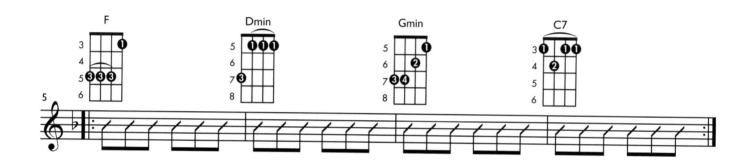

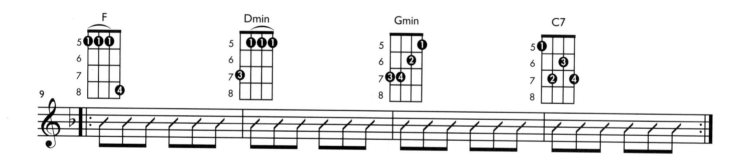

"All Along the Stairway" uses the progression of i–VII–VI–VII. In the key of Amin, the chords are Amin–G–F–G. You've heard this progression in songs by artists such as Bob Dylan and Led Zeppelin. Again, each two-measure segment should be considered a separate exercise.

ALL ALONG THE STAIRWAY

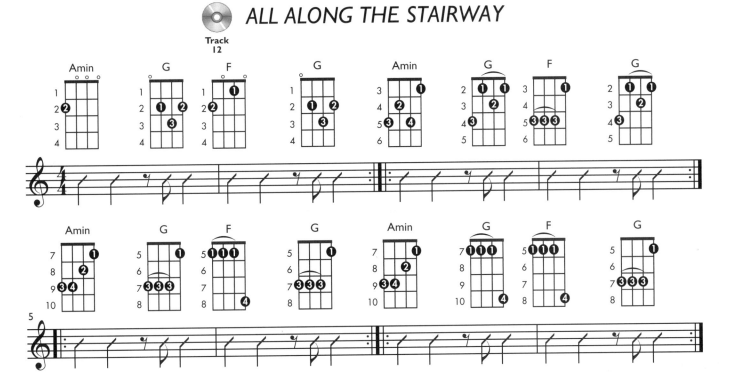

Now, we'll transpose "All Along the Stairway" into D Minor. Note that we're still using many of the same chord shapes but at different frets. Again, you can try transposing this progression into other keys or positions on the neck.

ALL ALONG THE STAIRWAY IN D MINOR

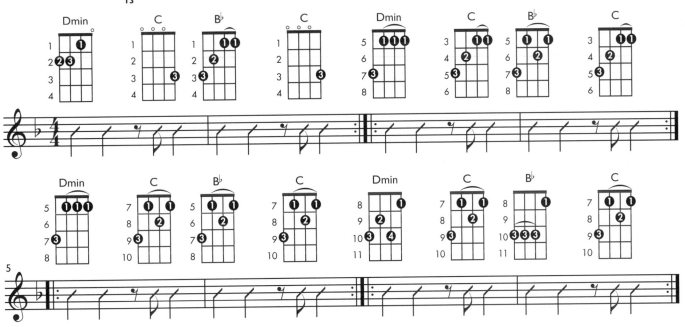

CHAPTER 2

Expanding Your Groove Palette

LESSON 1: GROOVE CONCEPTS

With a varied repertoire of more complex rhythm patterns and strums, you can make even the simplest chord progressions sound more interesting. In this chapter, we'll work on expanding your palette of strums.

To review a concept introduced in *Beginning Ukulele*, it's extremely important to align downstrums and upstrums with the correct beats (or parts of the beat), otherwise your strums won't have the right groove or feel for a song. There's a saying in real estate that there are three important things to consider when buying a house: location, location, location. For uke playing, the three most important things to remember are strum direction, strum direction, strum direction.

Although there are some exceptions to this rule, in general, when playing a $\frac{4}{4}$ rhythm, we'll use downstrums (toward the ground) on the *downbeats* (1, 2, 3, 4) and upstrums (toward the sky) on the *offbeats*, or *upbeats*, (the &'s). Notice that the names "downbeat" and "upbeat" are descriptive. If a rhythm has continuous eighth notes (1-&, 2-&, 3-&, 4-&), you'd play alternate strum directions (down-up, down-up, down-up, down-up). If a beat is left out, leave out its strum and use the appropriate direction for the next strum. So, you might end up with two upstrums or two downstrums in a row. For example, if the rhythm is 1, 2-&, 3-&, 4, you'd play down, down-up, down-up, down. Also, make it a point to tap your foot on the downbeats, as this will help you internalize where they should occur.

Sometimes, it's not what you play that makes a piece of music interesting, it's what you leave out. This next exercise demonstrates this concept. Play the first measure, repeating many times and getting a good groove going. Then, try the second measure, also repeating many times, leaving out the downbeat of beat 3, and accenting the up on the & of 2 (this produces a really energetic groove). Make sure to follow the downstrum and upstrum indications accurately. Next, do the same for measures 3 and 4. Also, try alternating the two measures, creating a two-measure strum pattern.

П = Downstrum
V = Upstrum

Many blues rhythms use triplets, so we'll look at those now. When playing triplets, we're fitting three eighth notes into the space of two normal eighth notes. If we were to follow strict alternate strumming, 1-&-a would be down-up-down, and then the second beat would start on an upstrum. However, that doesn't result in as strong a groove, so we're going to modify this by starting beat 2 on a downstrum. We'll do the same for the third and fourth downbeats, playing down-up-down, down-up-down, down-up-down, down-up-down for our count of 1-&-a, 2-&-a, 3-&-a, 4-&-a.

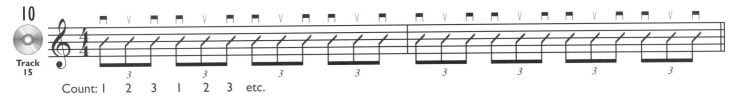

Often, triplet rhythms are juxtaposed with *duple* rhythms, or rhythms where the beat is divisible by 2 rather than 3. Following are some examples combining triplets and duple rhythms. The first example is reminiscent of Robert Johnson's "Sweet Home Chicago" and "Dust My Broom." The second example is a common rhythm and the third example is a variation of it, adding an offbeat on the "&" of 4. The fourth example is the rhythm from Robert Johnson's "Terraplane Blues" and the last example is a variation on it, again adding an offbeat on the "&" of 4.

LESSON 3: 3+3+2

So far, many of our $\frac{4}{4}$ rhythms have had a duple, or two, feel, with emphasis placed on the number counts. To explain this in more depth, if we think of a $\frac{4}{4}$ measure as eight eighth notes, then we've been subdividing them into twos: ONE-two (i.e., 1-&), ONE-two (2-&), etc.

However, this isn't the only way to subdivide the beats. If we create groupings of three eighth notes, we can subdivide eight eighth notes into two groups of three and one group of two: 3+3+2. Count out loud, "ONE-two-three, ONE-two-three, ONE-two," accenting each of the ONEs, and the result is an interesting *syncopation,* or shifting of the emphasis from strong beats to "weaker" beats. This rhythm is used in many styles around the world. Note that these groupings of three eighth notes are not triplets, so each group will add up to a total of a dotted quarter note (one and a half beats) not a quarter note.

12
Track 17
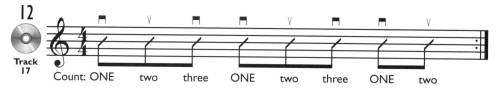

We can also play this rhythm without strumming every beat and create more cool syncopation, especially if a drummer or other instrument is playing quarter notes on the downbeats. When first learning the following rhythm, try counting all of the beats out loud, clapping only on the ONEs.

13
Track 18
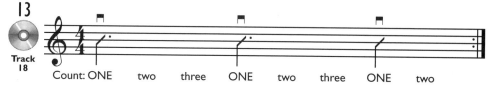

LESSON 4: SPLIT STRUM

Uke players like Roy Smeck and George Formby traditionally used this rhythm in the *split strum.* Try the exercise, using downstrums and upstrums exactly as indicated. To do the split strum, the first downstrum is across all four strings, the first upstrum is mostly brushing strings 1 and 2, and the next downstrum is mostly brushing strings 3 and 4. On the strumming hand, try using the index finger and thumb (*i-i-T-i-i-T-i-i*) or even just the thumb throughout. Also, as demonstrated in the video, you can strum down with *m* and *a*, then up with *i*, and down with *m* (*ma-i-m*). Here is the split strum, holding a C chord.

14
Track 19
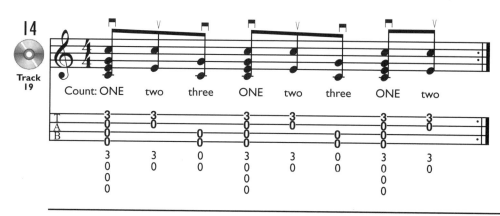

Now, we'll try adding a "tap" finger to the split strum, which brings out a ragtime type melody. To do this with a C chord, lift the left-hand 3rd finger off the fretboard to sound the open 1st string on the upstrums. This produces a tapping sensation and creates a three-note melody, the third note being on the 4th (high-G) string.

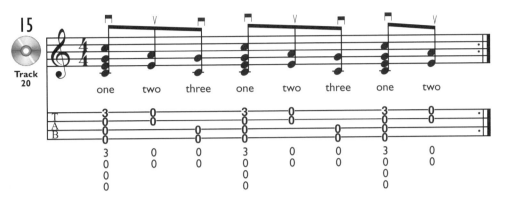

LESSON 5: BO DIDDLEY BEAT, OR CLAVE

The 3+3+2 subdivision is also the foundation of the classic Bo Diddley beat, a powerful two-bar pattern. This is also known as the *clave*, and it is a common rhythm found in both Latin American and African music. In the first measure, we play just the ONEs instead of playing all the eighth notes. In the second measure, there's a rest on beat 1, and then we play quarter notes on beats 2 and 3, and another rest on beat 4. Practice until you can keep this going with a good groove.

Now, we'll experiment with strumming continuous eighth notes, muting all the notes between the accented notes in the example below. Mute by slightly relieving pressure from your left hand while still holding the chord in place as you strum. This works best with *closed position chords*, which contain no open strings. This technique produces a cool, driving rhythm. Practice until you can keep this going with a good groove. Try it using a straight eight-note rhythm, and then try it using swing eighths.

In $\frac{3}{4}$ time, there are three beats per measure, with the quarter note receiving one beat. As with $\frac{4}{4}$, the downbeats (1, 2, 3) will all be played with downstrums and the "&'s" will be played with upstrums. Following are some $\frac{3}{4}$ strum patterns. Each measure is a complete exercise to be repeated many times before going on to the next measure. There will be opportunities to use these strums in songs in later chapters. Also, if you worked through *Beginning Ukulele*, you can incorporate these patterns into the $\frac{3}{4}$ songs you learned there.

18
Track 24

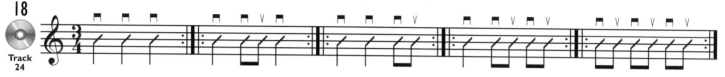

In $\frac{6}{8}$ time, there are six beats per measure, with the eighth note receiving one beat. Typically, in $\frac{6}{8}$ time, there are two accented beats, 1 and 4, so we would count: ONE-two-three, FOUR-five-six. In both $\frac{3}{4}$ and $\frac{6}{8}$, there are a total of six possible eighth notes per measure; however, the accents in each time signature are completely different. Think of $\frac{3}{4}$ as being three quarter-note beats per measure, whereas $\frac{6}{8}$ is two dotted quarter-note beats per measure.

There are a few different strumming approaches for $\frac{6}{8}$. The first is to divide beats into quarter-eighth, quarter-eighth, or ONE-(rest)-three, FOUR-(rest)-six. Play the "ONE" and "FOUR" as downstrums and the "three" and "six" as upstrums. The next approach is to strum all six eighth notes, and we can do this either as down-up-down, down-up-down or down-up-down, up-down-up. Each option has a slightly different feel—the first is more driving, while the latter seems airier. Choose whichever strum sounds best for the song you are playing. Another strum you can use (which was covered in *Beginning Ukulele*) is down-down-up, down-down-up. Whichever pattern you choose, always make sure to accent the "ONE" and "FOUR."

Here are some $\frac{6}{8}$ strums. Repeat each one many times before practicing the next measure.

19
Track 25

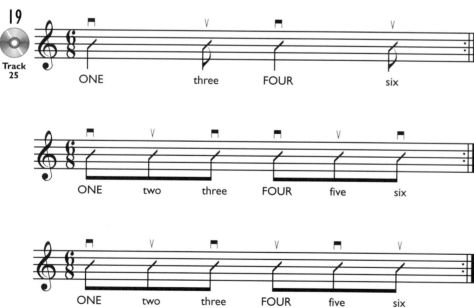

CHAPTER 3

Kind of Blue

When you go to a blues jam, the first song you'll often hear is a 12-bar blues. However, there are various other song forms used in blues. Being able to play these other blues forms will keep different songs from sounding too much the same. In Lesson 2, we'll start learning some of these other forms, but first, let's review the 12-bar blues.

LESSON 1: 12-BAR BLUES

As you'll recall from *Beginning Ukulele*, the 12-bar form is made up of three sung lines. The first line of lyrics repeats twice, and then it's "answered" with an ending line. Below is the chord progression for the 12-bar blues, shown with Roman numerals. Try it in different keys, using moveable chord forms from the previous chapter. Experiment using both major and dominant 7th chords, as they're often interchangeable in the blues. Also, try using some of the various rhythms from the previous chapter.

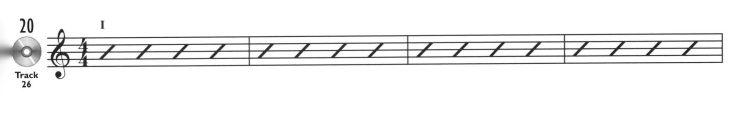

LESSON 2: 16-BAR BLUES

A common *16-bar blues* form has four sung lines. The first lyric line repeats three times instead of two, and then there's the ending line. Below is a sample progression, based on 16-bar tunes such as "Lonesome Road Blues." There are also ragtime-style 16-bar blues forms that we'll be discussing soon. Again, try the example below in different keys, using moveable chord forms and various rhythms.

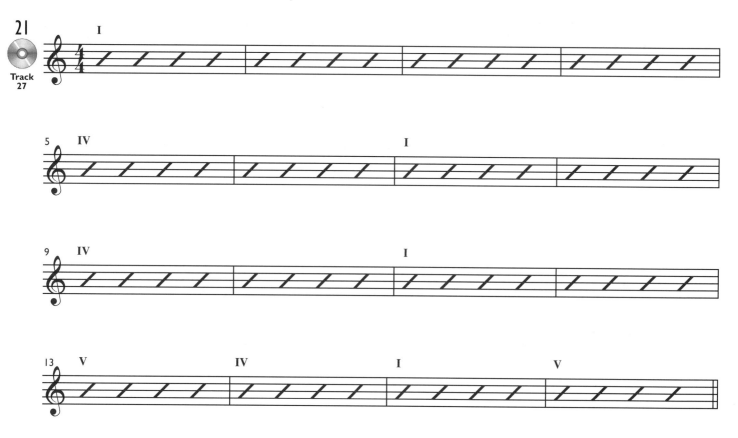

LESSON 3: 8-BAR BLUES

A common 8-bar form has two sung lines, the first lyric line doesn't repeat as it did in the other forms, and then there's an ending line. The example below is in the style of "Key to the Highway," a classic 8-bar blues in the key of A. It works well with the rhythm as notated, but also try using some of the rhythms we explored earlier.

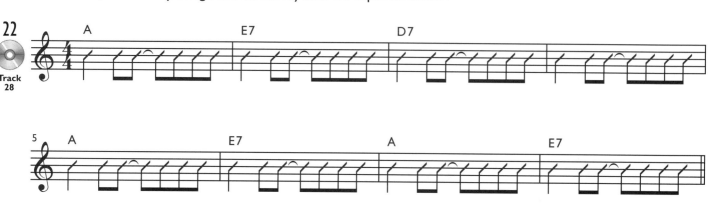

LESSON 4: TURNAROUNDS

Often, near the end of a verse in a song, you'll hear what is called a *turnaround*. A turnaround occurs during the last two measures of each *chorus* (repetition of the song form) and is an excellent way to add variety. At bar 11 (of a 12-bar form), instead of playing the I chord for a full four beats, we'll play one beat of the I chord, followed by a melodic line that leads up or down to the V chord. Below are three turnarounds in the key of A. Try using them in the last two measures of Example 22.

23
Track 29

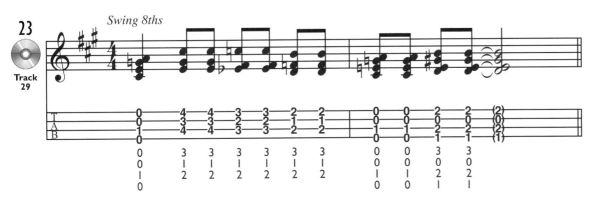

24
Track 30

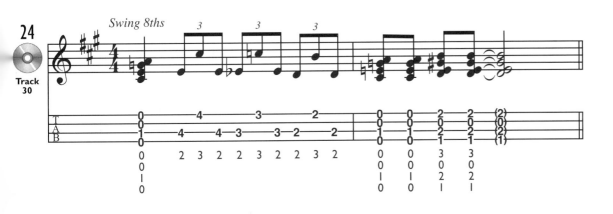

25
Track 31

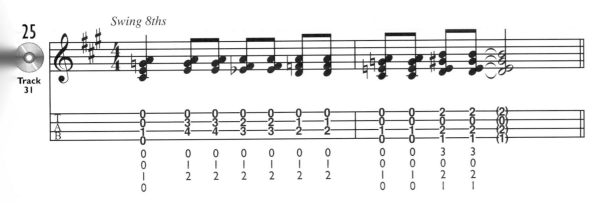

Following are some turnarounds in the key of C. Notice we're using the same shapes from the key of A but farther up the neck. You'll be able to transpose these ideas into other keys as needed.

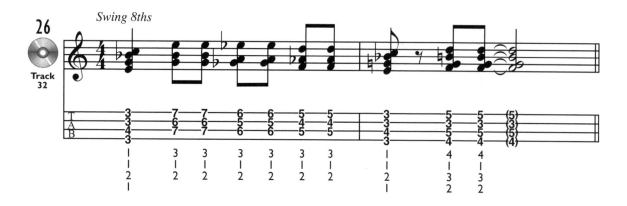

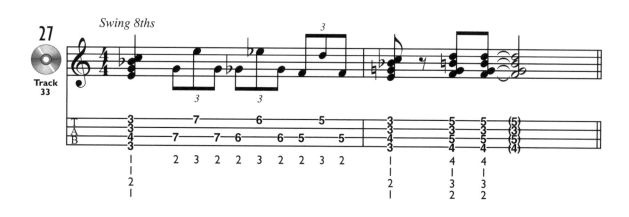

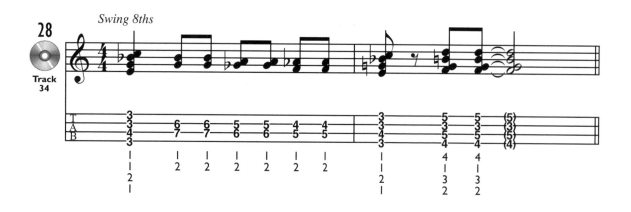

Here's a turnaround in the key of F.

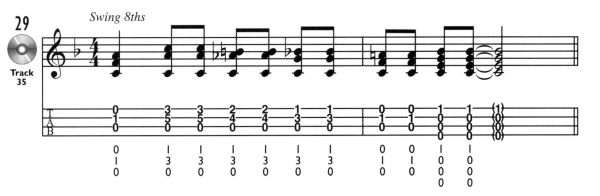

Below is that same turnaround but in the key of G. Again, notice we're using the same shapes but farther up the neck. You can try transposing these ideas into other keys. These same turnarounds will work for 12-, 8-, or 16-bar blues progressions.

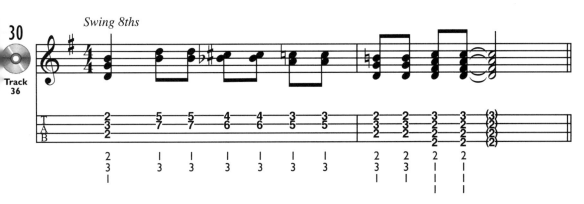

As you'll recall in *Beginning Ukulele*, we discussed chord progressions that cycle counterclockwise through the circle of 5ths. For example, in the key of G, D7 is the V chord. The secondary dominant, or V of the V, is A7, which naturally leads back to the D7. The secondary dominant of A7 (in other words, the V of the V of the V), is E7, which naturally leads back to the A7.

Let's play "Salty Dog Blues," a classic 16-bar blues progression using this counterclockwise circle of 5ths progression. Although the song is in G, we don't encounter the tonic chord until measure 7, and again at 15. Notice that some chords have notes that change on the 1st string, which brings out the melody of the song.

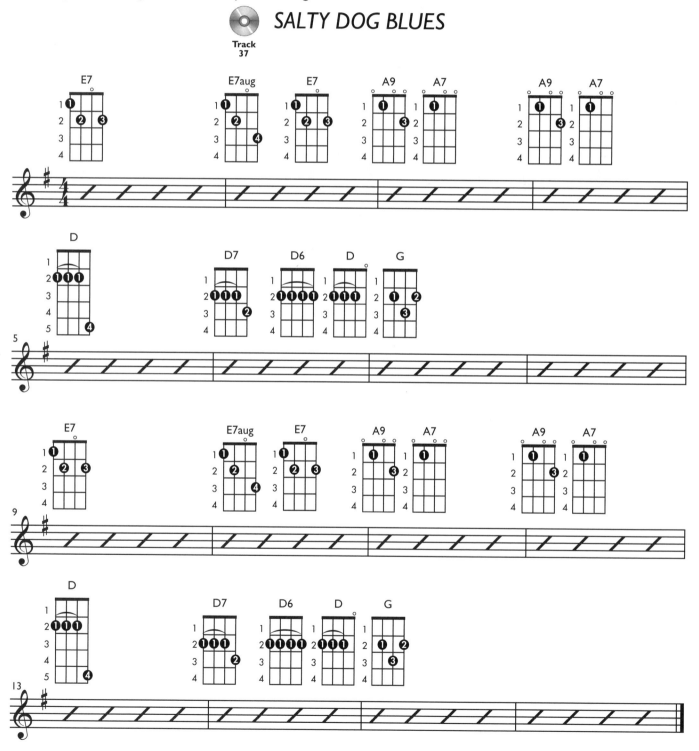

SALTY DOG BLUES

Track 37

LESSON 6: JAZZIN' THE BLUES

Now, we'll look at some ways to "jazz" up the blues. One common approach is to use secondary dominants as discussed in the previous lesson. We'll demonstrate using a standard 12-bar blues progression in the key of C. In C, the V chord is G7, the V of G7 is D7, and the V of D7 is A7.

Normally, measures 7–8 would be the I chord, leading to the V chord in measure 9. Instead, we'll cycle counterclockwise through the circle of 5ths, starting with A7 in measure 8. That leads us to D7 in measure 9, and, finally, the V chord, G7, in measure 10 (instead of its usual spot in measure 9).

Another variation is to play the IV chord in measure 2, and then go back to the I chord at measure 3, instead of staying on the I chord for the first four measures. We'll also play C7 at measure 4, which leads into the IV chord at measure 5. One more variation is to play a diminished chord on beats 3 and 4 of measure 2 and also at measure 6. In addition, you can use any of the turnarounds in the key of C for the last two measures.

As you'll notice when playing the following, it still sounds like the blues, but with more harmonically complex chord movement occurring in each measure.

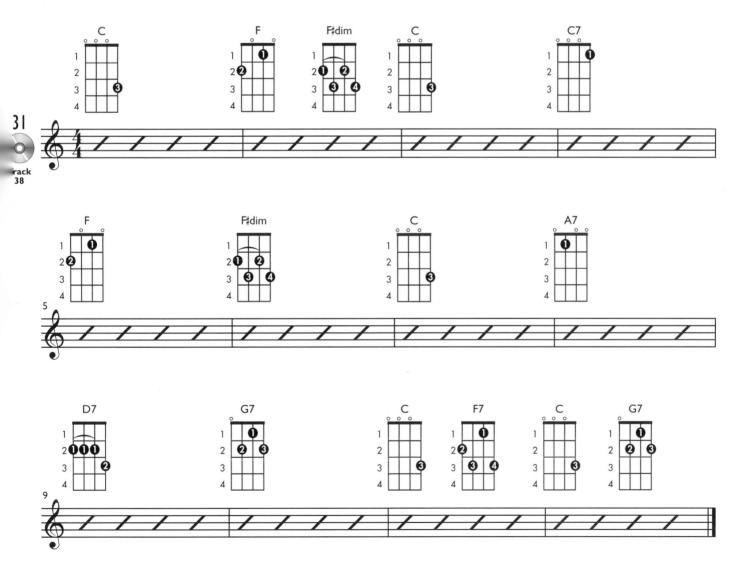

Now, we'll vary this progression even more, using some of the moveable chord shapes from Chapter 1 (starting on page 102). We'll also play C7 instead of C for the I chord, which sounds bluesier; and at measure 4, we'll play another voicing of C7 higher up on the neck to lead us into the IV chord.

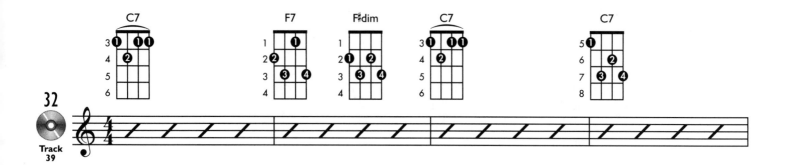

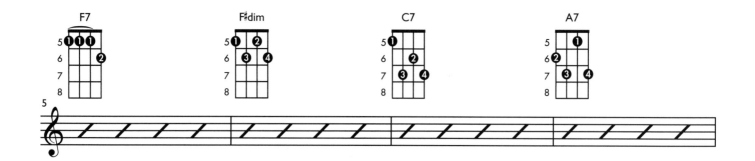

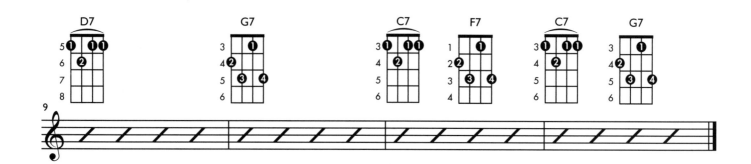

Now, were going to play "Alice's Red Hot Electric Rag," a 16-bar blues and ragtime progression that uses the counterclockwise circle of 5ths progression. A number of classic songs use this same chord progression, including Bessie Smith's " 'Lectric Chair Blues," Robert Johnson's "Red Hot," Sippie Wallace's "Women Be Wise," and Arlo Guthrie's "Alice's Restaurant."

In C, the V chord is G7, the V of G7 is D7, and the V of the D7 is A7. The A7 naturally leads back to the D7, and the D7 naturally leads back to the G7, our original V chord in C.

In the first four measures, we begin on C, and then jump to A7 to start working our way back through the cycle of 5ths to C. In the second four measures, we again begin on C, jumping to A7 to cycle back to G7, which then leads us to the third line. This third group of four measures is like a turnaround (I–I7–IV–IV°) and leads us to the final four measures, which are the same as the first.

Now, let's play "Alice's Red Hot Electric Rag."

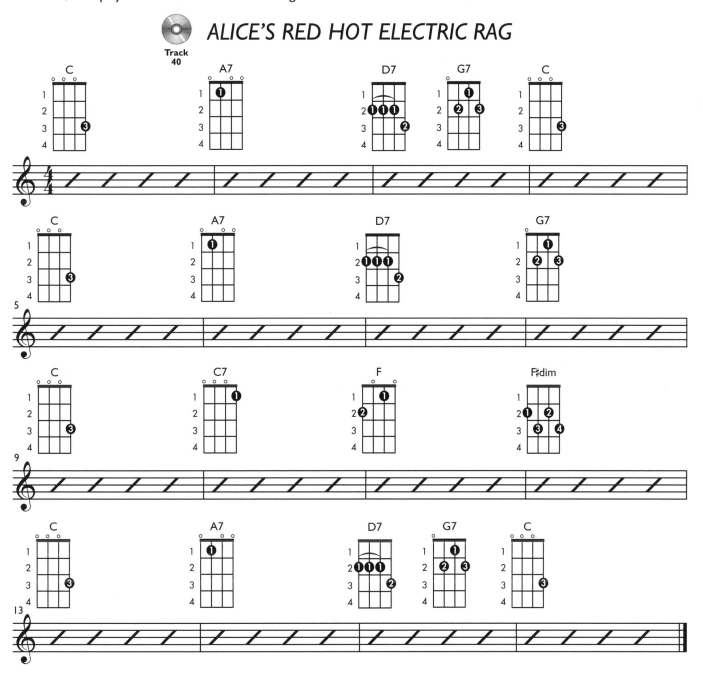

Track 40
ALICE'S RED HOT ELECTRIC RAG

CHAPTER 4

Melodic Playing

LESSON 1: OPEN-POSITION SCALES

The ukulele is versatile for playing single-line melodies. In *Beginning Ukulele*, we played some simple melodies in C—now we'll branch out and try playing in other keys as well. A good way to prepare for this is to practice the open-position scales for the new keys we will be playing in. The range of the uke covers one octave in open position. Because of this, not all these scales go from root to root; some start a few notes below or above the root. They all contain a full octave, however, some going from a 3rd below to a 3rd above, or a 5th below to a 5th above. (Note: Some ukulele players use a low-G bass tuning which extends the melodic range lower by a 4th. See the Appendix on page 95 for more about the low-G tuning.)

To finger the following scales (except for G Major and D Major), use the 1st finger for the 1st fret, the 2nd finger for the 2nd fret, the 3rd finger for the 3rd fret, and the 4th finger for the 4th and 5th frets. The G Major and D Major scales are played in 2nd position, so for them we'll use the 1st finger for the 2nd fret, the 2nd finger for the 3rd fret, the 3rd finger for the 4th fret, and the 4th finger for the 5th fret.

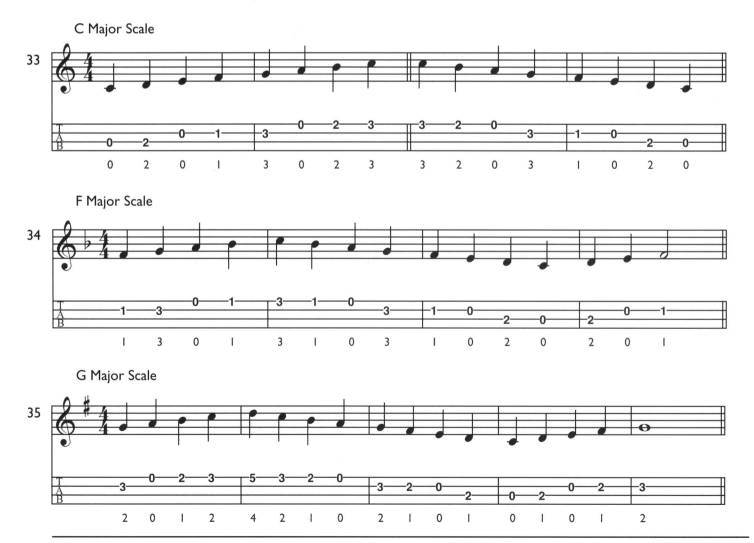

D Major Scale

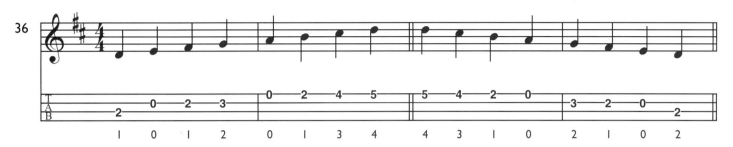

A Major Scale

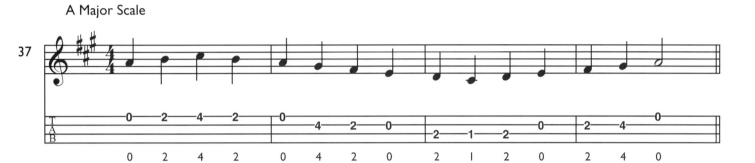

LESSON 2: PLAYING MELODIES

Now, we'll play some single-line melodies. Below is "Amazing Grace" in the key of G. Play the melody using downstrokes with the thumb. Chords are provided so you can also use this song to practice your strum patterns in $\frac{3}{4}$ time.

AMAZING GRACE

Track 41

Now, we'll play Red River Valley in the key of F. You can also use this song to practice your strums in $\frac{4}{4}$ time.

RED RIVER VALLEY

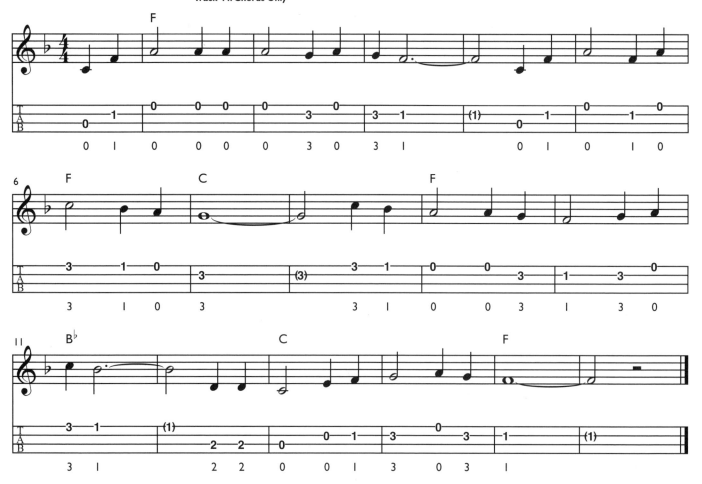

Track 42
Track 43: Melody Only
Track 44: Chords Only

LESSON 3: SCALES UP THE NECK

We're going to explore playing melodies higher up the neck. To do this, we'll use moveable scale positions, which will also be an important tool for improvisation.

Our first moveable scale form is based on the open-position C Major scale. The scale degrees are labeled inside the black dots. By moving the root (R) to any position on the neck, you can use this scale form to play a major scale in any of the 12 major keys. For example, if you place the root on the 2nd fret of the 3rd string, you get a D Major scale, if you place it at the 4th fret of the 3rd string, you get an E Major scale, etc.

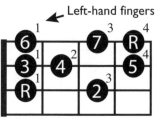

Next, we'll play a moveable form based on the open-position F Major scale. Now, the root is on the 2nd string and is played with the 2nd finger. This form also spans an octave, but instead of going from root to root, it goes from 5th to 5th. Move this scale form up or down the neck to play in any key.

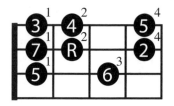

Let's try a well-known melody from the 1860s, "Aura Lee." This song will probably sound familiar, as it was the basis for Elvis Presley's "Love Me Tender." We'll play it in the key of C, using the "F shape" major-scale position starting at the 7th fret, which would be considered *7th position*. This "F shape" position is often used for playing melodies that go to the 5th below the root, as happens in "Aura Lee."

Once you've learned this melody, try transposing it to other keys by starting at other frets. For example, if we start at the 2nd fret, we would be in the key of G; if we start at the 5th fret, we would be in the key of B♭.

AURA LEE

Track 45
Track 46: Melody Only
Track 47: Chords Only

Now, we'll play "Oh! Susanna," using the "C Position" moveable scale to transpose the melody into the key of G. Again, we're in 7th position but in a different key than with "Aura Lee." Once you've learned this melody in G, you can use the exact same fingering to play it in D, starting at the 2nd fret, or F, starting at the 5th fret.

OH! SUSANNA

Track 48
Track 49: Melody Only
Track 50: Chords Only

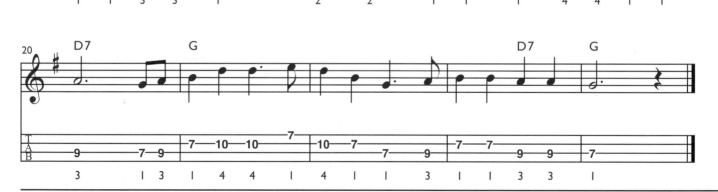

CHAPTER 5

3rds and 6ths

LESSON 1: 3RDS

It is possible to simultaneously play melody and harmony on the uke. Learning to play 3rds and 6ths will facilitate this. We'll harmonize each note of a scale by playing a 3rd above that note. Using the C Major scale as an example, play the open C string and harmonize it with the open E string—the interval between them is a major 3rd. Now, go up two frets on the C string to the D note and harmonize it with the F, 1st fret on the E string. The interval between those two notes is a minor 3rd. Below is a complete one-octave C scale, harmonized in 3rds. The first two measures are played on the middle strings (C and E), and the next two measures are on the high strings (E and A).

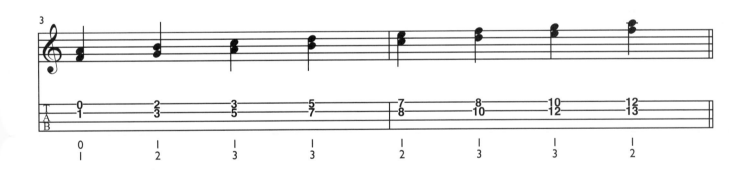

Now, we'll revisit "Ode to Joy" from *Beginning Ukulele*, this time harmonized in 3rds. Note that there are a few spots where the 3rd interval doesn't sound that good, as it doesn't fit the accompanying chord that would be played, so those notes are harmonized in 4ths instead.

ODE TO JOY (HARMONIZED IN 3RDS)

Track 52

Ludwig van Beethoven
(1770–1827)

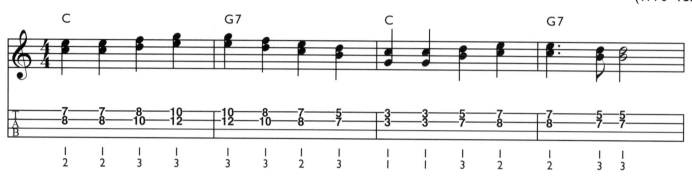

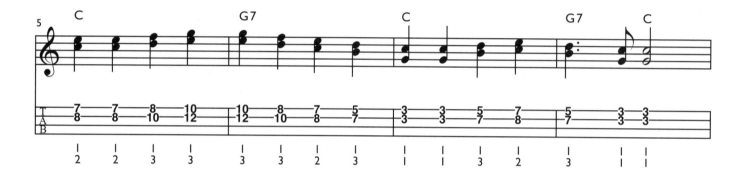

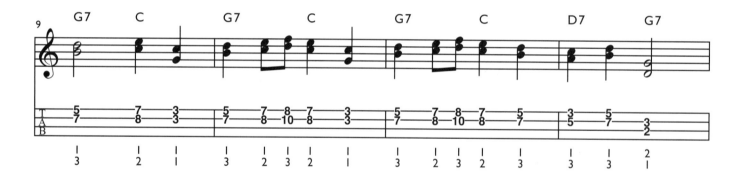

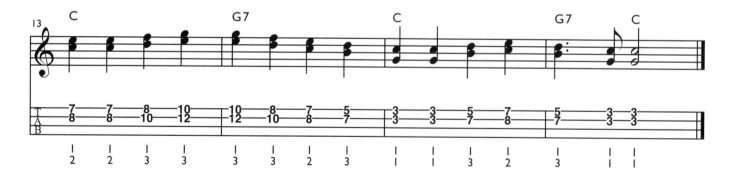

Now, we'll harmonize each note of a scale by playing a 6th above that note. To the right is a C Major scale harmonized in 6ths.

Now, we'll revisit "Ode to Joy," harmonized in 6ths. Note that there are a few spots where the 6th interval doesn't fit the chord that would be played, so those notes are harmonized in 5ths instead.

ODE TO JOY (HARMONIZED IN 6THS)

Ludwig van Beethoven
(1770–1827)

CHAPTER 6

Fingerstyle Uke

LESSON 1: FINGERPICKING PATTERNS

While the uke is most often heard strummed, it has a beautiful, harp-like sound when played fingerstyle. To play the uke fingerstyle, we'll be picking individual strings with the fingers of the right hand. Some picking patterns will use four fingers (thumb, index, middle, and ring), and others will use three fingers (thumb, index, and middle).

In classical guitar notation, the picking fingers are designated using the letters *p*, *i*, *m*, and *a*:
  p = thumb, *i* = index, *m* = middle, and *a* = ring.

In banjo notation, the letters *T*, *i*, and *m* are used:
  T = thumb, *i* = index, *m* = middle.

For this book, we're using a hybrid of the two, the letters *T*, *i*, *m*, and *a*:
  T = thumb, *i* = index, *m* = middle, and *a* = ring.

First, we'll explore some patterns in $\frac{4}{4}$ time. Each measure is an individual exercise, so repeat it until you can play it smoothly without mistakes. The exercises are written using a C chord, but once you get comfortable with that, try using other chords, keeping the pattern going smoothly as you change from chord to chord.

Our first exercise is a simple arpeggio using four fingers. The next pattern uses three fingers, with the thumb alternating between the 3rd and 4th strings. This is similar to a fingerstyle guitar pattern, and on the C chord, it creates the arpeggio root–3rd–5th–8th(root). The next two patterns use what is often called a *pinch*, plucking two strings together. In the first pinch exercise, the pinch is on the downbeat of the measure, and in the second pinch exercise, it occurs on the second beat. As you get proficient with these patterns, you can combine them into longer, two-measure patterns. The final exercise demonstrates a two-measure pattern. For those wishing guitar-like fingerstyle patterns with extended bass range, consider trying the low-G tuning. (For more about the low-G tuning, see Appendix on page 95.)

Now, we'll revisit "Alice's Red Hot Electric Rag," using a couple of the fingerpicking patterns just covered. As you become proficient with this song as written, try varying the patterns so that each pass through sounds slightly different.

Track
56

ALICE'S RED HOT ELECTRIC RAG (FINGERSTYLE VERSION)

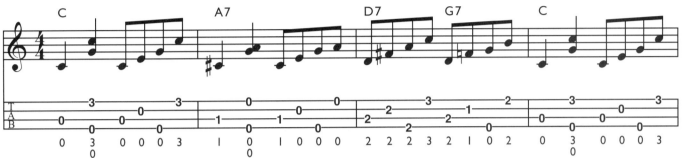

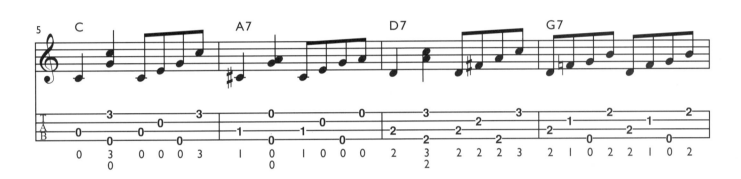

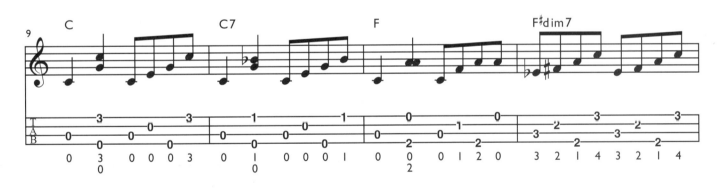

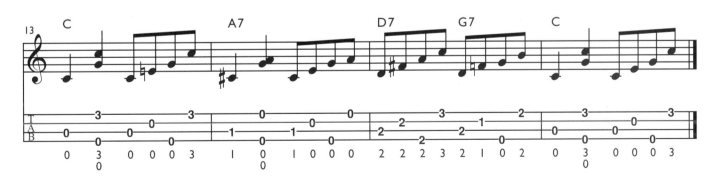

We can often adapt techniques from other fretted stringed instruments to the uke, and one instrument that offers considerable inspiration is the banjo. Banjo and uke both share a re-entrant string, in other words, a higher-pitched string placed where the lowest-pitched string would be on most other stringed instruments. Banjo pioneer Earl Scruggs used a three-finger technique to play syncopated banjo rolls, and it transfers well to uke.

Returning to our discussion from page 112 about 3+3+2 subdivisions in $\frac{4}{4}$ time, this rhythm is also the foundation of the banjo roll, now played fingerstyle instead of with strumming. We'll use the thumb, index, and middle fingers to play these rolls. The *forward roll* is played *T–i–m–T–i–m–T–m* or *T–i–m–T–i–m–T–i*. Accent the thumb notes to bring out the syncopation. Here's the forward roll on a couple of different string combinations.

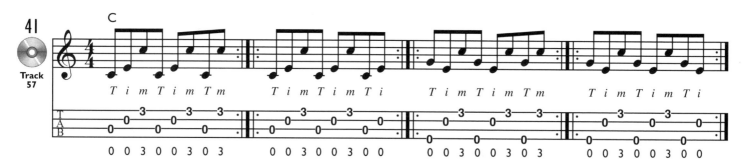

Next, we'll play the *backward roll*: *m–i–T–m–i–T–m–T*. This time, accent the middle finger (*m*) notes.

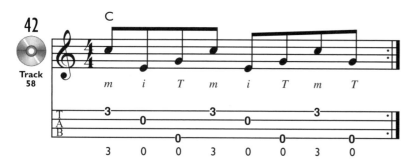

Now, we'll combine the two previous rolls into a *forward-backward roll*: *T–i–m–T–m–i–T–m* or *T–i–m–T–m–i–T–i*.

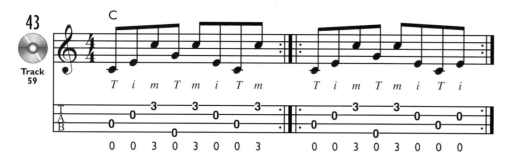

Now, we'll use some rolls in a song. We'll play "Rolling Down That Long Lonesome Road," a 16-bar blues form in the key of G. After playing it as written, pick another roll, any roll, and try to keep it going through the entire progression. As you master these, try to string together different rolls for variety.

Track 60

ROLLING DOWN THAT LONG LONESOME ROAD

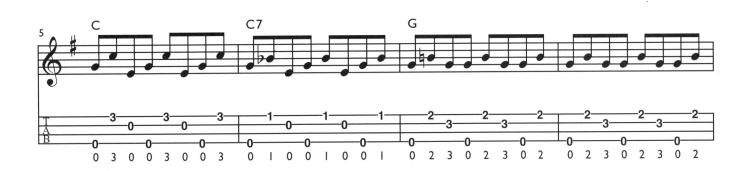

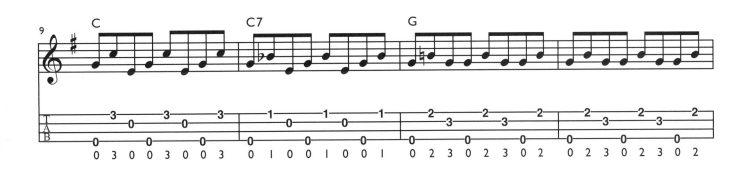

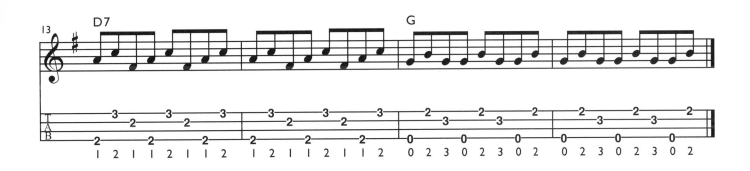

Now, we'll look at how to apply fingerpicking in ¾ and ⁶⁄₈ time. Be sure to check out the previous lesson on these time signatures on page 114 if you haven't read it yet.

Below are a couple of patterns in ¾ time. The first two incorporate pinches on beats 2 and 3. The third pattern is an arpeggio, with each finger playing one string. The final pattern is an arpeggio incorporating pinches on beats 2 and 3 and single notes on the "&'s" of those same beats. Try out these patterns on songs in ¾ that we've done previously. These patterns would also work for a ¾ version of "Fifty Ways to Leave the Fifties," playing a one-measure pattern per chord change.

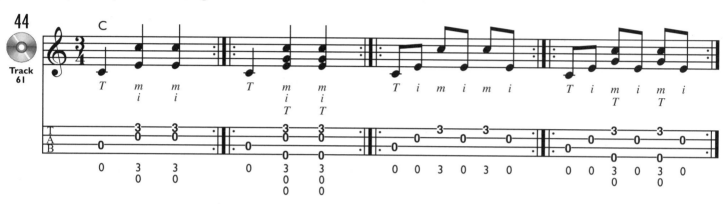

Here are a couple of patterns in ⁶⁄₈ time. The first pattern is an arpeggio, with each finger assigned to one string. The second pattern is also an arpeggio, however, this time we're only using thumb, index, and middle fingers. These patterns would also work for a ⁶⁄₈ version of "Fifty Ways to Leave the Fifties," playing a one-measure pattern per chord change.

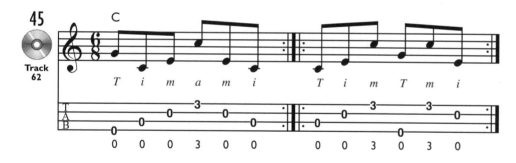

"House of the Rising Uke" uses the first $\frac{6}{8}$ pattern from the previous page throughout.

HOUSE OF THE RISING UKE

Track 63

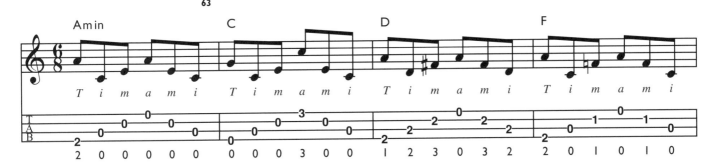

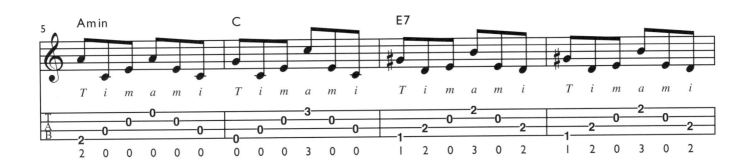

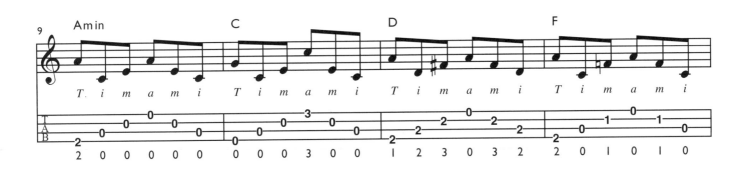

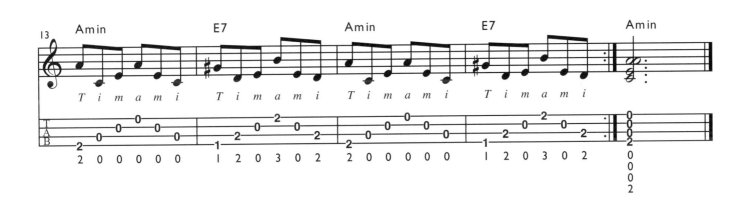

CHAPTER 7

On the Other Hand: Tricks and Techniques for the Fretting Hand

A way to add interest to your playing is by using *hammer-ons*, *pull-offs*, and *slides*. These fretting-hand techniques allow us to play more notes quickly, with maximum efficiency for the picking hand—and they also sound great!

LESSON 1: HAMMER-ONS

In written music, hammer-ons are notated by connecting two notes of differing pitch with a *slur* (⌒). To play a hammer-on, pick the first note of a pair with the picking hand, and then tap a fretting-hand finger onto the fret so that the second note sounds without plucking it.

The first four hammer-on exercises below use an open string for the first note, and then the second note is sounded by tapping a fretting-hand finger onto the designated fret. Don't lift the finger off the string after tapping or you'll lose the note's sustain. The rest of the exercises use a fretted string for the first note, and the second note is one or more frets higher. Leave the first finger down on the note as you hammer-on with the next finger—this will make it easier to play and sound smoother. It takes practice to do this firmly enough so that the second note is as clear and even in volume to the first plucked note. For these exercises, use the fretting-hand 1st finger for the 1st fret, the 2nd finger for the 2nd fret, the 3rd finger for the 3rd fret, and the 4th finger for the 4th fret. To get the most out of these exercises, try them on all four strings.

$\underset{\smile}{H}$ = Hammer-on

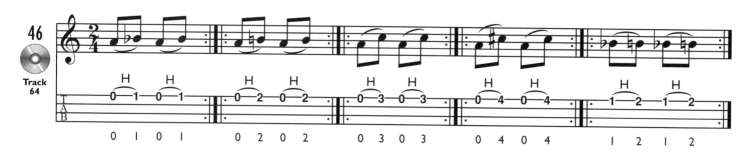

Pull-offs are also notated in written music by connecting two notes of differing pitch with a slur. To play a pull-off, pick the first note of a pair with the picking hand, and then pull off that fretting-hand finger from the fret so the second note sounds without using the picking hand.

The first four pull-off exercises below use a fretted string for the first note. After plucking the string to sound the first note, pull off that finger to sound the open string for the second note. Again, use all four fretting-hand fingers at their respective frets. The rest of the exercises use a fretted string for the first note, and the second note is one or more frets lower. Place both fingers onto the string, pluck the higher note, and then pull that note off, leaving the target-note finger in place—otherwise that second note won't be correct. Try these exercises on all four strings.

$\underset{\frown}{P}$ = Pull-off

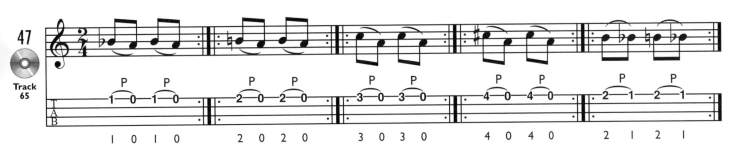

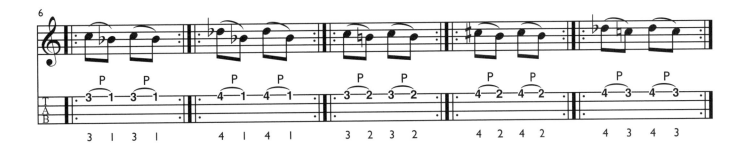

LESSON 3: COMBINING HAMMER-ONS AND PULL-OFFS

Now, we're going to combine hammer-ons and pull-offs into one exercise, getting three notes to sound while only picking once. Try these exercises on all four strings.

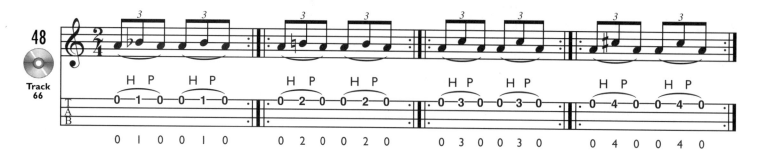

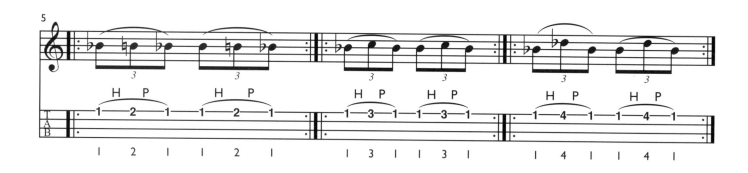

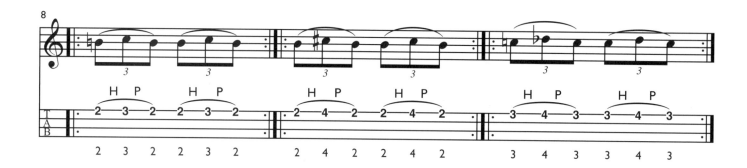

Below are two variations of a C Major scale; both are played using hammer-ons when ascending and pull-offs when descending.

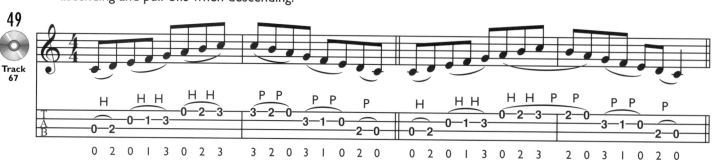

Like the previous techniques, slides consist of two notes that are both sounded while only the first note is plucked. However, for slides, we'll use the same finger for both notes. Play the first note, then, without lifting your finger from the string, slide across the string to the second note. Usually, slides span a distance of one or two frets, although it is possible to slide larger distances. Slides are notated by connecting two notes of differing pitch with a slur and a line.

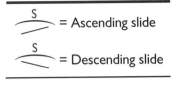

It's also possible to slide into chords. This works best with closed-position chords, as in the example below.

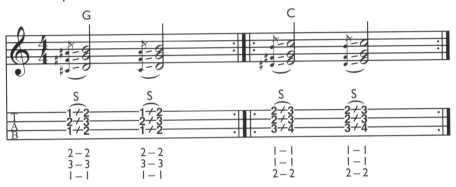

♪ = *Grace note.* An ornament played quickly before a main note or chord.

LESSON 5: BENDING STRINGS AND VIBRATO

Now, we'll try bending strings. On a nylon-stringed instrument, it's possible to bend a half step or even slightly farther higher up the neck. To bend, play a note and then—without releasing pressure—push the string up toward the next string. It's also possible to bend toward the floor except on the 1st string. When bending, the pitch will rise about a quarter to a half step. If you push the string even farther, you can bend toward a whole step, but this is more challenging on nylon-stringed instruments such as the ukulele. There are a few different methods for bending strings, depending on the desired musical result. One is to play the fretted note first, then bend up and hold the new pitch (this is a standard *bend*), or you can bring the bend back down to the original note (*bend and release*). Another method is to bend to the higher note before plucking the string, pluck, and then release to the original note (*pre-bend*). to the right are examples of these variations.

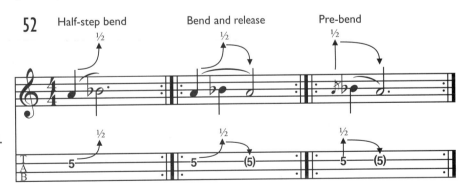

VIBRATO

We can make our melodies really sing with *vibrato*, a rapid variation in pitch slightly higher or lower than the main pitch. To achieve vibrato on the uke, gently rock a fretting finger back and forth on the string, making sure to not slide over onto another fret. Go easy—a common mistake is over-exertion, or shaking the finger or hand too hard. Practice doing vibrato on any string and at any fret, using each of your fingers.

LESSON 6: *ASHGROVE* (USING HAMMER-ONS AND PULL-OFFS)

This next piece, Ashgrove, is a traditional Welsh melody featuring hammer-ons and pull offs. Chords are provided so you can also use this song for $\frac{3}{4}$ strumming and fingerpicking accompaniment practice.

ASHGROVE

Track 68
Track 69: Melody Only
Track 70: Chords Only

Next, we'll play a blues melody, "Sitting on Top of the World," which features the sliding technique. Variations of this melody have been used for many classic blues songs, including "Things 'Bout Going My Way," "You Gotta Move," and "Come On Into My Kitchen." Try adding vibrato to the held notes to make them sing. Chords are provided so you can also use this song to practice $\frac{4}{4}$ strumming accompaniments.

 ## SITTING ON TOP OF THE WORLD

Track 71
Track 72: Melody Only
Track 73: Chords Only

CHAPTER 8

Chord-Melody

LESSON 1: CHORD-MELODY STYLE

In this chapter, we will explore *chord-melody* style. There is a long tradition of chord-melody style on ukulele, from traditional Hawaiian to modern rock. In this style, we combine melody and chordal accompaniment to create a full solo arrangement, instead of dividing these roles into separate instrumental parts as we've done so far.

Our first chord-melody arrangements will use what is called *thumb-style* in Hawaiian ukulele playing. To play in this style, strum a chord downward with the thumb, ending at whichever string contains the melody note. It's important not to play any strings above the melody, as the higher pitch can be confused with the melody notes. There can be exceptions to this when strumming the re-entrant string as part of the chord, if it's higher than the melody. In this case, strum the re-entrant string lightly, and then land a little louder on the melody string.

First, we'll play "Oh! Susanna," for which you learned to play the melody in *Beginning Ukulele*. In this arrangement, we'll add a chord at the beginning of each measure, followed by the remaining single-line melody notes. Try to hold the chord so its notes keep sustaining while you play the subsequent notes.

 OH! SUSANNA (CHORD-MELODY)

Track 74

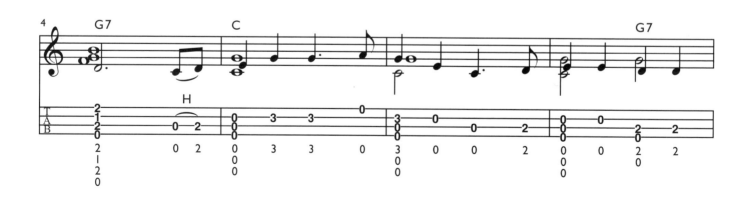

Next, we'll play a song for which you learned the melody on page 125, "Amazing Grace." In this arrangement, we'll incorporate some minor and 7th chords for more harmonic interest. As in the previous song, we'll add a chord to the melody note at the downbeat of each measure, which will be followed by the remaining single-line melody notes. Hold the chords to keep them ringing while you play the subsequent notes.

AMAZING GRACE (CHORD-MELODY)
Track 75

LESSON 3: ASHGROVE (CHORD-MELODY)

Our next chord-melody arrangement is "Ashgrove," which features hammer-ons and pull-offs. Make sure to hold down the notes of the chord so they sustain while you're playing the subsequent melody notes.

ASHGROVE (CHORD-MELODY)

LESSON 4: *GREENSLEEVES (CHORD-MELODY)*

We'll play one more chord-melody arrangement, "Greensleeves," in the key of D Minor.
Again, make sure to hold down the notes of the chord so they sustain while you're playing
the melody notes that follow.

GREENSLEEVES (CHORD-MELODY)

Track
77

CHAPTER 9

Getting Jazzy

LESSON 1: EVERYTHING YOU WANTED TO KNOW ABOUT JAZZ

The uke was a popular instrument at the beginning of the Jazz Age, and is it is well-suited for playing classics from the Great American Songbook. Many of these songs are 32 measures in length and follow a standard AABA form. The A part is 8 measures long, and it is repeated, sometimes with a second ending, bringing us to 16 bars. Then there is an 8-bar B part, which is followed by another repeat of the A part, sometimes with a final ending, totaling 32 bars.

Many of these songs use more sophisticated chords. You'll recall that we discussed the harmonized major scale on page 102, using triads. We will now revisit the harmonized major scale, this time building four-note chords on each degree of the scale. Here are the results in C.

CMaj7   Dmin7   Emin7   FMaj7   G7   Amin7   Bmin7♭5   CMaj7

Building four-note chords on each degree of the major scale results in four different types of 7th chords: *major 7th*, *dominant 7th*, *minor 7th*, and *minor 7th flat 5th*. Following are the formulas to construct these chords in any key.

Major 7th	root–3rd–5th–7th
Dominant 7th	root–3rd–5th–♭7th
Minor 7th	root–♭3rd–5th–♭7th
Minor 7th flat 5th	root–♭3rd–♭5th–♭7th

A common progression found in many jazz tunes is ii–V–I. This progression uses three out of the four types of 7th chords found in a harmonized major scale. The ii minor naturally leads to the V7 dominant, which leads back to the I. In the key of C, the ii chord is Dmin7, the V is G7 and the I is CMaj7. Here's an example:

Dmin7
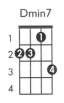

G7

CMaj7

53

Track 78

Now, we'll play "Has Anybody Seen My Uke?"—a chord progression based on a typical 32-bar AABA jazz standard in F. Remember our discussion about chord progressions using the circle of 5ths? In the key of F, C7 is the V chord; the secondary dominant, or V, of the C7, is G7. The secondary dominant of G7 is D7, and the secondary dominant of the D7 is A7. "Has Anybody Seen My Uke?" starts with an F chord. After one measure, it jumps to A7 and then starts cycling back counterclockwise toward the F over the course of the first eight measures. After returning to F, there is one measure of C7 leading to the second line, which is that same 8-bar progression repeated, this time ending at F. The B part jumps to the A7 to start and then cycles back to the C7, which leads to the final 8-bar A part.

 HAS ANYBODY SEEN MY UKE?

Track
79

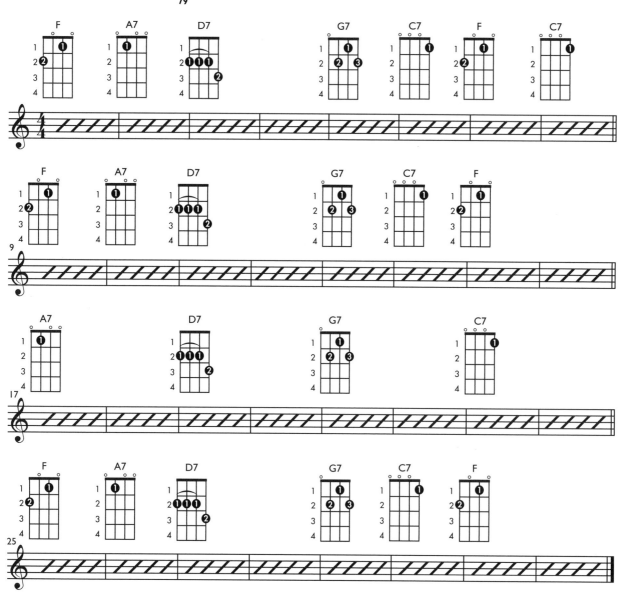

"Uke's Got Rhythm" is based on the chord progression for "I've Got Rhythm" by George Gershwin. This progression, known by jazz musicians as *rhythm changes*, is also the basis of numerous jazz tunes. In the first two measures, we play B♭, Gmin7, Cmin7, and F7, a I–vi–ii–V progression in the key of B♭. Bars 3 and 4 are a repeat of the first two measures. In measures 5–8, the progression is I–I7–IV–♯IV°7–I–V7–I. The B part (starting at measure 9) jumps right to D7, then cycles its way back counterclockwise to the F7, which leads us back to B♭ for the final 8 bars. Cool!

UKE'S GOT RHYTHM

Track 80

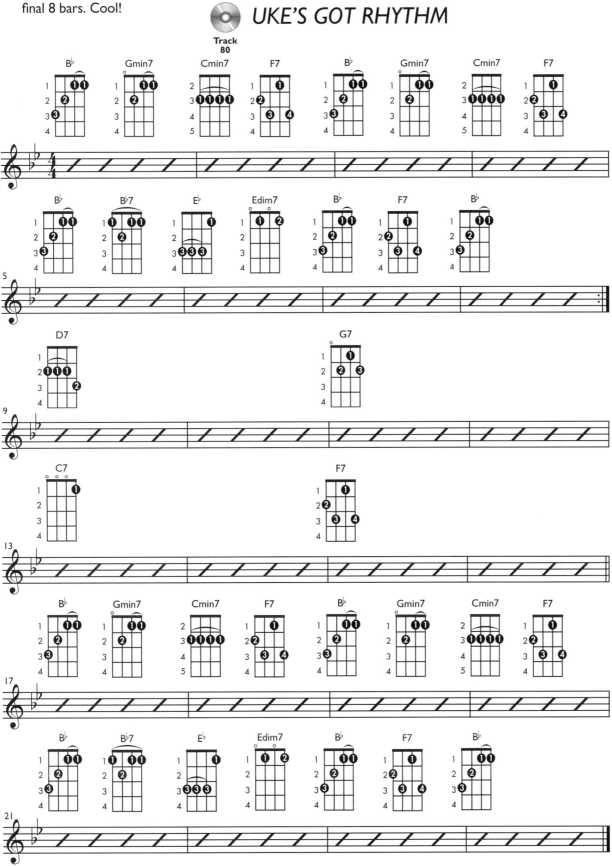

LESSON 4: GYPSY JAZZ

A popular jazz style known as Gypsy jazz was created by Django Reinhardt and the Hot Club of Paris during the 1930s. We'll play a 12-bar minor blues progression in this style. Instead of the minor 7th chords found in the harmonized scale, we'll play minor 6th chords, a common stylistic sound in Gypsy jazz.

To play a minor 6th chord, start with a minor 7th chord shape, and lower the ♭7th another half step to the major 6th. (Note: To end the song, leave out the A7 in the last measure.)

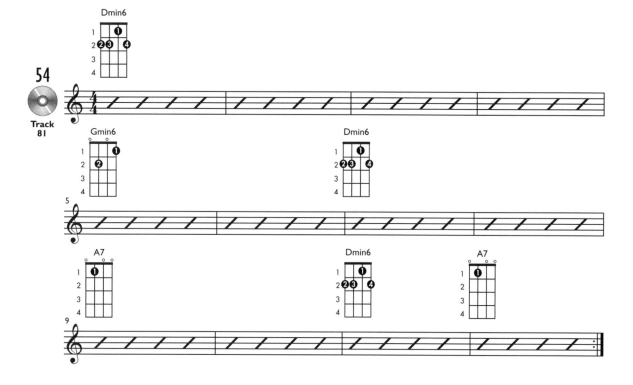

Here it is again, with chord inversions.

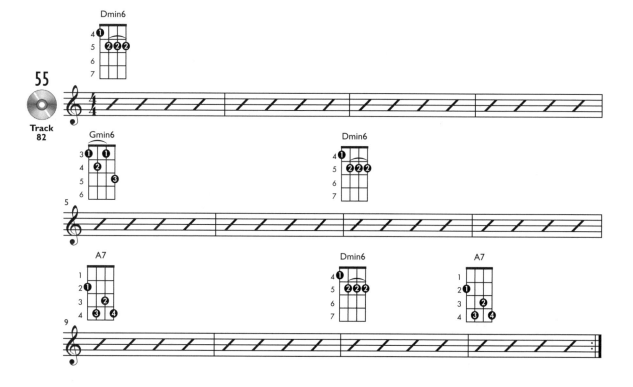

CHAPTER 10

Let's Jam

When learning to play an arranged song, you know what the song is supposed to sound like before playing it, thus you can practice the same thing over and over, working toward a clear goal. Because an improvised solo never comes out the same way twice, learning to improvise can feel a bit more abstract and elusive.

In this chapter, you will be learning pentatonic scales in various positions. Pick one position and practice improvising with it for a while. Just practicing a scale over and over can get monotonous, so try playing along with backing tracks to practice your soloing. In time, you'll get to know which finger movements will produce what kind of melodic movement within a position, eventually developing a sense for what something will sound like before you actually play it. Move on to the next adjacent position, and do the same. Notice the connecting notes in each position, then start to practice going between two positions during a solo.

A great solo tells a story and feels like it has a distinct beginning, middle, and end. We can achieve this goal by fully developing our melodic ideas, as opposed to just stringing together disparate riffs that don't relate to each other.

Great soloing is green and sustainable. Improvisers recycle and reuse ideas all the time. For example, play a short melodic phrase over the I chord, using just a few notes. When we get to the IV chord, play the same idea, slightly varying it rhythmically. When we get to the V chord, still use the basic shape of the original idea, but vary it even more to end the 12-bar phrase.

Call and response is a very effective technique. To use it, play the same original short idea, this time answering it with a different phrase that completes the sentence, so to speak. Now vary that idea as we discussed above, answering with the response, also varied, each time.

Finally, try singing your improvisational ideas, then see if you can find what you sang on your instrument. Often, what we sing comes out sounding better than the results we get from moving our fingers in familiar ways.

Jamming with other people is among the most fun musical things to do. We'll explore the tools you need for improvising creative solos.

Pentatonic scales sound great and are extremely useful when improvising. The word "pente," from the Greek, means "five," and "tonic" means "tones," or "notes." Thus, pentatonic scales are scales containing five notes, instead of the seven notes found in major and minor scales. Pentatonic scales are ancient and are used in musical styles around the world.

MAJOR PENTATONIC SCALE

Let's take a look at the *major pentatonic scale.* Leave out the 4th and 7th notes of the major scale, and the result is a major pentatonic scale. The formula to build a major pentatonic scale in any key is root–2nd–3rd–5th–6th. For example, a C Major scale is C–D–E–F–G–A–B–C. Leave out F (the 4th) and B (the 7th) and you get the C Major Pentatonic scale: C–D–E–G–A–C.

C Major Pentatonic Scale

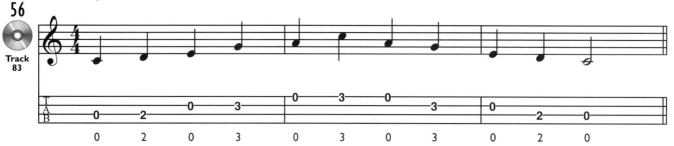

MINOR PENTATONIC SCALE

Using the exact same notes, but starting on A, the 6th degree of the scale, results in an A Minor Pentatonic scale: A–C–D–E–G–A. The A Minor scale is the *relative minor* of C Major. Notice the difference in sound, even though they use the same notes.

A Minor Pentatonic Scale

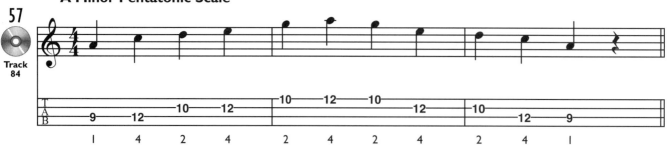

The formula to build a *minor pentatonic scale* in any key is: root–♭3rd–4th–5th–♭7th. We'll compare the two types of pentatonic scales from the same root, which will help you hear the differences. To construct a C Minor Pentatonic scale, start with a C Major scale. C is the root. Skip the 2nd degree of the scale, D. The 3rd is E—lower it by a half step, making it E♭. The 4th, F, and 5th, G, stay the same. Skip the 6th degree, A. The 7th note is B—lower it a half step, making it B♭. Here's the C Minor Pentatonic scale.

C Minor Pentatonic Scale

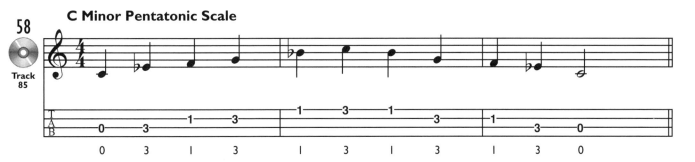

BLUES SCALE

There is also what is called the *blues scale*, which is a minor pentatonic scale plus one note, the ♭5th. In C, the 5th is G—lower it a half step and you get G♭.

C Blues Scale

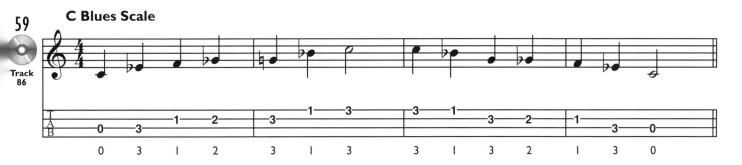

PENTATONIC SCALE POSITIONS

Below are moveable positions of the minor pentatonic scale that can be used to play up the neck and in any key. Each one connects with the next. Once you've learned all five positions, you can play the minor pentatonic scale spanning the entire fingerboard. (Note: To extend your improvisational range a 4th lower, consider trying the low-G tuning.)

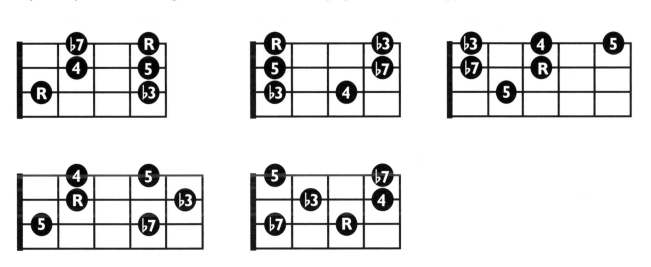

LESSON 3: SOLOING USING THE MINOR PENTATONIC SCALE

Using our 12-bar blues progression in C from page 115, we'll play a sample solo based on the minor pentatonic scale. Also, remember the syncopated rhythms using triplets that we covered on page 111? We'll use one of them to create the melodic idea. When we get to the V chord, we vary the original melodic idea by moving it up a whole step. Finally, we end with a slight variation of one of the turnarounds in C that we covered on page 118 (Example 27). Recycle and reuse!

60

Track 87

Track 88: Melody

Track 89: Chords

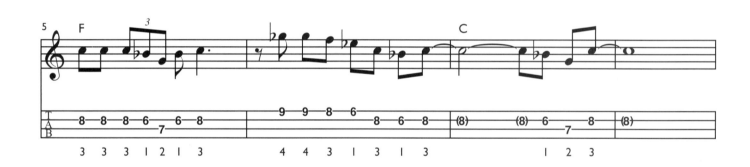

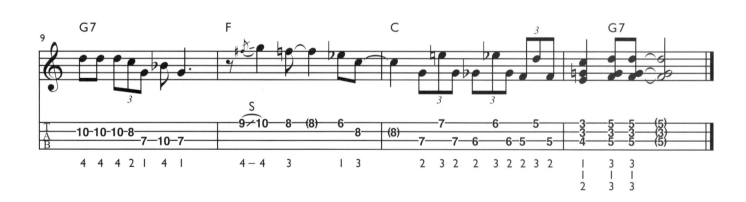

LESSON 4: SOLOING USING THE MAJOR PENTATONIC SCALE

The major pentatonic scale is a versatile scale for improvising and works in many styles from blues and bluegrass to country and rock. Recalling our discussion in the previous lesson on pentatonic scales, the major pentatonic scale contains the exact same notes as the minor pentatonic scale, just starting on a different root note. So the fingerings are easy to learn!

Let's improvise on a simplified version of the chord progression from "Rolling Down That Lonesome Road Blues" (from page 135), a 16-bar progression in G. Here's a sample solo using the G Major Pentatonic scale.

Now, let's explore changing major pentatonic scales over each chord. The G Major Pentatonic scale contains the following notes: G–A–B–D–E. The notes contained in a G chord are G–B–D, so the G Major Pentatonic scale contains all three chord tones. The notes in a C chord are C–E–G; the G Major Pentatonic scale contains the E and G, but not the C root. If we instead play the C Major Pentatonic scale, C–D–E–G–A, over the C chord, it contains all the chord tones.

The notes in a D chord are D–F♯–A. The G Major Pentatonic scale contains the D and A, but not the F♯, the 3rd of the chord. Similarly, if we play the D Major Pentatonic scale, D–E–F♯–A–B, over the D chord, it contains all the chord tones.

Perhaps the idea of changing scales over each chord sounds challenging, but it really isn't as difficult as it might seem. Looking again at the G Major pentatonic scale, it contains the following notes: G–A–B–D–E. The C Major Pentatonic scale contains C–D–E–G–A. Only one note changed, the B note moved up a half step to C. The D Major Pentatonic scale contains D–E–F♯–A–B. Comparing it to the G Major pentatonic, again, only one note changed, the G moved down a half step to F♯. Having these chord tones available for these chords really sounds great.

Below is another sample solo over the chord progression for "Rolling Down That Lonesome Road Blues," this time changing scales over each chord. Many of the melodic ideas from the previous version have been used so you can hear the difference between the two approaches.

LESSON 5: COMBINING MAJOR PENTATONIC, MINOR PENTATONIC, AND BLUES SCALES IN A SOLO

There is no magic formula to which pentatonic scale should be used to solo over a song. Try different scales over the same progression and see which you prefer. Each scale will yield a very different sound and feel. Sometimes, you'll notice that both approaches sound good, and, in fact, we can combine different scales into our solos. Before trying to combine multiple scales in a solo, I recommend spending a lot time practicing each scale individually.

We will now discuss how to combine scales in a solo. First, compare major pentatonic, minor pentatonic, and blues scales in the key of C.

C Major Pentatonic	C(R)–D(2)–E(3)–G(5)–A(6)
C Minor Pentatonic	C(R)–E♭(♭3)–F(4)–G(5)–B♭(♭7)
C Blues	C(R)–E♭(♭3)–F(4)–G♭(♭5)–G(5)–B♭(♭7)

Combine all the notes, and the composite scale contains: C(R)–D(2)–E♭(♭3)–E(3)–F(4)–G♭(♭5)–G(5)–A(6)–B♭(♭7). Here it is in open position.

The composite scale isn't really that useful to play exactly as it is over a progression; rather, it is a way to understand what notes are available to you within the overlapping scales. One approach you can use is to create a melodic idea from one pentatonic scale, and then answer it with an idea in another scale. Here's an example, using C and F Major Pentatonic for the "call" during the first two measures, and C Minor Pentatonic for the "response" in the next two measures.

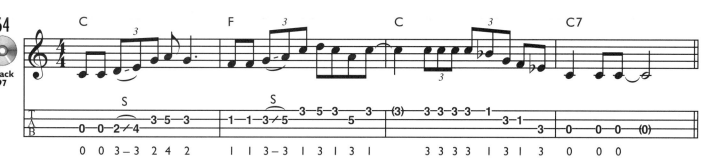

Below is a sample improvisation using our composite scale over a jazzy blues progression. A variation of Example 64 is the basis for this solo. Same as with our previous solos, we're recycling!

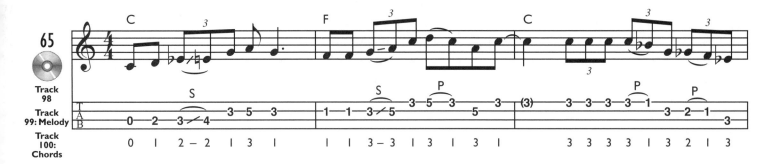

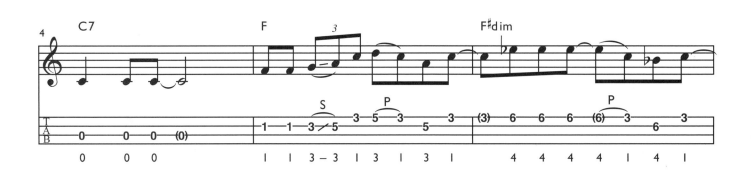

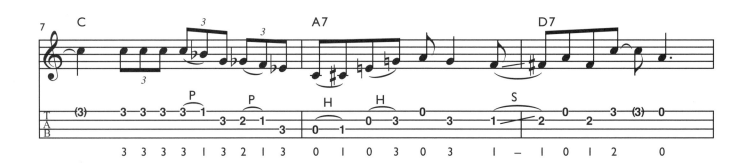

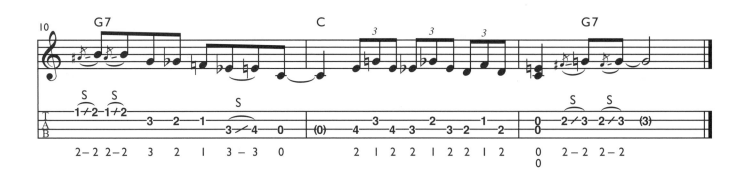

CONCLUSION

It's been a pleasure working together. Continue to practice and play with as many different musicians as you can. See you in *Mastering Ukulele*!

MASTERING UKULELE

CONTENTS

INTRODUCTION

Mastering Ukulele builds on what you learned in _Beginning Ukulele_ and _Intermediate Ukulele_. In this section, you will learn:

- How to construct and play more types of chords across the fretboard
- Major scales and modes
- Major and minor pentatonic scales
- Arpeggios
- Working your way up the neck using moveable positions
- Music theory applied to the ukulele
- Playing techniques including strums, fingerstyle, harmonics, and muting
- Playing and arranging chord-melody style
- Improvisation

We will venture into styles such as blues, jazz, rock, folk, classical, and fingerpicking. As you work through _Mastering Ukulele_, many songs and exercises can be combined to extend the range of possibilities. For example, try various rhythms learned in one chapter over a song or chord progression in another lesson. We will present ideas on how to progress and create your own style using the concepts presented in this section.

CHAPTER 1

The World A'Chording to Uke

To play more sophisticated chords, we will first review the four-note chords found in the harmonized major scale, since many *extended chords* (see page 168 for an explanation of extended chords) are built using them as a foundation. We discussed the harmonized major scale in *Beginning* and *Intermediate Ukulele*. Here are the four-note chords in the key of C.

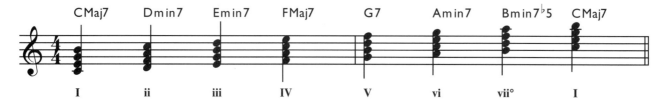

Building four-note chords in 3rds on each degree of the major scale results in four different types of 7th chords: *major 7th, dominant 7th, minor 7th,* and *minor 7th flat 5th*. The resulting chord types and order are the same in any key: the I and IV are both major 7ths; the V is a dominant 7th; the ii, iii, and vi are minor 7ths; and the vii chord is a minor 7th ♭5. All of these chords are very useful for playing many styles of music.

Here are the formulas to construct these chords in any key:

Major 7th	root–3rd–5th–7th
Dominant 7th	root–3rd–5th–♭7th
Minor 7th	root–♭3rd–5th–♭7th
Minor 7th flat 5th*	root–♭3rd–♭5th–♭7th

---

* The minor 7th flat 5th (min7♭5) is also known as a *half-diminished 7th chord*, since it contains a diminished triad but not a fully diminished, or double flatted, 7th (♭♭7).

7th chords contain four notes, and since the ukulele has four strings, we'll play these chords using one string per note. Below are four moveable inversions that can be used to play any major 7th chord. (Remember from *Beginning Ukulele* that root-position chords have the root at the bottom of the voicing, 1st inversion chords have the 3rd at the bottom, 2nd inversion chords have the 5th at the bottom, and 3rd inversion chords have the 7th at the bottom.) Each degree of the chord is listed below the string. Below, the inversions are presented according to the note on the 1st string: root, then 3rd, then 5th, and finally 7th. This order is useful for creating chord-melodies. In the first and third voicings, you'll notice a *dissonance* (clashing sound) due to the minor 2nd intervals contained within them. Let's look first at the major 7th shapes.

Major 7th Inversions (Maj7)

 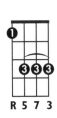 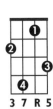 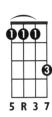

7 3 5 R   R 5 7 3   3 7 R 5   5 R 3 7

Once you've learned the major 7th shapes, simply flat the 7th degree in each of them and you get four dominant 7th inversions. These are presented in the same order as above.

Dominant 7th Inversions (7)

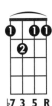 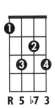 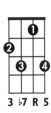 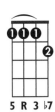

♭7 3 5 R   R 5 ♭7 3   3 ♭7 R 5   5 R 3 ♭7

Now, flat the major 3rd of each dominant 7th inversion and you get four minor 7th inversions, again presented in the same order as above.

Minor 7th Inversions (min7)

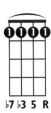 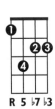 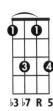 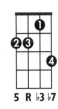

♭7 ♭3 5 R   R 5 ♭7 ♭3   ♭3 ♭7 R 5   5 R ♭3 ♭7

Finally, flat the 5th degree of the minor 7th inversions and you have four inversions of the minor 7th ♭5th.

Minor 7th Flat 5th Inversions (min7♭5)

 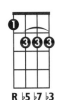 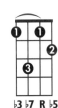 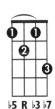

♭7 ♭3 ♭5 R   R ♭5 ♭7 ♭3   ♭3 ♭7 R ♭5   ♭5 R ♭3 ♭7

In addition to the four types of 7th chords, 6th chords are extremely useful. The formula for the major 6th chord is root–3rd–5th–6th. To build a major 6th chord, simply lower the ♭7th of the dominant chord by a half step to the 6th interval.

Major 6th Inversions (6)

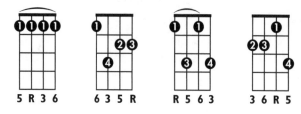

In addition to the four types of 7th chords, 6th chords are extremely useful. The formula for

Notice that the major 6th inversions above are the exact same shapes as the minor 7th inversions. The only thing that has changed is that each string is now labeled as a different interval. Using the C Major scale as an example, if we construct a C6, the notes contained are C–E–G–A. The notes in an A Minor 7th chord are A–C–E–G. C6 and Amin7 have the same exact notes but different chord names. Which name might be used in a song will depend on its context. One more thing to be aware of is that the ukulele is tuned G–C–E–A, the notes of a C6 chord.

The formula for the minor 6th chord is root–♭3rd–5th–6th. There are a couple of ways to build these from chords you've already learned. Flat the 3rd of a major 6th chord inversion, or, lower the ♭7th degree of the minor 7th chord by a half step to the sixth interval.

Notice that the minor 6th inversions below are the exact same shapes as the minor 7th flat 5th inversions. The only thing that changed is that each string is labeled as a different interval. Let's compare: An Amin6 contains A–C–E–F♯. The notes contained in an F♯min7♭5 are F♯–A–C–E; again, same exact notes, different chord name.

Minor 6th Inversions (min6)

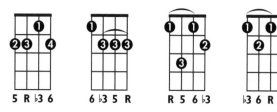

LESSON 4: SUSPENDED CHORDS

Suspended (or *sus*) *chords* are very useful. You've heard them used extensively by artists like Joni Mitchell, Pete Townshend, Pierre Bensusan, and others—and they often appear in traditional Hawaiian music as well. There are two types of suspended chords: the *suspended 4th* (sus4) and the *suspended 2nd* (sus2).

The most commonly used suspended chord is the sus4, which is constructed by raising the 3rd of a major triad by a half step to the 4th. For example, a C chord is made up of the notes C(root)–E(3rd)–G(5th). Raise the E(3rd) a half step to F(4th) and you get a Csus4.

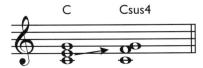

Because the suspended chord contains no 3rd, it is rather ambiguous and could be used in place of either a major or minor chord. Try this in some songs or progressions you already play. In *Intermediate Ukulele*, we looked at moveable major chord shapes. To create a moveable sus4 chord shape, simply raise the 3rd of any of those.

Now, we'll look at the suspended 2nd (or sus2) chord, which is constructed by lowering the 3rd of a major chord by a whole step to the 2nd. For example, a C chord is made up of the notes C(root)–E(3rd)–G(5th). Lower the E(3rd) a whole step to D(2nd) and you get a Csus2.

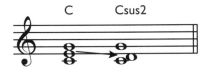

Like the sus4, the sus2 chord contains no 3rd, so it is also ambiguous and could be used in place of either a major or minor chord. Here's an interesting thing to consider. The notes contained in a Csus2 are C–D–G. The notes contained in a Gsus4 are G–C–D. Thus, any sus2 could also be considered an inversion of the sus4 chord.

Suspended chords often resolve to the major chord of the same name. Below are a couple of examples going from a sus4 to the major chord to the sus2 and then back to the major.

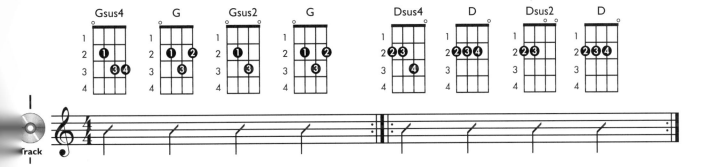

LESSON 5: WHAT ARE ALL THOSE OTHER NUMBERS, ANYWAY?

You've probably looked at some chord names and wondered about all those numbers such as 9, 11, and 13. The numbers themselves are *extensions*, and the chords that use them are *extended chords*. Let's look at how extended chords are constructed.

EXTENDED CHORDS

In the key of C, the V chord is G7. This dominant 7th chord was built by adding every other note from the C scale: G–B–D–F. If we keep adding consecutive notes in 3rds (G–B–D–F–A–C–E), the A is the 9th (also the 2nd an octave higher), the C is the 11th (also the 4th an octave higher), and E is the 13th (also the 6th an octave higher).

Root   3rd   5th   ♭7th   9th   11th   13th

Here's a handy way to think of extended chords, the combined numbers of 7th and extension conveniently add up. For example, if we add an E note to a G Major triad, it is G6; however if we add an E note to G7, it is now G13 (6 + 7 = 13). If we add an A (the 2nd) to a G Major triad, it is generally called Gadd9. If we add an A (the 2nd) to a G7 chord, it is now called G9 (2 + 7 = 9). Once you learn the formulas for the chord names, it is possible to construct any chord. This is better than trying to memorize a zillion chords.

In theory, an extended chord contains all the previous notes, so a G13 would contain root–3rd–5th–♭7th–9th–11th–13th. In common practice, however, we often just use the notes of the G7 chord (G–B–D–F) plus the 13th (or 6), E. If we wanted the chord to contain both the 9th and 13th, we could specify this in the chord's name: G9add13.

You might be wondering how we can play these extended chords on the uke—it only has four strings. We can leave out other notes to add in the extensions. The root and 5th are the most expendable notes. Another instrument in an ensemble, such as bass or guitar, might be playing those notes. The 3rd is important as it specifies whether the chord is major or minor. The 7th lets us know what type of 7th chord it is (dominant 7th, major 7th, or minor 7th). So, if we leave out both the root and 5th, we could play a G9 chord using only three notes: B(3rd), F(♭7th), and A(9th). Hmm...that left us an extra string...we could add in a 13th!

ALTERED DOMINANT CHORDS

In addition to the extended chords, there are *altered dominants*, which are dominant chords with the extensions either raised or lowered by a half step, for instance: ♭9, ♯9, ♯11, or ♭13. A common altered dominant chord is E7♯9, sometimes called the "Hendrix chord," as it was often used by Jimi Hendrix. When leaving out notes, we run into the possibility of certain combinations of notes having multiple chord names. For example, G7♭9 contains G–B–D–F–A♭. If we leave off the root note, it's a Bdim7 chord. This ♭9 chord is often used in Gypsy jazz.

You will have a chance to work with many of these chord types later in this book (for example, on page 173). Refer back to this lesson to review how the chords are constructed.

LESSON 6: ii–V–I PROGRESSION

A progression found in many jazz tunes is ii–V–I, or ii–V. The ii naturally leads to the V7, which leads us back to the I. The ii–V–I progression uses three of the four types of 7th chords that we found within a harmonized major scale, so it's a great practice exercise for learning to play these chords in context. In the key of C, the ii chord is Dmin7, the V is G7, and the I is CMaj7. Below is an example using moveable chord positions. Try transposing and practicing this exercise into other keys. In a later chapter, we will use some of these chords in songs.

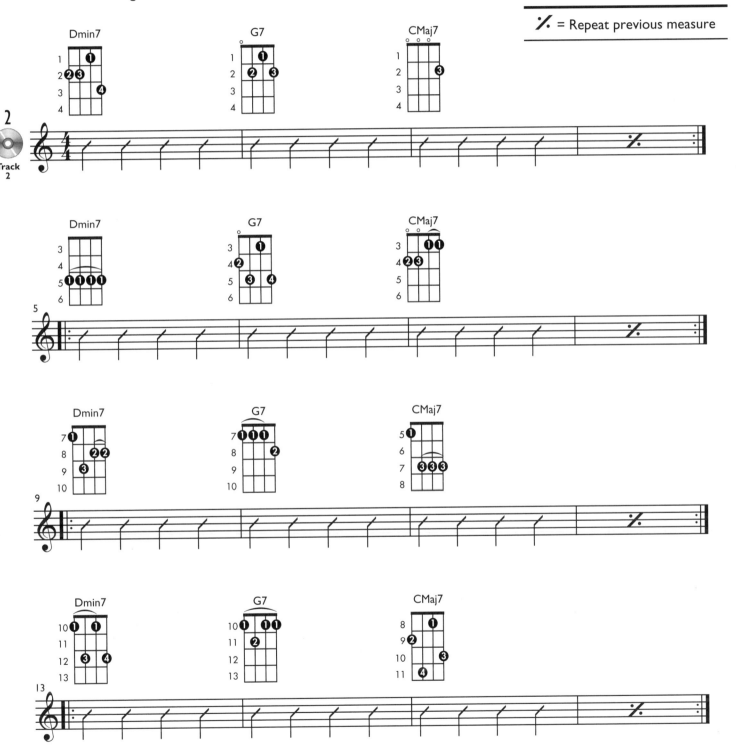

CHAPTER 2

Arranging Chord-Melody Style Up the Neck

LESSON 1: CHORD SCALE

Chord-melody style is where a song's accompaniment and melody are combined into a single solo arrangement, and it is among the most expressive styles on the ukulele. We'll explore arranging chord-melody style up the neck.

A fundamental tool for doing this is the *chord scale*, which is a major scale played on the 1st string with an inversion of the I, IV, or V chord underneath each note of the scale. This requires knowledge of the major triad inversions covered in *Intermediate Ukulele*, and also an understanding of what notes are in each chord and which interval is found on each string. In the key of C, our I, IV, and V chords are C, F, and G. To review:

	Root Position	1st Inversion	2nd Inversion
Notes in C Major	C–E–G	E–G–C	G–C–E
Notes in F Major	F–A–C	A–C–F	C–F–A
Notes in G Major	G–B–D	B–D–G	D–G–B

Below is a chord scale in the key of C. Practice it both ascending and descending.

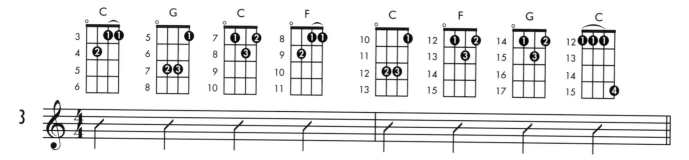

Now, we'll play "When the Saints Go Marching In," which was among the first songs you learned to play the melody for in *Beginning Ukulele*. This time, we're going up the neck and using the chord scale, which creates a very full-sounding arrangement. I advise playing the melody on one string first, just to get a feel for where the notes are, and then add in the chords. Once you've learned to play the chord-melody arrangement, try incorporating some of the strums we did in *Intermediate Ukulele* or from later chapters in this section.

WHEN THE SAINTS GO MARCHING IN (CHORD-MELODY)

Track 3

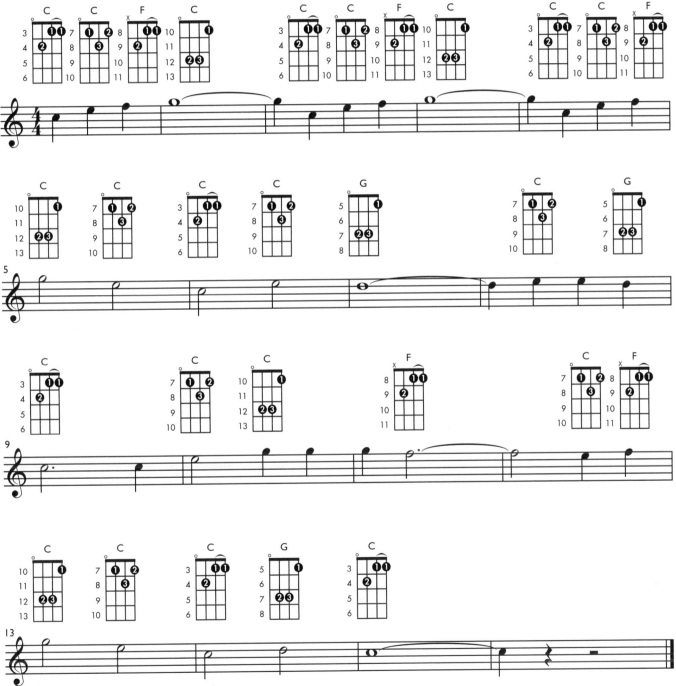

LESSON 3: *THE STAR-SPANGLED BANNER* (CHORD-MELODY)

As you get familiar with this technique of playing melodies with the chord scale, you can add in other types of chords. The following arrangement of "The Star-Spangled Banner" incorporates the major triad inversions we've already used plus a few minor and dominant 7th chord inversions. It also incorporates some single-note melody playing, rather than using chords for every note.

Track 4

THE STAR-SPANGLED BANNER (CHORD-MELODY)

As you get familiar with playing melodies using the chord scale, continue to add other types of chords. Let's revisit "Jazzin' the Blues" from *Intermediate Ukulele*. This arrangement uses the moveable dominant 7th inversions you've learned, and adds some extended and altered chords to create melodic interest.

In measure 5, an F9 is used instead of an F7. This isn't an arbitrary choice. The reason for the substitution is in the previous measure, where we played an inversion of C7 containing a G note on the 1st string. When switching to the F7, the G melody note was kept in the chord, turning it into an F9. Something similar is done in measure 7, where we use an inversion of C with E, the 3rd, on the 1st string. We keep that note constant throughout the next three measures, playing an A7 with that same E on the 1st string, then a D9 with that E now a 9th, and finally a D♭7♯9, in which that E note is the ♯9th.

Also featured is a *tritone substitution*, in which we substitute a chord whose root is a ♭5th away from that of the chord that was written. In measure 10, the original chord was G7, the V chord of the key. A ♭5th interval from G is D♭, so we play a D♭7 instead. For more color, the chord is further altered by adding a ♯9th. The tritone substitution is also used at the end, where a D♭9 takes the place of G7. Try using some of these concepts in other songs you play.

At the end of this piece, you can play a C or C7 chord for a sense of finality.

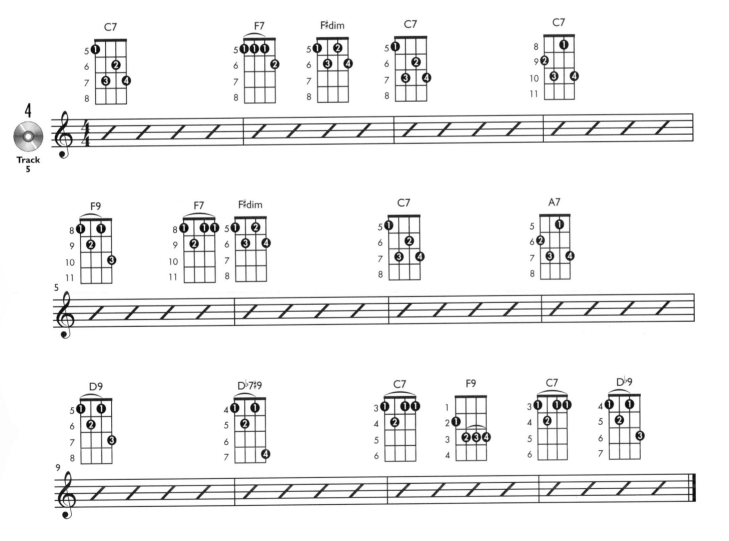

Track 5

CHAPTER 3

Yet More Strums and Techniques

LESSON 1: REVIEWING TRIPLES, BURSTS, AND SPLIT STRUMS

This lesson is a quick review of techniques covered in *Beginning* and *Intermediate Ukulele*. The lessons that follow will build on these techniques, and in the next chapter, you'll use many of them in larger musical examples.

Track 6

THE TRIPLE STRUM

The *triple strum* (also simply called a "triple") is a three-stroke pattern that can be executed a number of ways. A common approach is to begin with a downstroke of the index finger (*i*), followed by a downstroke of the thumb (*T*), then an upstroke of the index finger. The first part of Example 5 shows the triple in a *3+3+2 rhythm* (two triples and a single down-up strum in eighth notes).

Track 7

THE TRIPLE BURST

The *triple burst* uses the triple strum as a flourish to set up a strong downstroke on the next beat. At slow tempos, it sounds like a triplet, but at faster tempos it sounds like quick burst of strums. The second part of Example 5 shows the triple burst.

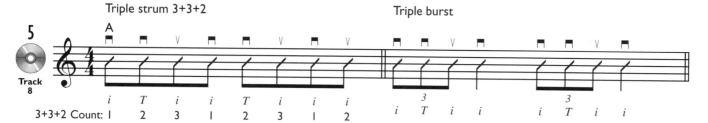

THE SPLIT STRUM

The *split strum* is often associated with British uke star George Formby. It produces a three-stroke rhythm, all with the index finger. The first stroke is a full downstroke. The second stroke is an upstroke that just hits the first two strings. The third stroke is a downstroke that just hits strings 3 and 4. Split strums often appear in a 3+3+2 rhythm of eighth notes. It is very common with split strums to lift a left-hand finger on and off one of the notes of the chord. This technique can be called a *tap finger*.

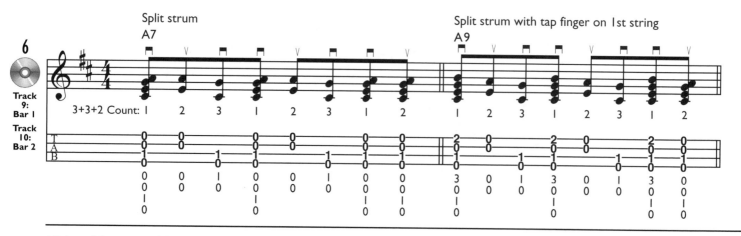

The *fan stroke* is one of many special strums made famous by George Formby in many films. It is a type of triple strum that also creates a visual effect for your audience. The best way to learn it is to break it down into three steps.

STEP 1

Start with your hand in a normal strumming position, ready to do a downstroke on all four strings. Your fingers should be curled in slightly, as they normally would be. The first part of the fan stroke could be done with the pinky (as Formby did), or the ring finger, which makes a more consistent sound. We will use the ring finger here.

Use your ring finger (labeled in music as "*a*") to make a downstroke across the strings, somewhere over the fretboard. As you make the downstroke, allow your fingers to fan out in a circular motion. If your uke was a clock, and the neck was at 12 o'clock, the path of your ring finger would be roughly 10:00 to 2:00. As you make the stroke, let your thumb stick out—you'll need it next.

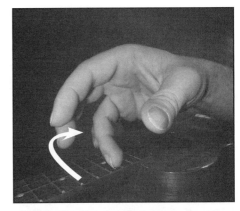

Step 1: Ring-finger downstroke.

STEP 2

Follow the ring-finger downstroke with a downstroke of the thumb (*T*). Follow the same path of 10:00 to 2:00 as in Step 1, allowing the thumb motion to push the rest of your hand farther around the circle. Your fingers will naturally curl back into your palm.

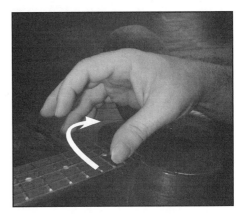

Step 2: Thumb downstroke.

STEP 3

Finish the fan stroke with an upstroke of your index finger (*i*), following a path of 4:00 to 7:00 around your imaginary clock. This part of the stroke is hard to see from the front and helps create the illusion that you are making magical sounds happen just by whirling your hand around the strings in a circle.

The fan stroke can be used like a triple strum to make various rhythms, or it can be done in a solid stream of fast triplets for a tremolo or rolling effect. Try practicing the fan stroke in slow quarter notes, then in triplets. Make sure each part of the strum is a distinct rhythmic sound.

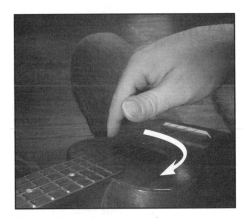

Step 3: Index-finger upstroke.

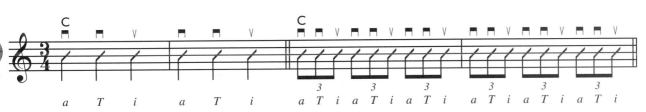

LESSON 3: THE FAN STROKE CONTINUED

It may take quite a bit of practice to get a good fan stroke going. Try watching yourself in a mirror and aiming for a smooth, fluid, "round-the-clock" look while producing the sound of three distinct strums. You can use the fan stroke in the same way you would use a triple strum. It can be combined with normal down-up strums and other combinations. One common way to use it is in a 3+3+2 rhythm, where you are strumming in eighth notes but the fan stroke groups the eighth notes into threes. Do two fan strokes then one down-up strum with the index finger for a 3+3+2 grouping. Try counting the rhythm two ways, as "1 & 2 & 3 & 4 &" and "1 2 3 1 2 3 1 2."

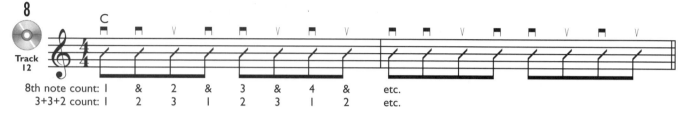

You'll get to employ your new fan stroke in some upcoming lessons. Here are some other fun things you can try:

- Try other combinations of fan strokes and normal strums, like 2+3+3.

- Try lifting a finger on and off of the chord while you play, as you would with a "tap finger" in a split strum.

- Try building up your speed so you can do a steady roll of fan-stroke triplets. At higher tempos this can sound like a machine gun! Be sure to grin maniacally as you execute this move.

- Try initiating the fan stroke on unusual beats of the bar, or starting the fan stroke with the thumb so that the whole sequence moves over by one stroke.

- Make up other variations or develop your own signature moves!

LESSON 4: ONE-FINGER TREMOLO

The *tremolo* effect is achieved by strumming very rapidly back and forth across the strings. Tremolo is indicated by two or three diagonal slashes (𝄍) above or below the note head. This lesson will focus on tremolo while strumming with the index finger. You can adapt the move to a pick as well. One-finger tremolo comes in two flavors:

- *Soft tremolo*—Use the skin of your fingertip (where your fingerprint is) to lightly brush across the strings. The movement is more back-and-forth than down-and-up. Try it with your fingertip over the soundhole or fretboard for a sweeter sound. Move from the wrist or elbow.

- *Hard tremolo*—Use the nail of your index finger in a down-up strumming motion. Instead of moving from your finger, hold the finger steady and wiggle your forearm back and forth from your elbow.

To get an idea of how tremolo works, try building up to the tremolo by starting with eighths, then sixteenths, then thirty-second notes. Try to stay loose and relaxed.

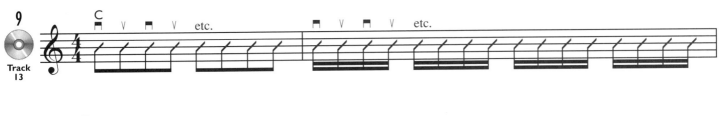

Try the following progression to a slow, steady beat. You can be very expressive by varying the speed of the tremolo and the intensity or volume. Try this progression with both soft and hard tremolo.

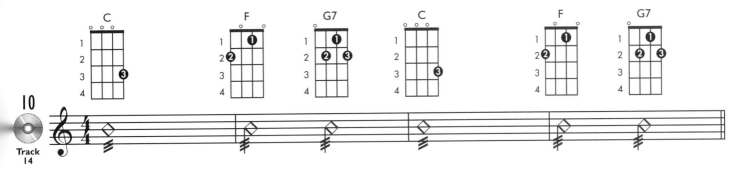

To develop your tremolo technique, plan to practice tremolo for a small portion of your regular practice time for many sessions in a row. It can take lots of time and patience for the technique to become smooth and even. Slides combine well with tremolo. In the progression below, the C and G7 chords are played in two inversions. As you tremolo, slide up the neck to the new inversion. You can drag out the slide slowly, or move more quickly to slide on the beat.

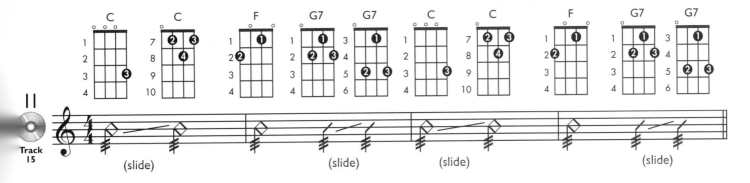

Now, we'll look to flamenco guitar music for a virtuosic strumming technique that translates well to the ukulele. The *rasgueado* is a rapid strum using multiple fingers in succession. There are a number of different ways to play a rasgueado, and we'll try some of the variations.

The first part of Example 12 is all downstrums using four fingers. The letter "*c*" indicates the pinky and "*a*" indicates the ring finger. Hold down an A Major chord, and then, one at a time, strum downward with the pinky, followed in succession by ring, middle, and finally index. Brush quickly across the strings with each finger, the next finger starting to brush before the previous finger is done. It isn't necessary to brush all four strings with each finger. You may want to try starting with all fingers held in a loose fist, and then flick them out one at a time. Practice this slowly at first, getting the right sound before speeding it up. The second part of Example 12 builds on the first part, adding an upstrum with the index finger at the end of each group of notes. In this example, we're fitting five sixteenth notes into the space of four—this is known as a *quintuplet*.

Right-Hand Review
T = Thumb
i = index finger
m = middle finger
a = ring finger
c = pinky

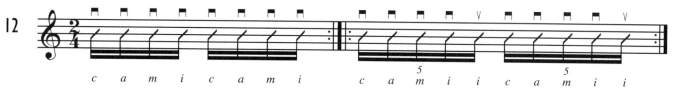

The first part of Example 13 is all upstrums using four fingers. Hold down an A Major chord, then, one at a time, strum upward with the pinky, followed by ring, middle, and index fingers. Brush quickly across the strings with each finger, the next finger starting to brush before the previous finger is done. The second part of Example 13 builds on the first part, adding a downstrum with the index finger at the end of each quintuplet.

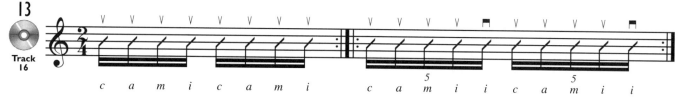

There are various other ways to play rasgueados—some using less fingers, others including the thumb. Experiment with different combinations, and try incorporating rasgueados into your arrangements and pieces that you already play. You can use an occasional rasgueado as a flourish, or use them throughout entire passages.

There are several possible variations and augmentations to the basic rasgueado technique.

- In the five-stroke rasgueado (*c-a-m-i-i*), the final stroke can be played with the thumb instead of the index finger. The thumb or index finger could be used in a downstroke or an upstroke. An upstroke of the thumb can be very powerful as it makes use of the broad surface of the thumbnail.

- Rasgueado can be a steady, machine-gun like division of the beat into four or five strokes, or it can be used to *roll* a chord. In a roll, the final stroke of the rasgueado is the downbeat of the chord. The following example illustrates the notation for this usage.

Below is an opportunity to try out your rasgueados and other techniques from this chapter. A popular progression in Spanish flamenco music uses a major chord, followed by another one a half step up, then another a whole step up, as in A–B♭–C. Note the special fingering of the A chord that allows you to move the 2nd and 3rd fingers up the strings into the other chords. The first exercise establishes the chord progression, then you can try out the various techniques. You can practice them as separate exercises or run them together, building speed as you repeat the whole sequence.

BIG FLAMENCO WORKOUT

Track 17

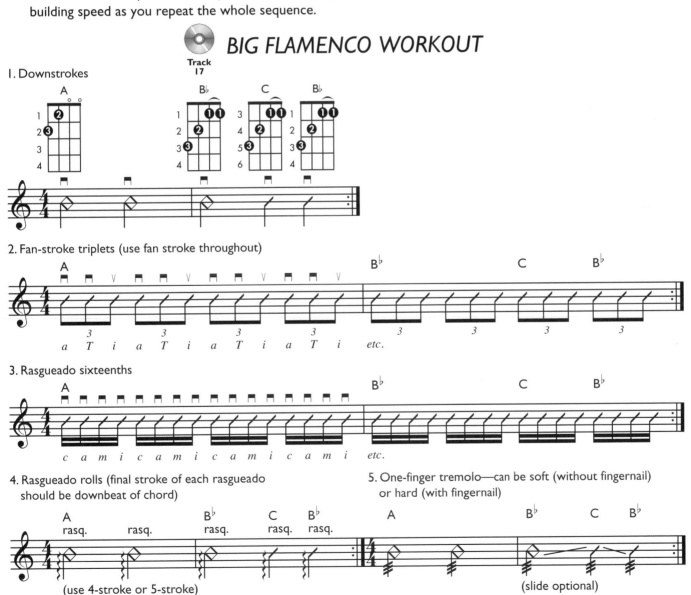

CHAPTER 4

Old-School Fancy: Traditional Ragtime, Jazz, and Hawaiian

LESSON 1: ALOHA 'OE

We're going to revisit "Aloha 'Oe," which you learned in *Beginning Ukulele*. This time, we'll play a chord-melody arrangement, utilizing chord shapes up the neck and harmonized 3rds. Make sure to hold chords throughout the measure so they will keep sustaining while you're playing the melody. First, learn the basic chord-melody arrangement, then try playing it utilizing the one-finger tremolo technique explained on pages 176–177. You can add in more tremolo if you wish, or use less. It's a great expressive tool.

This beautiful Hawaiian song was composed in 1878 by Queen Lili'uokalani, the last monarch of Hawaii. The lyrics tell of a parting embrace, which has come to symbolize longing for loved ones and for homeland. There are countless recordings of this song, from Hawaiian steel guitarists to Elvis Presley.

ALOHA 'OE

Track 18

Here's a piece based on chord changes from the ragtime era classic "12th Street Rag." Many uke players such as Roy Smeck played these types of ragtime showpieces.

This piece uses the tap finger techniques we discussed earlier. Once you get comfortable with this piece, try adding in some other occasional flourishes and fancy strums from the preceding chapter.

RAGGIN' ON 12TH STREET

Track 19

Here is a ragtime-style tune that will give you a chance to try some more of the special tricks and techniques you've been learning. "George on Holiday" pays tribute to the banjo ukulele–toting British movie star of the 1930s George Formby. His style paired upbeat comedic songs with a trick-bag of special effects like split strums, triples, and fan strokes.

"George on Holiday" opens with triple bursts that were first shown in *Beginning Ukulele*. A triple burst is a fast triple strum that leads into a strong downbeat. At a slow tempo, these bursts will sound like triplet eighth notes, but at a faster tempos they will turn into a flamenco-style burst of chords. A tip that might help is to hold your thumb and index finger a couple of inches apart and use a shake of the wrist to do the triple burst. This helps the burst feel like one quick motion instead of three distinct finger strokes.

Also, keep an eye out for the fan strokes. As indicated, the first stroke of the fan stroke is a downstroke of the ring (*a*) finger. You could use your pinky instead, or the pinky and ring together. Remember, for the fan stroke, you should slightly fan out your fingers as you come across the strings. The sections that use fan strokes, triple bursts, and split strums are labeled in the music.

GEORGE ON HOLIDAY

Track 20

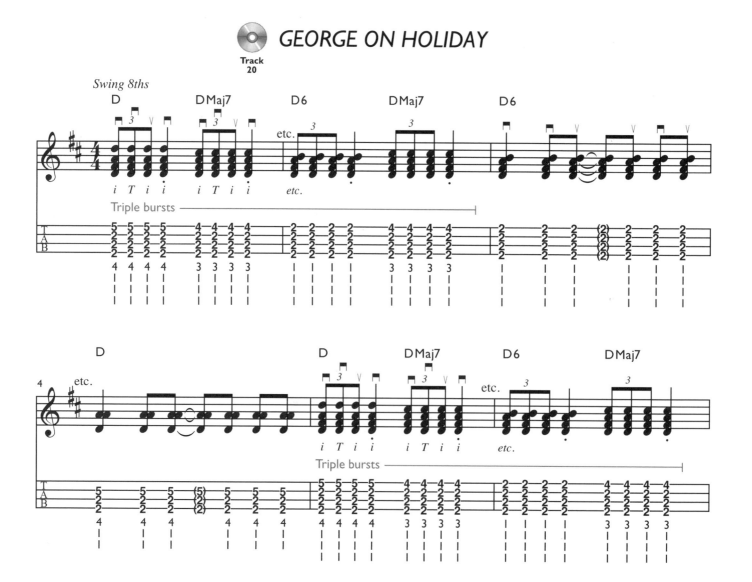

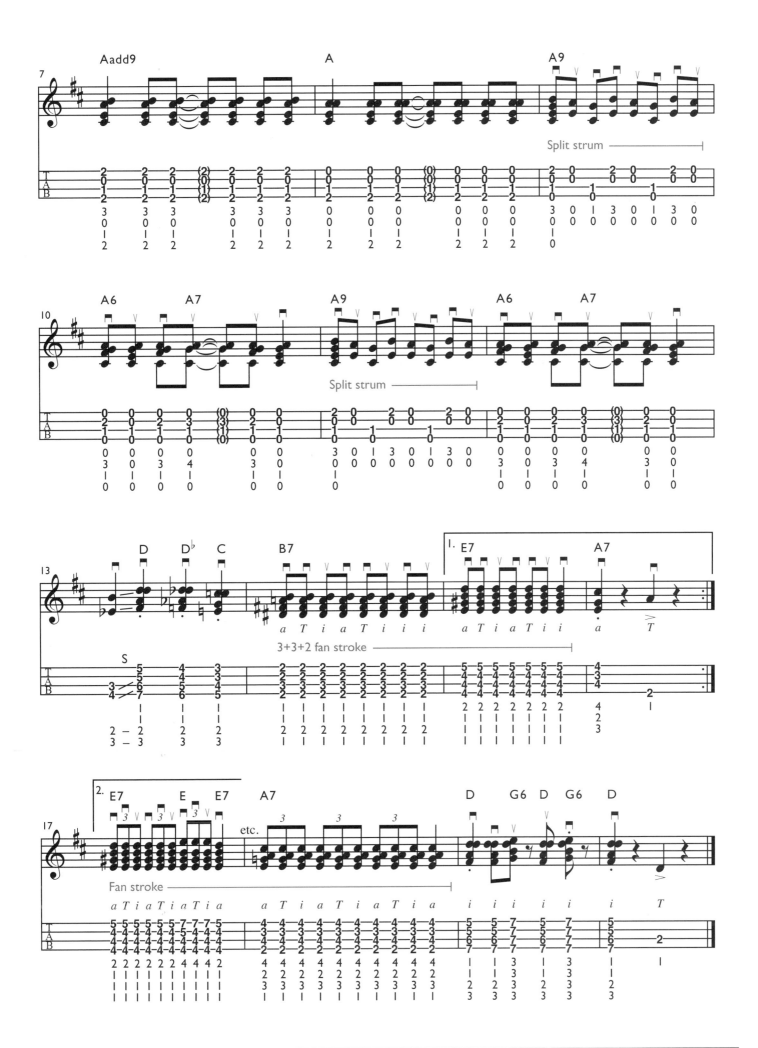

Next, we'll play a piece based on the chord progression from "Autumn Leaves," using four types of 7th chord inversions found in a harmonized major or minor scale. This song features ii–V progressions, which we discussed earlier. An interesting thing about this chord progression is that it uses a chord for every degree of the harmonized scale, with one slight exception. In the key of E Minor, the i is Emin, ii is F#min7♭5, III is GMaj7, iv is Amin7, v is Bmin7, VI is CMaj7, and VII is D7. Instead of the v minor, which would be Bmin7, the song uses a dominant 7th, B7, in its place. We're sometimes altering this chord as well, playing a ♭9 or #9, which sounds much jazzier.

AUTUMN HAS LEFT

Track 21

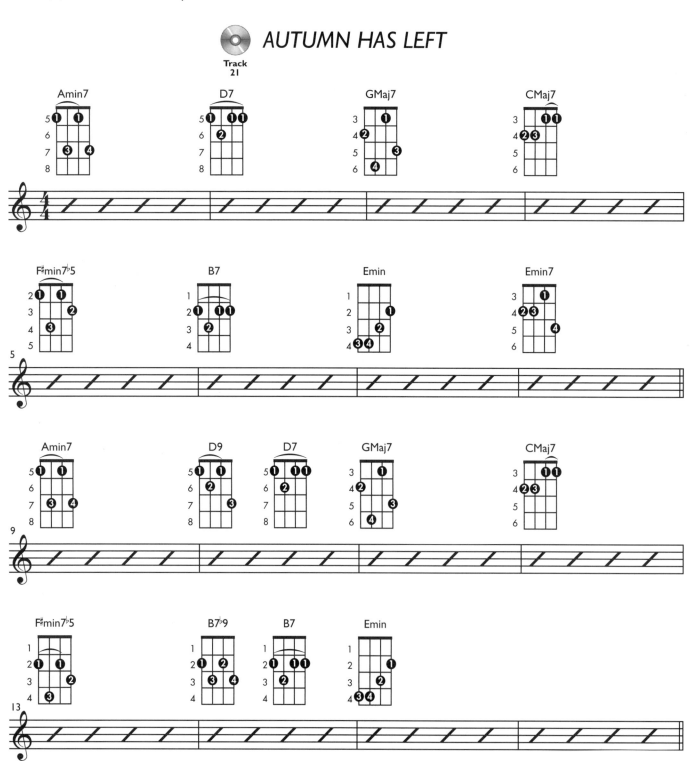

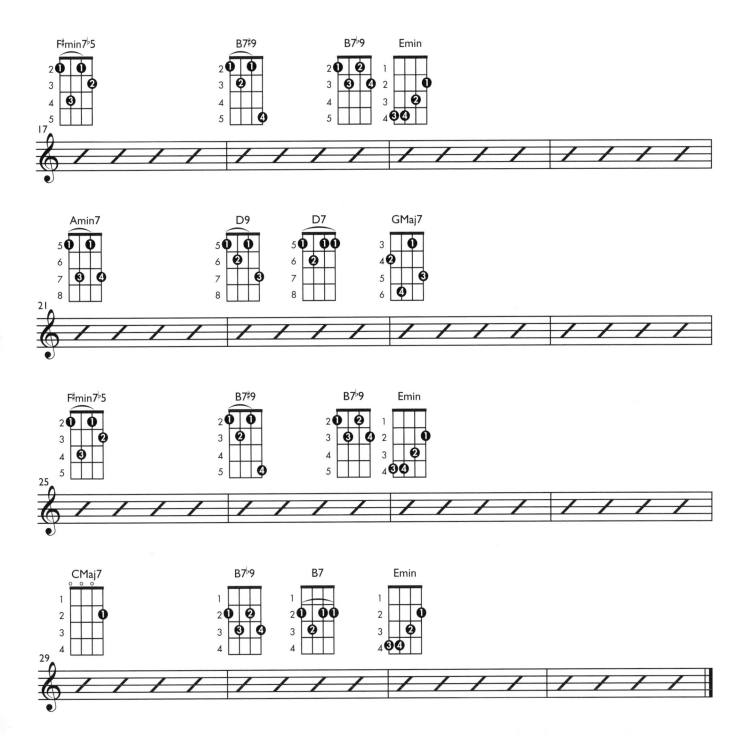

Now, we'll play "Has Anybody Seen My Uke?"—a chord progression based on a typical 32-bar AABA jazz standard in F. In *Intermediate Ukulele*, we discussed chord progressions that cycle through the circle of 5ths, and played a simpler version of this song. In this arrangement, we're using dominant 7th chord inversions up the neck and also some extended chords. Additionally, this song contains a C7aug (augmented), which is a dominant 7th chord with a raised, or augmented, 5th (♯5).

HAS ANYBODY SEEN MY UKE?

Track 22

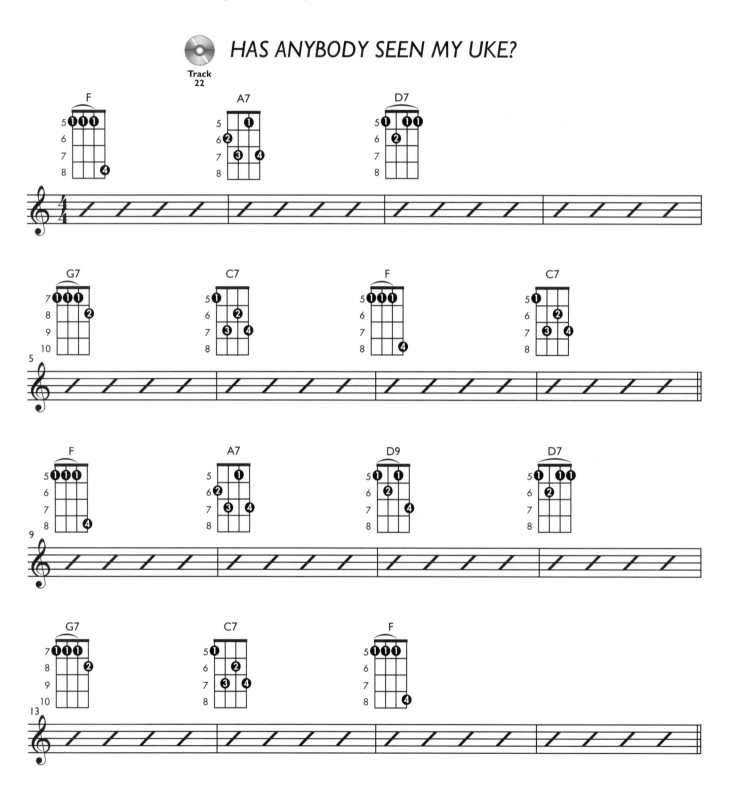

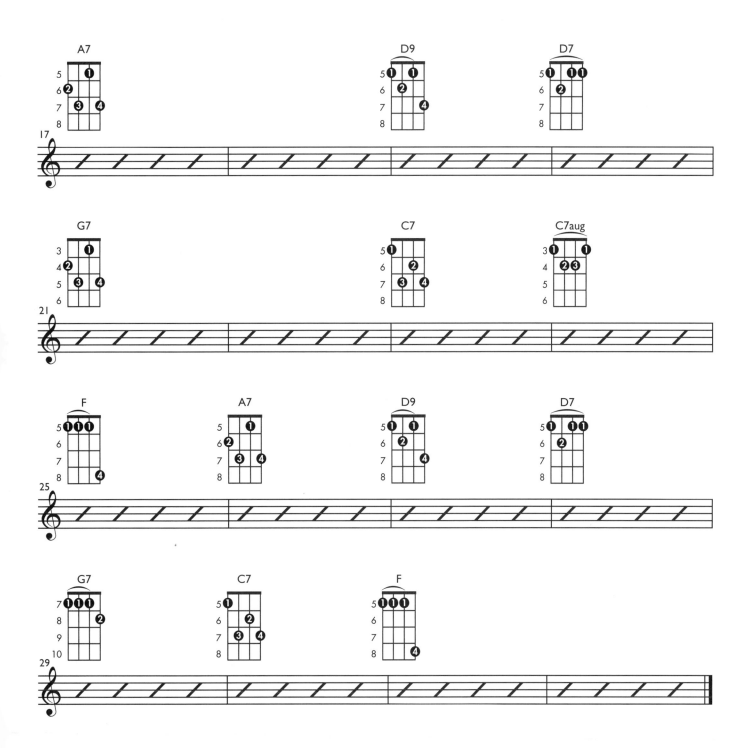

There is a great deal of crossover between jazz/swing techniques and the vocabulary of Hawaiian music. In this lesson, you will learn a strum pattern that incorporates a triple stroke and a new flourish based on a "rake." The patterns shown in this lesson are inspired by the playing of master Hawaiian falsetto singer Richard Hoʻopiʻi. He uses the gentle roll of patterns like these to accompany his singing.

The first step is to learn the following strum pattern, which alternates between a simple down-up stroke and a triple stroke. Note that all examples in this lesson are counted in swing eighths, so the triplet feel is present in every beat. The triple strum shown on beat 2 and 4 of each measure begins with a downstroke of the index finger (*i*), usually just hitting strings 3 and 4, like you would with a split strum. Follow this short downstroke with a full downstroke of the thumb. On the last beat of the triplet, return with an upstroke of the index finger. You may want to try this triple stroke by itself several times before incorporating it into the full pattern.

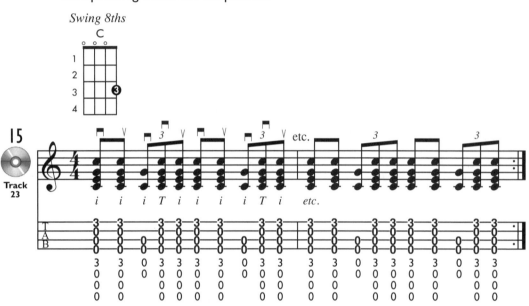

The second step is to learn a special flourish, adapted from a *rake stroke* (where the strum drags through the strings so that the notes sound individually). The stroke begins with an upstroke of the thumb, using the back of the thumbnail. Use one continuous motion, but drag through the strings so the notes of the first three strings sound like a quick triplet. Practice this move with your ring finger (*a*) slightly curled up in your palm. Once you've got the thumb move down, finish the stroke with a downward rake of the ring finger (*a*). All together it should sound like one stroke that sort of goes "whoosh," like a wind chime or a harp. Below are two ways to illustrate the move using a C chord.

THE "WHOOSH"
How it sounds: How it is shown:

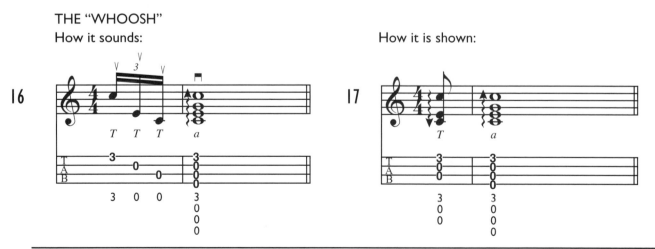

You wouldn't have to use the ring finger to make the main downstroke of this move, but it does have benefits. One reason is that this finger will only have that one job to do, making it easier to incorporate with the other fingers in the strum pattern. The other reason is that, once you practice the move enough to make it easy, it looks like a sleight of hand trick from the front. You hear this sound, but the fingers that produced it are a bit hidden from view.

To put it all together, you will start the "whoosh" move on the last part of each triple stroke (replacing the upstroke of the index finger), so that it accentuates the strong downbeats on beats 1 and 3. Go very slowly at first, and keep the triplet feel throughout.

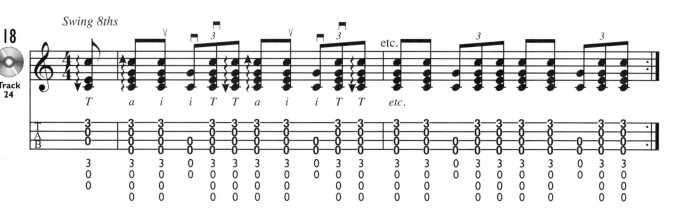

Below is a Hawaiian-style progression you can use to practice this strum pattern. You can also play through it without the flourishes, using the simpler triple pattern from the beginning of the lesson. Go at a slow, easy tempo. The pattern should remind you of an island breeze or of gentle waves breaking on the beach. To fully get in the mood, keep an open bottle of sunscreen nearby while you practice.

THE BREEZE THROUGH THE TREES BLOWS WITH EASE

Track
25

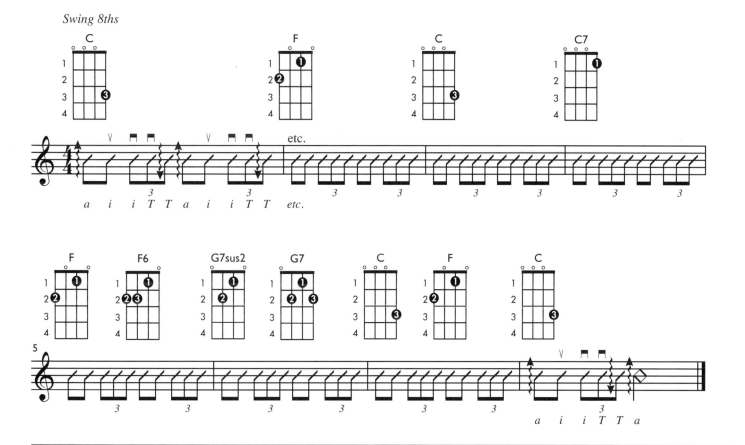

CHAPTER 5

Scales and Arpeggios: Positions Up the Neck

LESSON 1: MAJOR SCALE POSITIONS

All melodies—composed or improvised—are created using notes from scales and arpeggios, so these are important to learn on the ukulele. We'll start with the major scale, as it is considered the foundation of Western music. It will also be used to further explain other aspects of music theory. We have discussed major scales previously in *Beginning* and *Intermediate Ukulele*, so you can look back at those to refresh your skills. We used two positions of the major scale in *Intermediate Ukulele*, now we'll add the rest of the positions, ultimately increasing your knowledge of the entire fretboard.

Essentially, there are seven positions of any diatonic scale, one position starting from each note of the scale. So in C Major, the first scale position would start on C, the root, next position would start on D, the 2nd, next on E, the 3rd, and so on, using the same seven notes each time. Below are the seven positions, presented in that order, with the starting note on the 3rd string. By learning them this way, each position overlaps the previous and next fingering positions. Once you learn all the positions in any key, it is possible to shift easily between them when playing melodies.

For many players, it is most intuitive to play the scales on just three strings—C, E, and A—not using the re-entrant G string (because of jumping octaves). However, the fingering for that string has been included below because it is useful to know all the notes available to you. If you have a ukulele in low-G tuning, the 4th string will extend the melodic range of these scale positions by a 4th.

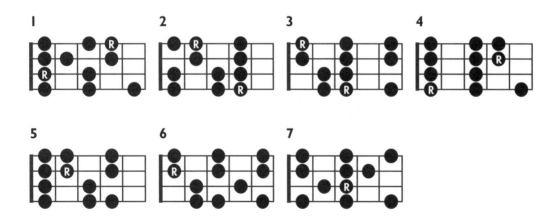

LESSON 2: À LA MODE

Modes are extremely useful scales for expanding your improvisational skills. The word "mode" derives from "mood," and each mode does evoke different moods and feelings. There are seven modes contained within any major scale. In C Major, start on the 5th, G, and go up one octave from G to G, using only the notes contained in the C scale—the result is the *Mixolydian mode*. Essentially, the relationships of the intervals between each degree of the scale have shifted places—now there's a half step between the 6th and 7th notes instead of 7th and octave. Another way to understand this scale is by comparing it to the key of G Major.

G Major scale: G–A–B–C–D–E–F♯–G.
G Mixolydian scale: G–A–B–C–D–E–F–G.

There is one note difference between them: the F♯ changed to F. Thus, any Mixolydian scale can be constructed by flatting the 7th degree of a major scale. This is an intuitive method for understanding the modes and being able to access them quickly.

Below are all seven modes, presented first in order, from one parent major scale, C. Note, the Ionian mode is also known as the major scale, and the Aeolian mode is also known as natural minor.

Ionian (major scale): C–D–E–F–G–A–B–C (step formula: W–W–H–W–W–W–H)

Dorian: D–E–F–G–A–B–C–D (W–H–W–W–W–H–W)

Phrygian: E–F–G–A–B–C–D–E (H–W–W–W–H–W–W)

Lydian: F–G–A–B–C–D–E–F (W–W–W–H–W–W–H)

Mixolydian: G–A–B–C–D–E–F–G (W–W–H–W–W–H–W)

Aeolian (natural minor scale): A–B–C–D–E–F–G–A (W–H–W–W–H–W–W)

Locrian: B–C–D–E–F–G–A–B (H–W–W–H–W–W–W)

Here are all seven modes again, this time with formulas for building each from a major scale. They are presented in a different order, each altering one note of the previous mode. A great way to compare these is to build them all from the same root note, so an example for each is provided, starting on C.

Lydian: R–2–3–♯4–5–6–7 (C–D–E–F♯–G–A–B–C)

Ionian: R–2–3–4–5–6–7 (C–D–E–F–G–A–B–C)

Mixolydian: R–2–3–4–5–6–♭7 (C–D–E–F–G–A–B♭–C)

Dorian: R–2–♭3–4–5–6–♭7 (C–D–E♭–F–G–A–B♭–C)

Aeolian: R–2–♭3–4–5–♭6–♭7 (C–D–E♭–F–G–A♭–B♭–C)

Phrygian: R–♭2–♭3–4–5–♭6–♭7 (C–D♭–E♭–F–G–A♭–B♭–C)

Locrian: R–♭2–♭3–4–♭5–♭6–♭7 (C–D♭–E♭–F–G♭–A♭–B♭–C)

Below are the fingering positions for the modes, starting with the root note on the 3rd string. Try playing them all in the same key for comparison.

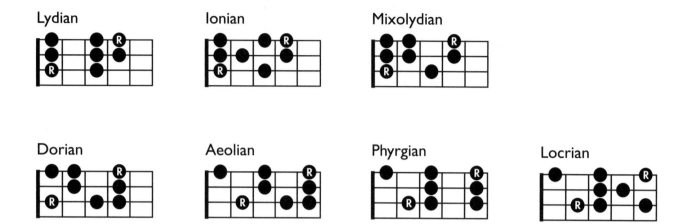

Lydian   Ionian   Mixolydian

Dorian   Aeolian   Phyrgian   Locrian

MODAL MUSIC

There are many beautiful modal melodies found in traditional Celtic and Appalachian music, particularly using Dorian and Mixolydian modes. In modal tunes, an entire melody might use only the notes from that particular mode; however, notes outside the mode are also occasionally used. The Phrygian mode is often used in flamenco music.

CHORDS AND MODES

Looking at chords, the Lydian, Ionian, and Mixolydian modes all contain the notes of a major triad, and thus can be used to improvise over major chords, each with different results. In addition, Lydian and Ionian both contain a major 7th interval, so they can also be used for improvising over major 7th chords. Mixolydian contains a ♭7th interval, so it can be used to improvise over the dominant 7th chord.

The Dorian, Aeolian, and Phrygian modes all contain the notes found in minor triads and minor 7th chords, and could be used to improvise over these chords. The Locrian mode contains a ♭5th in addition to the ♭3rd and could be played over a min7♭5 chord.

Besides using modes to solo over particular chords, it is possible to use one mode through an entire progression, if those chords are all contained within the scale. In a later chapter, we will explore using some of the modes to improvise.

LESSON 3: MAJOR AND MINOR PENTATONIC SCALES

Let's review pentatonic scales, which were covered in *Beginning* and *Intermediate Ukulele*.

MAJOR PENTATONIC SCALE

A *major pentatonic scale* is constructed by leaving out the 4th and 7th notes of the major scale. The formula to build a major pentatonic scale in any key is: root–2nd–3rd–5th–6th. For example, the notes of a C Major scale are: C–D–E–F–G–A–B–C. Leave out F (the 4th) and B (the 7th), and you have the notes of the C Major Pentatonic scale: C–D–E–G–A–C.

Using the major scale positions we discussed earlier in this chapter, you can easily find fingerings for the corresponding major pentatonic scales. Below are five positions of the major pentatonic scale (in parentheses are numbers of the corresponding major scale positions from page 192). Each one connects with the next. Once you've learned all five positions, you will be able to play the major pentatonic scale spanning the entire fretboard.

1 (1)

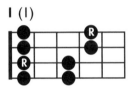

2 (2)

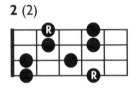

3 (3)

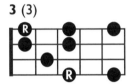

4 (5)

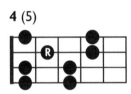

5 (7)

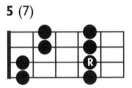

MINOR PENTATONIC SCALE

The *minor pentatonic scale* can be considered a mode of the major pentatonic scale. Using the exact same notes, but starting on A, the 6th degree of the scale, results in an A Minor Pentatonic scale: A–C–D–E–G–A. The A Minor Pentatonic scale is the relative minor of C Major Pentatonic. The formula for a minor pentatonic scale is: 1–♭3–4–5–♭7.

Below are moveable positions of the minor pentatonic scale that can be used to play up and down the neck and in any key. Notice that these scales use the same fingerings as the major pentatonic—the only difference is which note is the root.

1

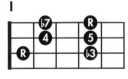

2

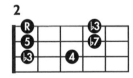

3

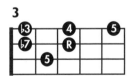

4

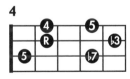

5

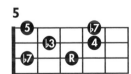

Arpeggios are a useful tool for playing melodies and improvising. An arpeggio contains all the notes of a chord played individually in succession.

MAJOR TRIAD ARPEGGIO FINGERINGS

A major triad arpeggio contains root–3rd–5th. Below are four major arpeggio fingerings.

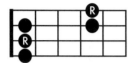 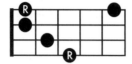

 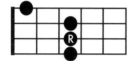

MINOR TRIAD ARPEGGIO FINGERINGS

A minor triad arpeggio contains root–♭3rd–5th. Simply flat the 3rd of the major arpeggio fingerings, and this results in minor arpeggios. Here are four minor arpeggio positions.

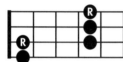 

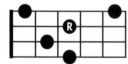 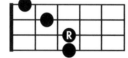

Now, we'll look at three types of 7th arpeggios.

MAJOR 7TH ARPEGGIO FINGERINGS
To create any major 7th arpeggio, add the 7th note of the major scale to the major arpeggio.

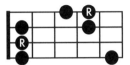

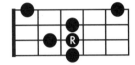

DOMINANT 7TH ARPEGGIO FINGERINGS
To create any dominant 7th arpeggio fingering, flat the 7th note of a major 7th arpeggio.

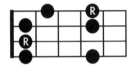
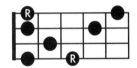

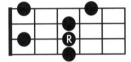

MINOR 7TH ARPEGGIO FINGERINGS
Finally, to create any minor 7th arpeggio, add a ♭7th to the minor arpeggio.

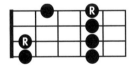
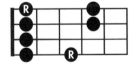

LESSON 5: SCALE AND ARPEGGIO PRACTICE IDEAS

PRACTICE USING MELODIES

As you learn your way around the scale and arpeggio positions, practice them in different ways to increase your fretboard knowledge. A great way to get to know your scales is to pick simple melodies—perhaps some you learned in *Beginning* or *Intermediate Ukulele*—and try playing them up the neck, using all the different scale positions we've covered.

PRACTICE BY IMPROVISING

Another great way to explore scales, modes, and arpeggios is to improvise using them, either over a practice chord progression, such as ii–V–I or I–IV–V, or over a drone. As an example, pick any scale with C as the root note, and improvise using the low C string as a root drone note. In C, the 5th is G, so you can use both of those strings as drones.

PRACTICE USING SEQUENCES

If we only practice a scale going straight up and down, then our improvisational ideas will often sound like we're just running scales. Let's use *sequences* to add some variety to our lines. A sequence is the repetition of a pattern or phrase at different pitch levels. We'll refer to these sequences using scale degrees. (Note: Another way to refer to the root is with the number "1.")

Following are sequence examples using a C Major scale in open position; however, you should also try them in different keys and positions. First, we'll play 1–3, 2–4, 3–5, 4–6, etc., in eighth notes. Start on the root (1), skip to the 3rd, then go back a step to the 2nd, and skip up to the 4th, etc. Then descend the sequence.

Now, we'll add the note to the sequence that we previously skipped and play 1–2–3, 2–3–4, 3–4–5, etc., ascending and descending in triplets.

Next, we'll play the scale in groups of four notes: 1–2–3–4, 2–3–4–5, 3–4–5–6, etc.

21
Track 28

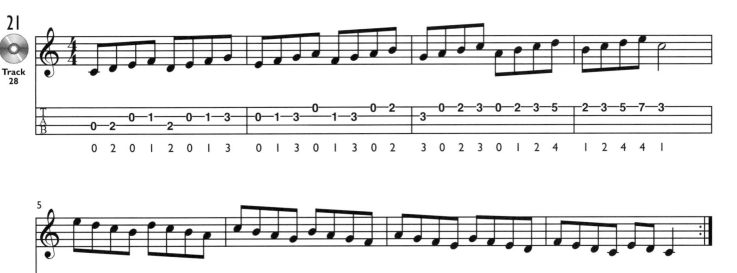

```
0 2 0 1 2 0 1 3   0 1 3 0 1 3 0 2   3 0 2 3 0 1 2 4   1 2 4 4 1
```

```
4 2 1 1 4 2 1 0   3 2 0 3 2 0 3 1   0 3 1 0 3 1 0 2   1 0 2 0 0 2 0
```

Try these practice ideas with any of the modes, pentatonic scales, or arpeggios. It really makes them come alive in very usable and interesting musical patterns. For example, here's the 1–2–3, 2–3–4, 3–4–5 exercise, transposed into the major pentatonic scale. Using only notes from the scale, the sequence would actually be 1–2–3, 2–3–5, 3–5–6, 5–6–8, etc.

22
Track 29

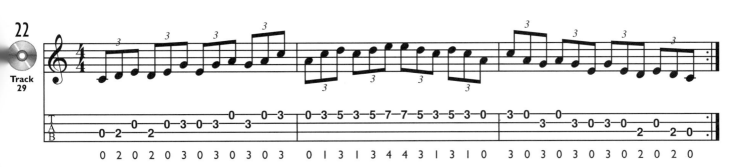

```
0 2 0 2 0 3 0 3 0 3 0 3   0 1 3 1 3 4 4 3 1 3 1 0   3 0 3 0 3 0 3 0 2 0 2 0
```

CHAPTER 6

Fingerstyle

LESSON 1: *HOUSE OF THE RISING SUN* (CHORD-MELODY)

Here's a chord-melody arrangement of "House of the Rising Sun," which utilizes chord inversions up the neck and fingerstyle concepts previously introduced in *Beginning* and *Intermediate Ukulele*. In this first pass through the song, the melody is primarily played on the 1st string, with plucked chords beneath. You can pluck the chords using thumb, index, middle, and ring fingers—one finger per string. Also, make sure to hold chords down for the full measure so they continue to ring out as you play the melody notes. It's important to learn this section well, as the next two variations will build on the same chord shapes.

 HOUSE OF THE RISING SUN (CHORD-MELODY)

Track 30

In this first variation, we'll incorporate a $\frac{6}{8}$ fingerstyle arpeggio accompaniment that we played in *Intermediate Ukulele*, this time combining melody and chords. We will use the exact same chord shapes as we played on the previous page. Again, make sure to hold chords down for the full measure so they continue to ring out as you play the melody notes.

HOUSE OF THE RISING SUN (VARIATION I)

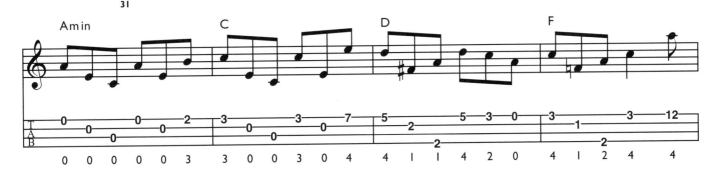

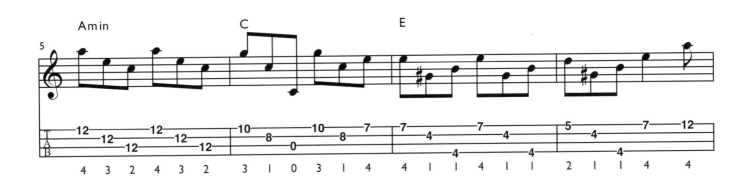

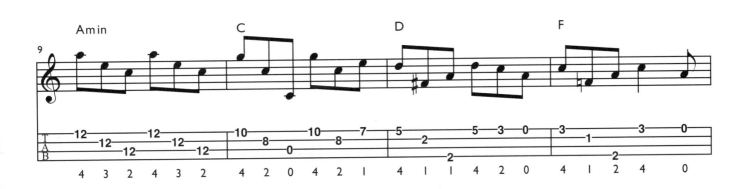

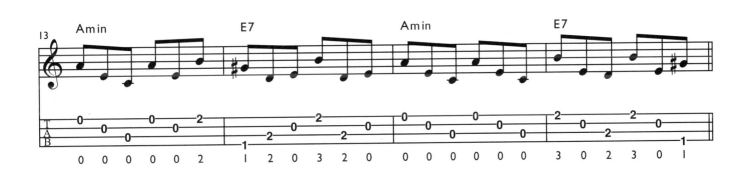

In the second variation, we'll incorporate the $\frac{6}{8}$ strum we played in *Intermediate Ukulele*, again combining melody and chords. You could use an alternating stroke or one of the triple strum patterns. We're still using the same chord shapes as played on the previous page.

HOUSE OF THE RISING SUN (VARIATION 2)

Track 32

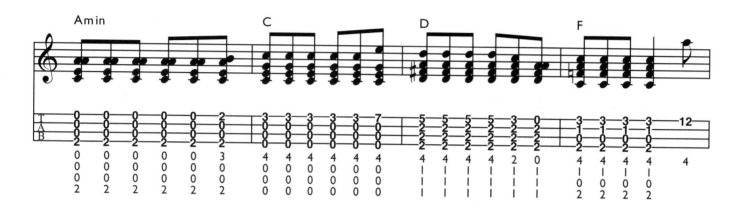

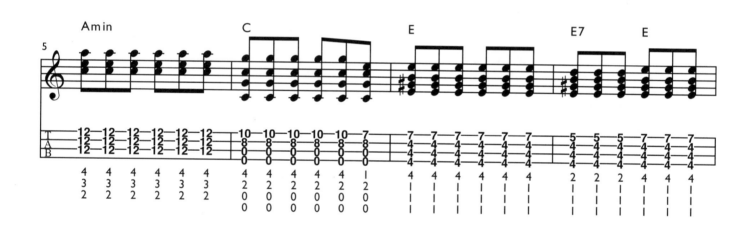

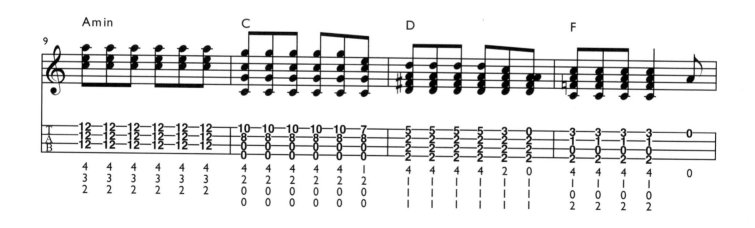

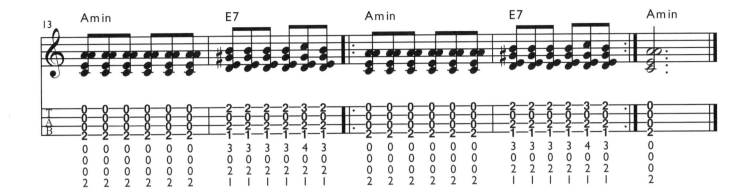

For a final variation, play the preceding example using the strum pattern below, incorporating a rasgueado, as discussed on pages 178–179.

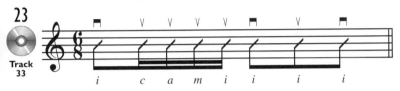

LESSON 2: CROSS-STRING FINGERING

An interesting aspect of the uke is the re-entrant string. The 4th string, G, is tuned only a whole step apart from the 1st string, A. This allows us to easily play what is called *cross-string fingering*, or *harp style*, which means that we play 2, 3, or more consecutive notes of a melodic passage on different strings, rather than all the notes on the same string. Playing this way results in a harp-like effect, with various notes sustaining and blending together.

Below is a C Major scale, demonstrating cross-string fingering. Hold down notes whenever possible so that they keep sustaining as you're playing consecutive notes. The first four ascending notes utilize hammer-ons, and the same descending notes utilize pull-offs.

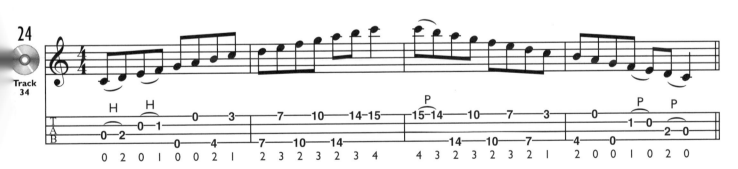

When arranging melodic passages, you don't need to follow this exact scale fingering; instead, decide which notes you want to have sustaining, and work out fingerings to allow that.

LESSON 3: *ARPEGGI-UKE* (CROSS-STRING)

"Arpeggi-uke" is in the key of D Minor, and it utilizes cross-string fingering techniques. The theme encompasses the first 16 measures, and a variation on the same chord progression takes up the next 16 measures. We return briefly to the original theme before ending. Make sure to hold down notes whenever possible, so that they will keep sustaining as you're playing consecutive notes in the measure.

ARPEGGI-UKE (CROSS-STRING)

Track 35

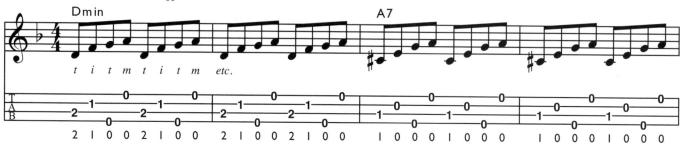

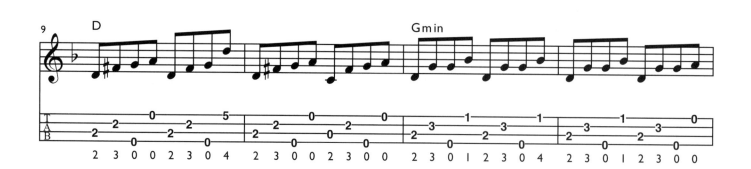

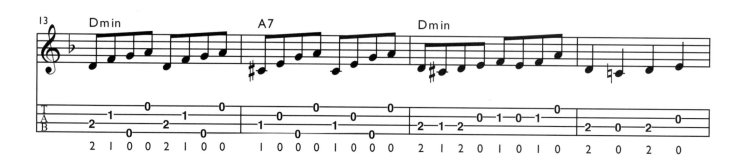

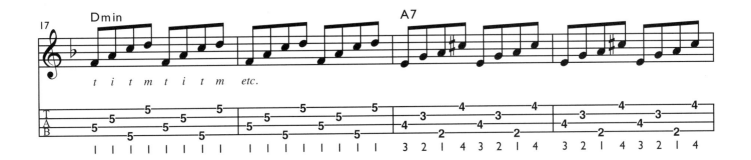

t i t m t i t m etc.

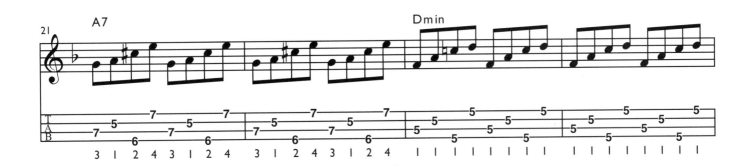

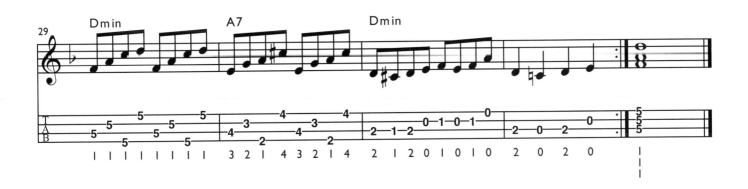

Now, we'll play a ragtime piece, "Cross-String Rag," which utilizes cross-string fingering techniques as demonstrated with the C Major scale on page 203. Make sure to hold down notes whenever possible so that they keep sustaining as you're playing consecutive notes.

 CROSS-STRING RAG

Track 36

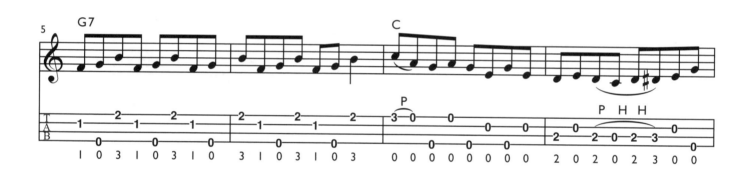

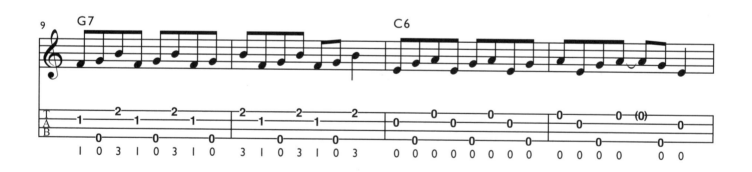

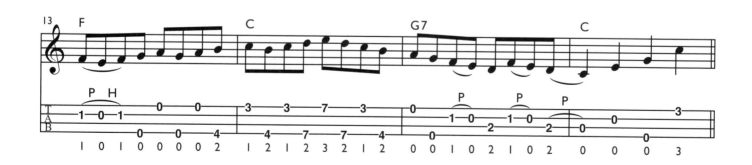

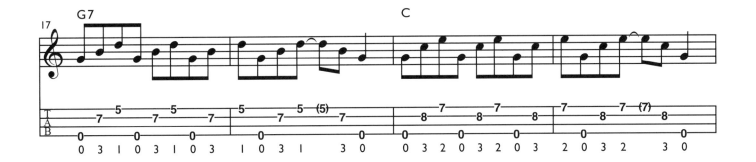

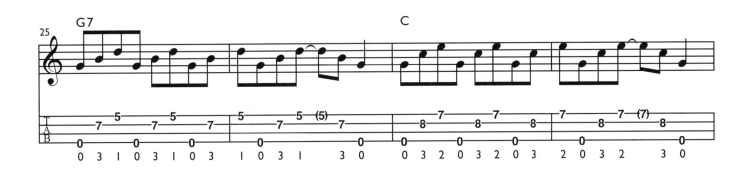

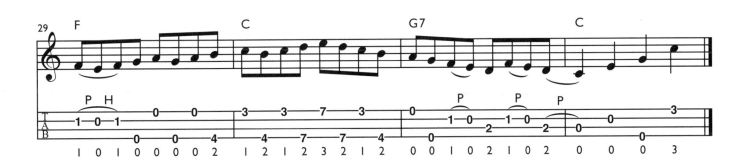

"Miss McLeod's Reel" is a popular fiddle tune that originated in Scotland, played in the key of A. In America, it's most often played in G and is also known as "Hop High Ladies" or "Did You Ever See the Devil, Uncle Joe?" This fingerstyle arrangement in C utilizes cross-string fingering, hammer-ons, and pull-offs.

 MISS MCLEOD'S REEL

Track 37

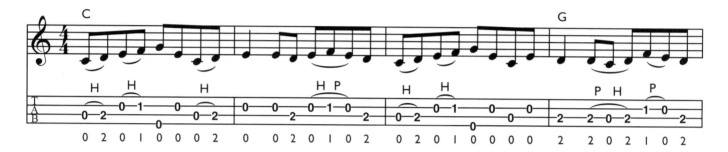

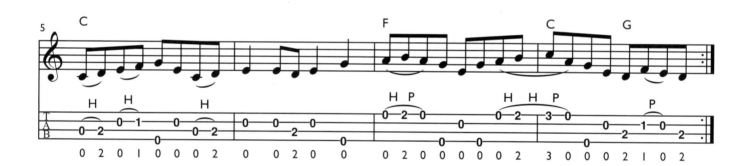

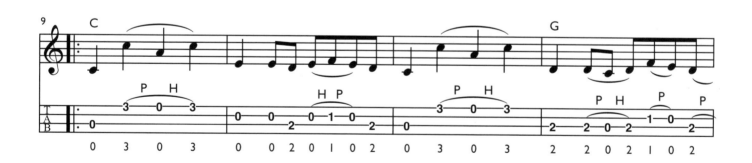

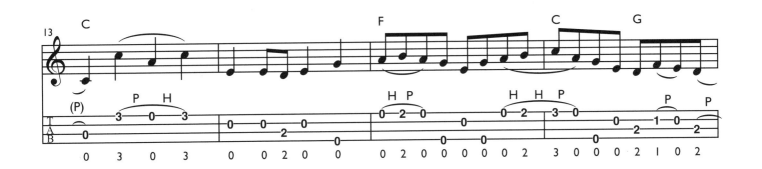

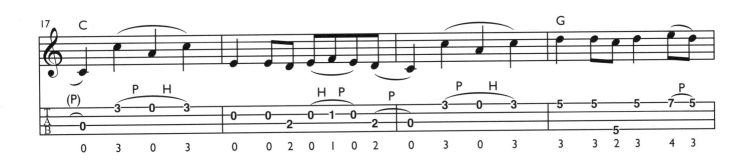

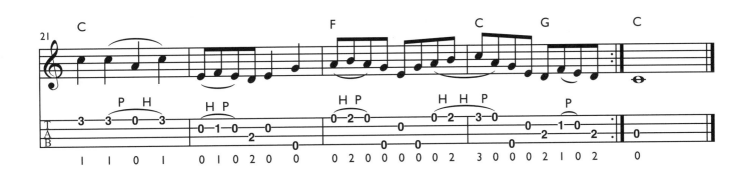

CHAPTER 7

Rockin' the Uke

LESSON 1: SONG FOR GEORGE

Beatles songs sound great on the ukulele. George Harrison was a uke enthusiast, so this is an homage to him. The 16-measure verse of "Song for George" uses a chord progression found within the harmonized major scale in key of A. In the chorus, we step outside the key, which The Beatles often did in their songs. Make sure to carefully follow the down-up strum shown in measure 1, and continue throughout the piece. Once you've learned the song, try incorporating some different strums from Chapter 3 (page 174–179) to create a variety of rhythmic textures.

SONG FOR GEORGE

Track 38

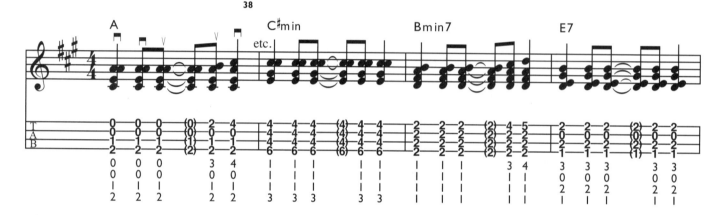

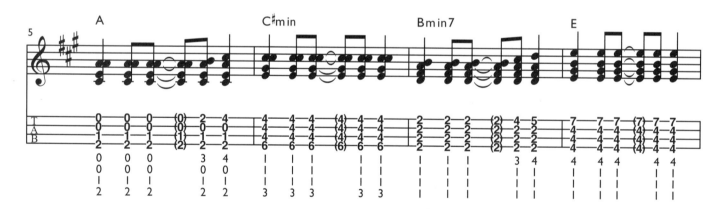

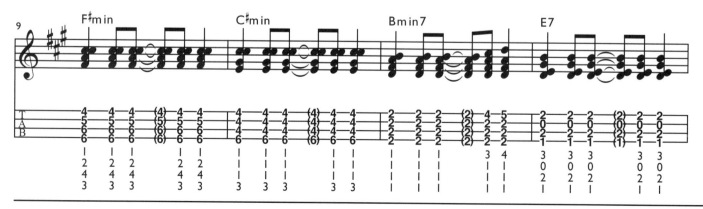

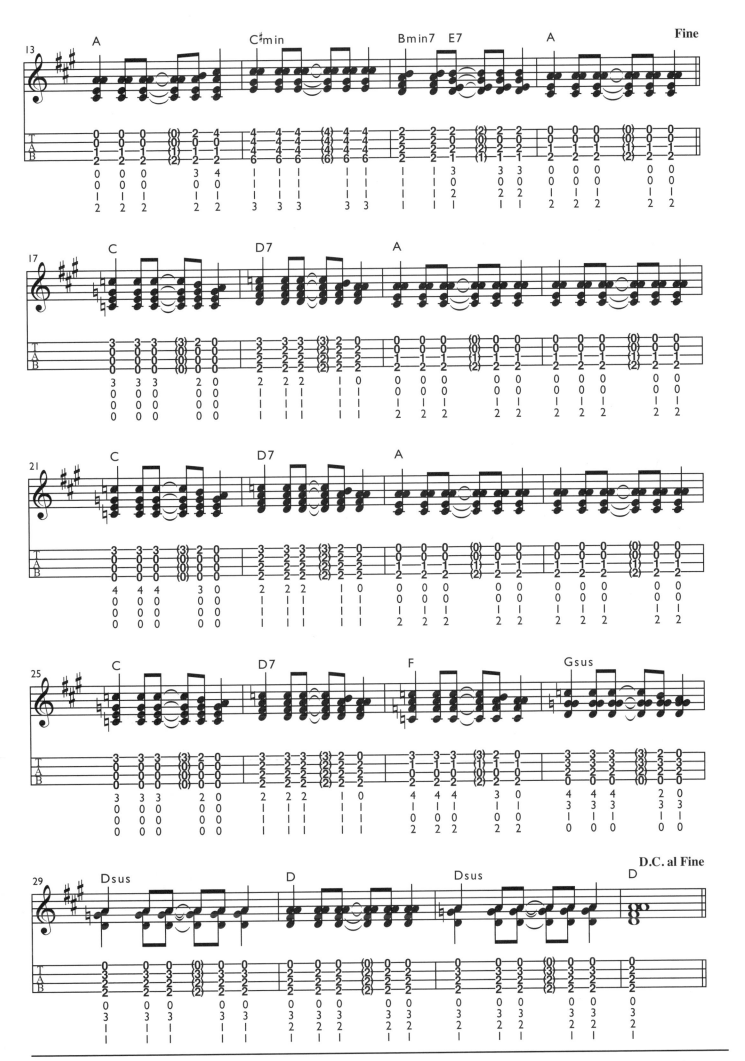

LESSON 2: BODY PERCUSSION

There are more sounds in a ukulele than just those that come from strings. Most ukes are very lightly built, very resonant wooden boxes. You can make lots of percussive tones by lightly tapping, thumping, or flicking various parts of the uke. As long as you don't go after it with too much force, your uke can be a little drum kit for your fingers. Here are a few techniques to try, some of which will be used in a later lesson.

Track 39

THE BODY OR BRIDGE TAP

You can use the pad of your index or middle finger to tap at various places on the body, bridge, or saddle (where the strings sit on the bridge). Nearer to the bridge, you get bassier sounds, while in other spots, you get higher-pitched sounds. You can also tap or thump with your thumb (keep it light and bouncy), or even lightly with your nails. But beware, if you do a lot of enthusiastic work with your nails on the top of the uke, you may end up with a scratched finish.

THE FLICK

For the *flick*, the back of your fingernail lightly bounces on the wood of the top, creating a sound like a woodblock. The key words here are "lightly" and "bounce." If you flick too hard and don't bounce, you could hurt your knuckles, or even knock a brace loose in your uke. But don't be afraid! Below are some tips to help you figure out the technique before you even try it on the uke.

NOTE

Try the following flick techniques on a wooden table, notebook, or magazine until you figure out the right amount of force and bounce. Once you move to the uke, try it on the upper bout of the uke top, on the 4th string side. You can try it other places for other tones, but we'll use this spot as home base.

Index Finger Flick

If you imagine a normal flick of the index finger, you would curl up the finger and hold the back of the nail with the end of your thumb. As you push your finger against your thumb, it builds up force until the finger pops past the thumb: FLICK! This move gives you the idea, but produces a flick that is too forceful to control musically. Instead, curl your index finger behind the middle joint of your thumb. Then, instead of building up a lot of opposing force, just build up a little and roll your thumb away sideways, producing a gentler flick. Try this on a flat surface. Keep your index finger curled up (don't extend as it flicks) so that it bounces lightly on the surface, making a light knocking sound. When you can do this several times in a row without knocking your knuckle into the table, try it lightly on your uke.

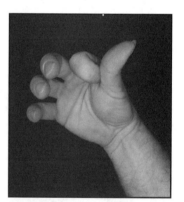
Index finger flick position.

Middle Finger Flick

This version gets even better results with less force. Use your middle finger for the flick, and curl it under the ball of your thumb. To get the position right, try this: make a fist and turn it palm-up so you can see your fingers. Release your index, ring, and pinky fingers from the fist, but leave your middle finger and thumb in place. That's the flick position. Turn it over and lightly flick a flat surface. Make sure to bounce off the surface lightly—don't drive it in like a nail. It takes very little force to get a nice little "knock" out of this move. Once you've got it, try it on the uke.

Work on your taps and flicks, then later in Lesson 4, you'll see how we can notate these techniques and put them into practice.

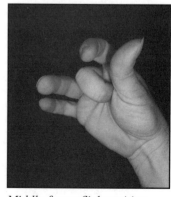
Middle finger flick position.

Funk strumming is usually based in a sixteenth-note groove (count 1–e–&–ah, 2–e–&–ah, 3–e–&–ah, 4–e–&–ah). A great way to approach it is to use closed-position moveable chords, or, chords that have no open strings. This allows you to keep the right hand going the whole time, using the left hand to mute or squeeze the strings and create different rhythms. One way to think of it is: "squeezing and scratching." The scratches are strokes that are muted by relaxing the pressure of your left hand without lifting off the string. The scratches are marked with an X instead of a note head. Try this rhythm with a C chord in a closed fingering.

Track 40: Scratching

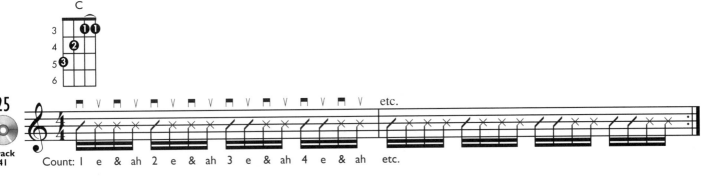

Track 41

You can make up endless variations of squeezes and scratches in a sixteenth-note groove. Try writing out a couple of bars of sixteenth-note counts, scattering X's and notes across the counts to find new grooves!

Funk music—as played by artists ranging from James Brown to Parliament to Prince, combines influences of jazz, R&B, and blues. Complex chords help spice up the harmony. Dominant chords like 7ths, 9ths, and 13ths are often used instead of simple major chords.

SLIDING INTO CHORDS

An easy technique that sounds cool is to begin strumming a chord one fret lower, then slide it up to the correct fret. This is called a *half-step approach* and can move up from below, or down from above. Following is a groove using a G9 chord with a half-step approach. A G9 contains the notes of G7 (G–B–D–F) and the 9th above G, which is an A note. When we play chords like this on the uke, some notes get left out of our voicing because we only have four strings. This version of G9 is missing the root. From the 4th to the 1st string, the notes are: B–F–A–D. Find a friend to play the missing G and you'll hear the whole chord! This strumming technique will be put into practice in the next lesson.

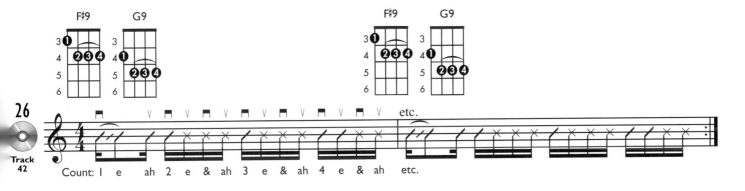

Track 42

A great way to build an arrangement is to layer simple ideas, the way some musicians layer short electronic loops to build a complex groove. Ukulele virtuoso James Hill used this approach to build a cool arrangement of Michael Jackson's hit "Billie Jean." Hill's arrangement pulls together a bass riff, a body percussion groove, and a chord sequence. We'll take a similar approach to build a groove for this lesson called "Gloves Off." Your strumming in this piece will mainly be with your index finger.

First, learn this little percussion groove. The top line shows the "flick" you learned on page 212. The lower line shows a light finger tap on the top. Make these sounds in the area of the upper bout of the uke, on the side above the 4th string. This will make it easier to integrate with the strums. Flick with your middle finger, so your index will be free for the tap.

27
Track 43

After you've got the percussion groove, put it aside and work on this chord progression that goes up the neck. Watch out for the pull off in the first chord of the four-chord pattern.

28
Track 44

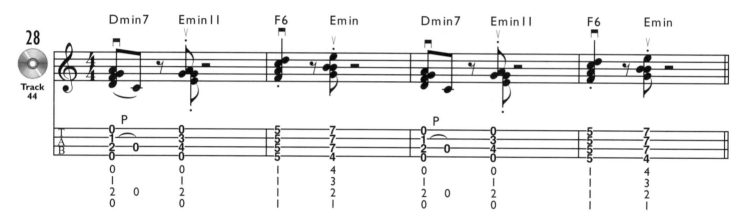

Now, try integrating both moves together. You'll find that the rests in one part line up with the moves in the other part. Later in the tune, you get to incorporate those sliding funk chords from the previous lesson, plus a couple of single-note runs.

🄫 GLOVES OFF

Track 45

CHAPTER 8

Jazz Improvisation

LESSON 1: IMPROVISING OVER DOMINANT 7TH CHORDS

Incorporating chord tones into your improvisation is a great way to make your solos sound more interesting. We'll practice this concept with "Has Anybody Seen My Uke?" using the arpeggios we covered in Chapter 5 (pages 196–199). Except for the I chord, F, for which we'll use an Fmaj6 arpeggio, we'll use dominant 7th arpeggios to improvise over the rest of the chords. Here's a sample solo over an eight-bar section of the song. After you play this, try coming up with your own solos over the full progression using these arpeggios.

Looking deeper into these arpeggios, we discover some interesting possibilities for melodic movement. Here are the notes contained within each chord:

A7 (A–C♯–E–G)
D7 (D–F♯–A–C)
G7 (G–B–D–F)
C7 (C–E–G–B♭)
F6 (F–A–C–D)

Notice that C♯, the 3rd of the A7 chord, moves down a half step to C, the 7th degree of the D7 chord. This movement continues through the progression, alternating 3rds and 7ths. The C in the D7 chord moves down a half step to B, the 3rd of the G7 chord. The B moves down a half step to B♭, the 7th of the C7 chord. Finally, the B♭ moves down a half step to A, the 3rd of the F chord. Now look at the 7th of the A7 chord, the G moves down a half step to F♯, the 3rd of the D7 chord. The F♯ moves down a half step to F, the 7th of the G7 chord. F moves down a half step to E, the 3rd of the C7 chord. Finally, E moves down a whole step to D, the 6th of the F6 chord. Pretty fascinating!

While we can play decent-sounding solos using only arpeggios, the chord tones are considered safe notes, in that they don't clash against the accompanying chords. We can make things more interesting by adding more notes, still using these chord tones as a foundation. Look at the Mixolydian mode (covered on page 193), and notice that it contains all four notes of a dominant 7th arpeggio plus three other notes. We'll use that mode to augment the ideas originally created from the arpeggios. On the I chord, F, we'll play the F Major scale—for all other chords, we'll use Mixolydian. In addition, we'll play a few ♭3rds (blue notes) to add some flair.

Here's a sample solo over a 16-bar section of the song, building on the ideas from the previous eight-bar example. After you play it, try coming up with your own solos over the full progression, incorporating these ideas.

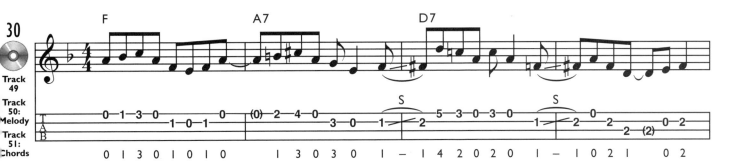

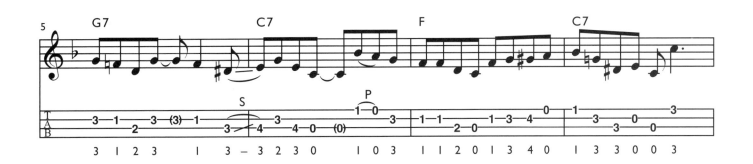

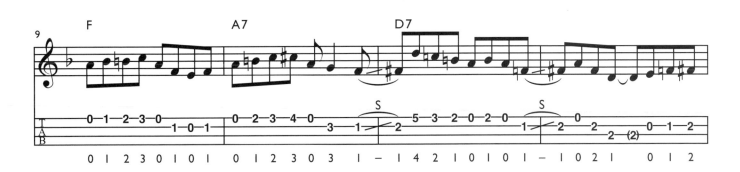

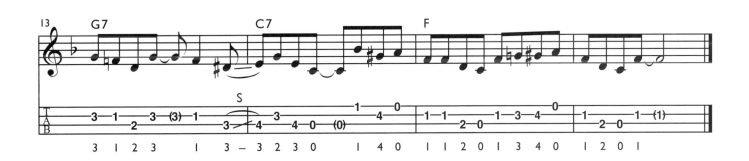

LESSON 2: IMPROVISING OVER OTHER TYPES OF 7TH CHORDS

Now, we'll use the same concept of using arpeggios on a song that has other types of 7th chords. We'll play "Autumn Has Left," which uses four different kinds of 7th chords: major 7th, dominant 7th, minor 7th, and minor 7th♭5th. Again, we'll take a look at the notes contained within each chord:

Amin7 (A–C–E–G)
D7 (D–F♯–A–C)
GMaj7 (G–B–D–F♯)
CMaj7 (C–E–G–B)
F♯min7♭5 (F♯–A–C–E)
B7 (B–D♯–F♯–A)
Emin7 (E–G–B–D)

This time, the C note, the 3rd of Amin7, stays the same note, becoming the 7th of D7. Then the C of the D7 chord moves down a half step to B, the 3rd of GMaj7. The B then stays the same note and becomes the 7th degree of CMaj7. Now, B moves down a whole step to A, the 3rd of F♯min7♭5. The A note remains the same for B7, now becoming the 7th of the chord. Finally, the A moves down a whole step to G, the 3rd of Emin7. The movement is slightly different than before, but still alternating 3rds and 7ths throughout the progression.

Now look at the 7th of the Amin7 chord—the G moves down a half step to F♯, the 3rd of D7. Then F♯ stays the same note, becoming the 7th of GMaj7. Then, F♯ moves down a whole step to E, the 3rd of CMaj7. The E note remains in the F♯min7♭5, but is that chord's 7th. Next, the E note moves down a half step to D♯, the 3rd of B7. Finally, the D♯ moves down a half step to D, the 7th of Emin7. We can utilize these movements in interesting ways when creating our solos. Below is a sample solo over the first eight measures of "Autumn Has Left," using arpeggios.

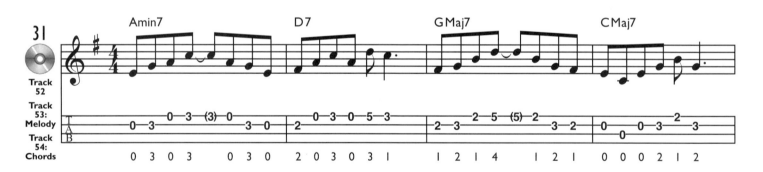

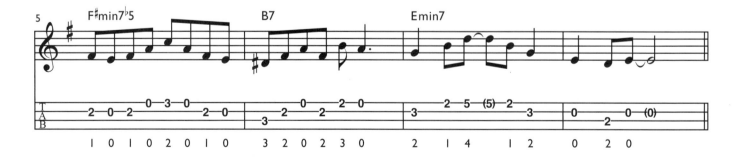

Now, we'll expand the solo, incorporating modes and blues notes. Recalling our previous chapter on modes, each mode contains a type of 7th chord within, thus you can use that mode to improvise over that type of chord. The notes of a major 7th arpeggio can be found within both Lydian and Ionian modes, so either of those scales can be used to improvise over the major 7th chord. The dominant 7th arpeggio is found within Mixolydian; the minor 7th arpeggio is found within Aeolian, Dorian, and Phrygian. And the minor 7th ♭5th is contained within the Locrian mode. Once you've played through this 16-bar example, try improvising and working out solos over the full 32-bar song.

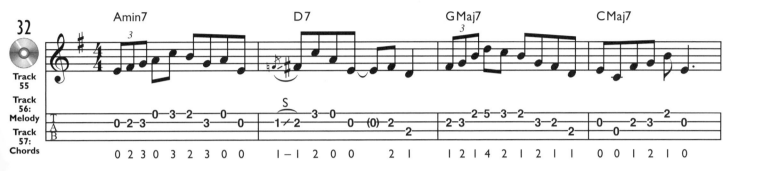

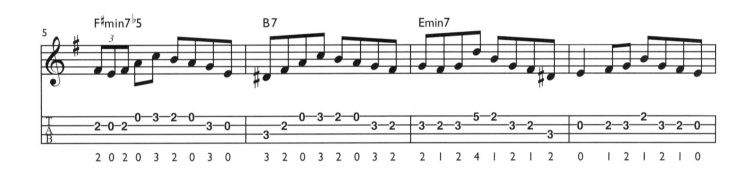

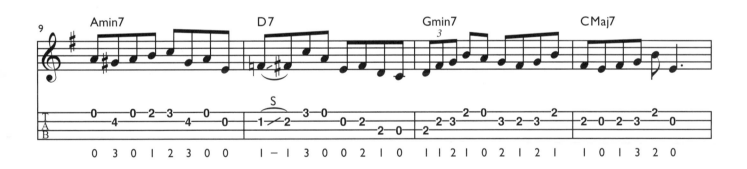

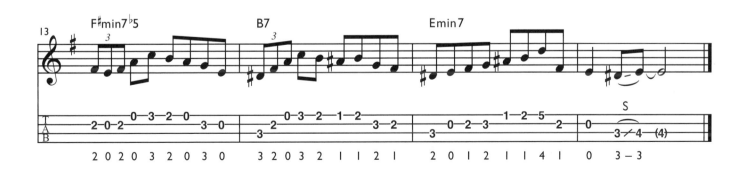

CHAPTER 9

World Rhythms and Scales

LESSON 1: ODD TIME SIGNATURES

When exploring music from other parts of the world, we encounter time signatures like $\frac{5}{4}$, $\frac{7}{8}$, and $\frac{11}{8}$. These rhythms are exciting to play on ukulele. Essentially, any odd time signature can be subdivided into groups of twos or threes. For example, in $\frac{7}{8}$, there is a possible total of seven eighth notes per measure. Instead of counting "one two three four five six seven," we break them up into groups of twos and threes. A typical way of counting $\frac{7}{8}$ is "ONE two three ONE two ONE two," accenting each group on its downbeat, the ONE. Another common way to subdivide is "ONE two ONE two ONE two three." The most intuitive way to strum these rhythms is to play the groups of three notes down-up-down, and the groups of two notes down-up. Below are some $\frac{7}{8}$ strums that are common rhythms in Greek and Balkan music.

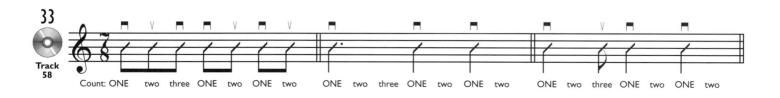

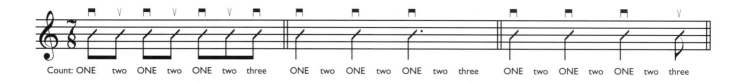

To play in $\frac{11}{8}$, we build on the 4th example of $\frac{7}{8}$ and add two more groups of two: ONE two ONE two ONE two three ONE two ONE two. Here are some $\frac{11}{8}$ strums.

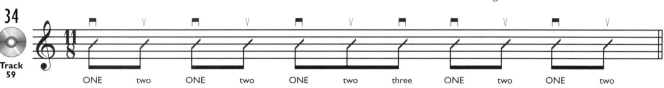

ONE   two   ONE   two   ONE   two   three   ONE   two   ONE   two

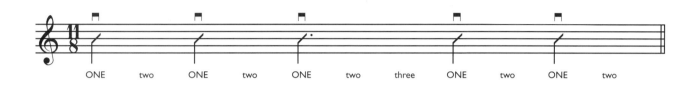

ONE   two   ONE   two   ONE   two   three   ONE   two   ONE   two

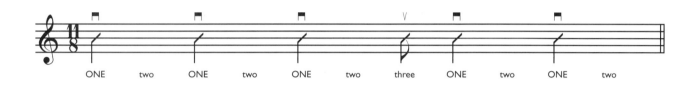

ONE   two   ONE   two   ONE   two   three   ONE   two   ONE   two

Here's an example of $\frac{5}{4}$, which is counted: ONE two three ONE two.

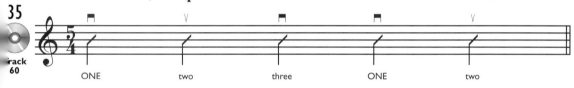

ONE   two   three   ONE   two

LESSON 2: HARMONIC MINOR AND ITS MODES

Exploring music of Eastern Europe and the Middle East, we encounter many different sounding scales, including some modes of the *harmonic minor scale*. The harmonic minor scale is constructed by raising the 7th degree of the natural minor scale by half a step (in other words, using a major 7th scale degree). The notes in A Natural Minor are: A–B–C–D–E–F–G–A. Raise the 7th and we get: A–B–C–D–E–F–G♯–A. The formula for the harmonic minor scale is: root–2nd–♭3rd–4th–5th–♭6th–7th. A significant feature of the harmonic minor scale is that it contains a minor 3rd interval between two consecutive notes. The modes we used previously only contained consecutive intervals of half and whole steps. In addition, the harmonic minor scale contains three half-step intervals rather than two.

A Harmonic Minor Scale

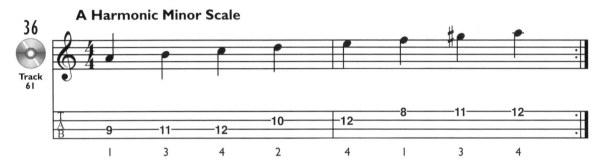

By starting on the 5th note of the harmonic minor scale, we get an exotic mode often used in klezmer, the traditional Jewish music of Eastern Europe. This mode is called *freygish*. In Arabic music, it is called *Hijaz*. You'll also hear this mode used in flamenco guitar. The formula for this 5th mode of the harmonic minor scale is root–♭2nd–3rd–4th–5th–♭6th–♭7th. Another way to think of it is being similar to the Phrygian mode, but with a major 3rd.

E Freygish (or Hijaz) Scale

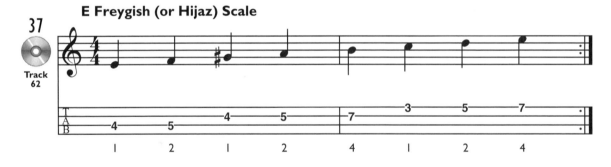

Start on the 4th note of the harmonic minor scale, and the result is another beautiful mode commonly referred to as the *Dorian ♯4*. The formula for this 4th mode of the harmonic minor scale is root–2nd–♭3rd–♯4th–5th–6th–♭7th. It is similar to the Dorian mode, but with a raised 4th, like Lydian. The Dorian ♯4 is often called the *Ukrainian Dorian scale* or *altered Dorian scale*, and it also used in klezmer.

D Dorian ♯4

Here's an original piece combining the freygish klezmer scale in A with Balkan $\frac{7}{8}$ rhythms.

BALKAN UP THE WRONG TREE!

Track
64

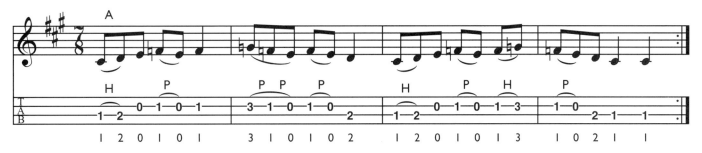

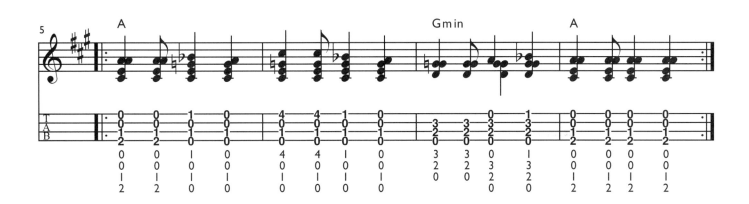

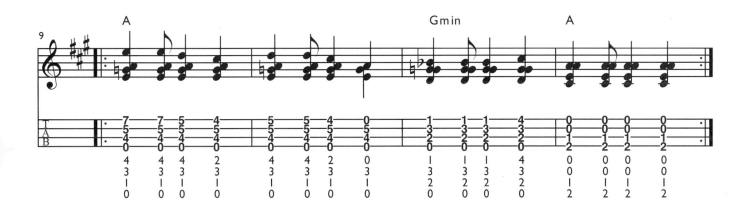

CONCLUSION

Thanks for joining us on this exploration of the ukulele. We hope you keep practicing,
playing, and coming up with your own music on the uke!